WORKSHOP SHORTCUTS

Tips, Tricks, Jigs & Aids for Woodworkers

Graham McCulloch

Sterling Publishing Co., Inc. New York

Library of Congress Cataloging-in-Publication Data

McCulloch, Graham.
    Workshop shortcuts : tips, tricks, jigs & aids for woodworkers /
Graham McCulloch.
        p.   cm.
    Includes index.
    ISBN 0-8069-0650-2
    1. Woodwork.   2. Woodworking tools.   3. Workshops—Equipment and
supplies.   I. Title.
TT185.M377   1994
684'.08—dc20
                                    93-44539
                                         CIP

10 9 8 7 6 5 4 3 2 1

Published by Sterling Publishing Company, Inc.
387 Park Avenue South, New York, N.Y. 10016
© 1994 by Graham McCulloch
Distributed in Canada by Sterling Publishing
% Canadian Manda Group, P.O. Box 920, Station U
Toronto, Ontario, Canada M8Z 5P9
Distributed in Great Britain and Europe by Cassell PLC
Villiers House, 41/47 Strand, London WC2N 5JE, England
Distributed in Australia by Capricorn Link (Australia) Pty Ltd.
P.O. Box 6651, Baulkham Hills, Business Centre, NSW 2153, Australia
Manufactured in the United States of America
All rights reserved

Sterling ISBN 0-8069-0650-2

Dedication

To my wife, Gwen, for persevering yet another writing.

Special Acknowledgments

Wilf "Woody" Woods has been a great help to me in putting this book together. Woody has done the photography for this book and my first book, *Ingenious Shop Aids & Jigs*. His work did not just stop at clicking the camera button; he did the lighting setups, and the printing, developing, and cropping. Woody also assisted in the setting up of the various jigs and shop aids that appear in the following pages. Many thanks, Woody.

Contents

Introduction 9

Workshop Safety 10
Kids in the Workshop 10
The Environment 10

Workshop Shortcuts 12
Abrasives 12
   New Types of Abrasives 12
   Sandpaper 14
Adhesives 14
   Glue, Removing 14
   Epoxy, Mixing 15
   Properly Applying Adhesives 16
Adze 17
Aluminum, Grinding and Filing 17
Angles, Drawing 18
Band Saw 19
   Description of a Band Saw 19
   Selecting Band Saws 19
   Angle Jigs for the Band Saw 20
   Backtracking 21
   Bevel-Cutting with a Band Saw 22
   Rounding Band-Saw Blades 22
   Selecting Band-Saw Blades 23
   Tensioning Band-Saw Blades 23
   Circle-Cutting with the Band Saw 24
   Cutting Compound Mitres with a
      Band Saw 25
   A Jig for Copying Parts 25
   Cutting Accurately with a Band Saw . . . 26
   Flush Fence for a Band Saw 27
   Crosscutting Dowels With a Band Saw . . 28

   Guide Blocks for the Band Saw 28
   Making Long Crosscuts with a
      Band Saw 29
   Shop-Made Out-Feed Roller for a
      Band Saw 30
   Proper Cutting Techniques with a
      Band Saw 31
   Relief Cutting with a Band Saw 31
   Resawing with a Band Saw 32
   Commercial Rip Fence for a Band Saw . . 32
   Safe and Accurate Cutting Techniques . . 33
   Scoring for a Straight Line 33
Bar Clamps, Gripping 34
Bench-Top Power Tools 35
   Band Saw 35
   1" Belt/Disc Sander 36
   4"–6" Belt/Disc Sander 36
   Bench Grinder 36
   Compound Mitre Saw/Sliding Compound
      Mitre Saw 36
   Drill Press 37
   Lathe 38
   Router/Shaper Table 38
   Scroll Saw 39
   Table Saw 40
Bench Vise 40
Bolts 40
Brace 41
Caulk 42
Centers, Drawing 42
Chair and Table Legs, Fitting 42
Chalk Line 42

Chisels, Maintaining 44
Circular Saw 45
   Circular-Saw Blades, Cleaning 45
   Shop-Made Cutting Guide 45
Clamps 46
   Long-Reaching Clamps 46
   Shop-Made Rubberband Clamps 46
   Shop-Made Mini-Clamps 46
   Protecting Your Workpiece from Clamps 46
Compass Cutter 47
Compasses 48
   Types of Compasses 48
   Shop-Made Compasses 49
Coping Saw Jig, Shop-Made 50
Depth Gauge 50
Dimples, Removing 51
Doors, Installing 51
Dowel Joints 52
Dowels, Hiding 52
Drawer Handle Jigs 52
   Method #1 52
   Method #2 53
Drill Bits 53
   Sharpening Drill Bits 53
   Truing Drill Bits 54
Drilling Techniques 54
   Drilling Around Corners 54
   Drilling Holes in Tight Spots 55
Drill Press 55
   Angle Jigs for the Drill Press 55
   Tightening Bits in a Drill Press 55
   Drilling into Spheres with a Drill
     Press 56
   Drill Press as a Lathe 56
   Setting Angles on a Drill Press Table . . . 56
   Raising the Table on a Drill Press 57
Dust 58
Files, Cleaning 58
Files and Rasps, Making Handles for 58
Filters, Disposable 59

Flooring in the Workshop 59
Foam, Cutting 60
Folding Rule, Description 61
Framing Clamps, Shop-Made 61
Framing Nailer, Shop-Made 61
Geometry 62
Handsaw 63
   Shop-Made Handsaw 63
   Japanese Handsaw 63
Hand Tools 64
   Clamping Tools 64
   Chisels 67
   Cutting Tools 67
   Fastening Tools 67
   Filing Tools 67
   Gripping Tools 67
   Hammering Tools 67
   Levelling Tools 69
   Marking Tools 69
   Measuring Tools 69
   Pliers 69
   Prying Tools 72
   Punches 72
   Scraping Tools 72
   Screwdrivers 72
   Nailsets 72
   Sharpening Tools 72
   Smoothing Tools 74
   Turning Tools 74
   Wrenches 74
Hinges, Types of 77
   Backlap Hinge 77
   Butt Hinge 77
   Concealed Hinges 77
   Piano Hinge 78
   SOSS Hinges 78
   Strap Hinges 78
Hole Saw 78
   Using Hole Saws to Make Rings 78
   Releasing Drilled-Out Plugs 79

Joints, Identifying 81
Laminating, Safety Techniques for 81
Lathe 82
   Description and Use 82
   Tools for the Lathe 85
   Lathe Duplicator 86
   Prolonging the Life of a Lathe 86
   Shop-Made Lathe Safety Guard 86
   Shop-Made Sanding Drums for
      the Lathe 88
   Sanding with the Lathe 89
Levelling Scribe 91
Lighting for the Workshop 91
Mallet, Shop-Made 91
Marking Gauge 92
Mathematic and Geometric Formulas for
   the Woodworker 93
   Arc 93
   Cube Area 93
   Circle Area 93
   Circle Circumference 93
   Parallelogram Area 93
   Polygon Area 93
   Rectangle Area 93
   Square Area 93
   Trapezoid Area 93
   Triangle Area 94
   Dividing a Line into Equal Parts 94
   Making an Equilateral Triangle 94
   Making a Pentagon Within a Circle 94
   Making a Hexagon Within a Circle 95
   Making Octagons 95
   Making an Ellipse 95
Measuring Techniques 96
Mitre Gauge 97
   Extending a Mitre Gauge 97
   Fitting a Mitre Gauge 97
Mitres, Hand-Cutting 98
Murphy's Laws of Woodworking 102
   The Law of the Clamps 102

The Ladder Law 102
The Screw Law 102
The Law of the Nail 102
Nailing Techniques 102
   Nailing Close to the Edges 102
   Nailing in Close Quarters 103
   Nailing Guards 103
   Toenailing Techniques 104
   Nailing the Correct Way 104
Nails 105
   Past Cost of Nails 105
   Common Nails 106
   Penny System 106
Paint 106
   Paint for Shop Floors 106
   Mixing Small Amounts of Paint 107
   Paintbrushes, Cleaning 107
   Removing Paint Inexpensively 108
   Paint Rollers, Cleaning 108
   Paint Roller Trays, Cleaning 110
   Estimating the Amount of Paint 110
Paint Thinner, Recycling 111
Patterns, Transferring 112
Pegboard 112
   Placement and Installation of
      Pegboard 112
   Uses of Pegboard 113
   Securing Hooks on Pegboard 113
Pencils, How to Use 114
Planes 114
   Description and Use of Planes 114
Plastics 116
   Bending Plastics 116
   Cutting Plastics 116
   History of Plastics 116
   Safety Techniques 118
   Types of Plastics 118
Plexiglas, Welding 119
Plywood, Preventing Tear-Out in 119
Polygons 119

Pop or Blind Riveter, Description
    and Uses 121
Portable Drill 122
    Shop-Made Depth Stop 122
    Drilling Perpendicular Holes with a
        Portable Drill 122
    Making Repeat Holes with a Portable
        Drill 123
Portable Power Tools 123
    Portable Power Tools for the
        Workshop 123
    Selecting Portable Power Tools 129
Pulleys, Sizing 130
Radial Arm Saw 130
    Checking a Radial Arm Saw for
        Square 130
    Adjusting the Depth of Cut on a
        Radial Arm Saw 131
    Extension Table for the Radial
        Arm Saw 132
    Mitre Cuts 132
    Mortise-and-Tenon Jig 133
    Setting Up the Radial Arm Saw 134
    Stop Block 134
    Swinging Fence for the Radial
        Arm Saw 134
    True Crosscutting with the Radial
        Arm Saw 136
Rasp, Shop-Made 136
Refinishing, Methods 136
Rotary Tools 141
    Sears Craftsman® Rotary Tools 141
    Rotary Tool Bits 142
Router 142
    Shop-Made Cross-Grain Jig 142
    Trimming Laminates with the Router . . . 142
Rust, Preventing 142
Sanders, Safety Guard for 143
Sanding Discs 144
    Refurbishing Sanding Discs 144

Removing Sanding Discs 145
Sawdust, Removing 146
Screwdrivers, Reusing 147
Screws 147
    Countersinking Screws 147
    Driving Screws into Hardwood 148
    Driving Screws into Wood in
        Tight Spots 149
    Measuring Screws 149
    Wood-Screw Pilot Holes 150
    Selecting Screws 151
Scroll Saw, Sanding with a 151
Seat, Shop-Built 153
Sharpening 153
    Aids for Sharpening 153
    How to Sharpen Tools 155
    Maintaining Your Temper 156
Shelf Brackets, Making 156
Shelves 157
    Making Shelves 157
    Painting and Finishing Shelves 157
Shooting Board 158
Shop Cleaning 159
Sliding T Bevel 159
Solvents 162
    Safely Disposing of Solvents 162
    Properly Storing Solvents 162
Spirals, Making 163
Spokeshave 164
Spray-Painting Small Parts 164
    Method #1 164
    Method #2 166
Squaring 166
Stains 167
    Wiping and Applying Stains 167
    Water-Soluble Wood Stains 167
Stationary Power Tools, Keeping Them
    Stationary 168
Steel Square 169
    Definition of a Steel Square 169

Measuring with a Steel Square 169
Table Saw 170
Tape Measure and Inside Measurements .. 170
Thickness Planer 170
    Making a Thickness Planer Work
       Better 170
    Making Tapered Legs with a Thickness
       Planer 173
Try Square 174
Vacuum 176
    Picking Up Nails with a Vacuum 176
Veneer 176
    Cutting Veneer 176
    Working Safely with Veneer 176
Vise 178
    Framing Vise 178
    Vertical Planing Vise 178
Wheels, Shop-Made 178
Wood, Sources of 181
Wooden Balls, Shop-Made 181
Wood Filler, Applying 184

Wood Scraps, Using 184
Wood Storage 184
Woodworking Trivia 184
Workbench, Bench Hooks 185
Workmate® 186
    Enlarging the Size of the Workmate 186
    Nail Support Bin for the Workmate 189
    Tool Rack for the Workmate 189
    Workshelf for the Workmate 189
Workshop, Remodelling a 191

Glossary of Woodworking

  Terms 200
APPENDICES 209
Weights and Measures 211
Metric System 212
Index 213
Acknowledgments 223
About the Author 224

Introduction

Ingenious Shop Aids & Jigs was my first attempt at writing a book. It started out purely as a personal reference guide. I wanted to write down all of the various shortcuts that I had learned over the years and kept in a file in my workshop. It was then that I realized that maybe other woodworkers would like to make use of them as well. Thus, the book. If you have read it, I hope you had as much fun as I did when writing it.

Well, not all of my shortcuts made it into that book, mostly because I didn't have all of them written down. In fact, I'm still writing them down. *Workshop Shortcuts: Tips, Tricks, Jigs & Aids for the Woodworker* contains more useful advice.

This book, like the first, is aimed at the home woodworker. It follows the same basic format as the first one, introducing in encyclopedic fashion and high-lighting through illustrations a wide variety of information that will help woodworkers work more easily and effectively. This includes the indispensable information such as tables containing metric conversions, nail and screw sizes, and the grit sizes of different abrasives, as well as many creative approaches to solving certain problems in the workshop. There is even a glossary of woodworking terms in the back of the book that should prove helpful to novice and more experienced woodworkers.

This book also contains information on the various assortment of hand tools and portable, bench-top, and stationary power tools that I suggest you have for a well-rounded workshop, including some of the features I would look for when purchasing them. The tools that are listed are meant to be a *guideline* only. It is not necessary to go running out immediately with this one book in hand and credit card in your other to your local hardware store.

One final point: If you have some shortcuts of your own that you would like to share with our readers, please send them to me c/o Shortcuts, P.O. Box 721, Halifax, Nova Scotia, Canada, B3J 2T3. The shortcuts have to work. They will be tried out in my workshop. Acknowledgement will be given in my next book for all of those that are accepted and published.

Workshop Safety

I know that the following information might seem redundant for most home woodworkers, but based on what is reported from the emergency departments at the hospitals, it bears repeating:

1. Read and fully understand the safety instructions that come with your tools. Always wear the required safety gear and make sure that the safety gear that you have is approved. Never use a tool in a way that it was not designed for.

2. *Never* take your frustrations out in the workshop. If you are angry about something, go for a walk. Simple over-the-counter drugs can also be a safety risk if they make you drowsy or if they affect your judgment.

3. Noise and dust can be safety hazards as well, so wear approved hearing protection and dust masks. Make sure that your shop is well-ventilated to the outside.

4. Wear the proper eye protection. A number of people that I know insist that plastic lenses in eyeglasses are as safe to wear around the shop as safety glasses. I recently had an opportunity to talk to an ophthalmologist regarding this and he told me these people are wrong. First, there is no side protection to prevent flying particles from entering the corners of the eyes. Second, safety glasses are usually made of a polycarbonate plastic, which will not shatter. The lenses usually sit deeper in the frames and the frames themselves are usually heavier. So please do not go into your shop wearing *only* your plastic prescription glasses.

5. The photographs in this book show some procedures that could be potentially dangerous. Do not attempt them unless you are fully aware of the safety hazards and take the necessary steps to eliminate them. Some tools may be shown without the required safety guards in place. This is done purely to get a clear photograph and should not be construed as the normal procedure.

6. *Never* change blades or make any adjustments to your power tools with the power switch turned on or with the tool plugged in. There are some who think that turning the tool off is all that is required. Please believe me, this is not so. Your hand could slip and accidentally hit the switch. There is also the possibility of a power surge that will turn the tool on. Why take a chance? Woodworking is a lot more fun with ten fingers.

Kids in the Workshop

One of the greatest things you can do is pass on your knowledge of woodworking to your children. Encourage them to work with you in the workshop. First and foremost, teach them to respect the inherent dangers involved in the handling of all tools and other materials. Teach them to respect the tools and appreciate their usefulness and emphasize to them that adult and/or parental supervision is required (Illus. 1). With proper guidance, you'll have your child making compound mitres and dovetail joints in no time at all.

The Environment

This is a topic that I could write volumes on. Other people have, so I won't. There are many pros and cons regarding the woodworker and his/her use of our natural resources. When a craftsperson produces a fine piece of furniture with intricate details and precision joinery, I can't help but sit back in awe of the work. But another part of me wonders how long it took for the tree that was used for the

Illus. 1. Kids love to follow their parents' examples. Teach your children the proper wood-working safety techniques and maybe start them off with a tool kit like this.

project to grow, and whether it can be replaced. This is a conundrum for most of us. We hate to see destruction of our forests similar to that which is going on in Brazil and the clear-cutting that is going on in parts of North America, but we as woodworkers still love to work with wood.

There has to be an answer that will satisfy us *and* the environment. My guess is that we all have to have a lot more respect for the 150-year-old tree. Any wood that we get from that tree has to be used wisely and diligently. I'm trying to do my part. I trust you are too. Some of the ways of doing this are through the use of veneers, plywoods, and particleboard. There is a lot less waste when these products are produced. Another way is to use the product economically. Plan your project in advance, using your material sparingly. A third approach is to *never* throw away any wood that is over 12″ long. I save the sawdust and use it for compost and the small scraps of wood for kindling, but I suppose that they can be recycled too.

I think I'll get off my environmentally friendly soapbox now and move on to the **workshop shortcuts**. Enjoy!

Workshop Shortcuts

Abrasives

New Types of Adhesives

The days of sandpaper and steel wool for finishing and between-coat sanding are just about over. Enter synthetic abrasives (Illus. 2 and 3). Bear-Tex® by Norton and Scotch-Brite® by 3M are two of the brands that come to mind, but I'm sure that there are others. These materials resemble pot scrubbers and work very well as finishing abrasives. There's very little residue to worry about. They do a nice clean job, especially between finishing coats, and do not leave any rust or black spots. These synthetics are *not* designed for heavy stock removal; they are *finishing* abrasives only.

Bear-Tex consists of a nonwoven web of nylon fibres that are impregnated with an abrasive grain (either silicon carbide or aluminum oxide) and then bonded with synthetic resins. The main advantage here is that Bear-Tex may be used in either *wet* or *dry* sanding situations.

These products are available in a wide range of grades. Norton uses two grading systems. The more accurate one uses the actual mesh number and grit size impregnated into the pad. The finest grit size is 1,000 and the coarsest 40, a system not unlike normal abrasive (sandpaper) grading. Remember, though, a number 40 Bear-Tex pad will be considerably *less* abrasive than number 40 sandpaper.

The other system that Norton uses is a simplified grading system: Micro-fine (MF), Ultra-Fine (UF), Very Fine (VF), Fine (F), Medium (M), and Coarse (C).

Bear-Tex is available in ⅜″ thick sheets of various sizes. An Olfa®-type utility knife or a pair of scissors will

Illus. 2. An array of synthetic sanding pads by Norton.

12

Illus. 3. A Norton synthetic sanding pad on a random orbital sander.

easily cut the product to the size desired.

One major advantage is the fact that these products will work on a sander equipped with a hook-and-loop-type pad (not unlike Velcro®) without any modification to the machine. Another plus is that they will work well in sanders that have "through-the-pad" dust pickups.

Another type of synthetic abrasive recently introduced on the market is Durite® screen by Norton. This is a product that is primarily designed for the drywall and plaster trades for smoothing out joints. The substrate (backing) is a synthetic screen. The screen is impregnated with a 120- or 150-grit abrasive. Durite is only available in a die-cut form that fits a drywall sander. However, this happens to be about one-third of a normal sheet of sandpaper, so it will fit many orbital sanders.

The main advantage of this product is the fact that it is a screen and is therefore extremely porous. As a result, when the screen is used with a very hard abrasive, it will last about five times as long as sandpaper. Try it on your finishing sander.

Illus. 4. This screen-type abrasive called Durite® by Norton is extremely efficient when installed on a finishing sander.

Sandpaper

Description

Modern, coated abrasives (sandpaper) have a flexible or semi-rigid backing to which abrasive grains are bonded by an adhesive. The usual backings used in the manufacture of sandpaper are cloth, paper, vulcanized fibre, polyester film, or a combination. The most common abrasives being used today are zirconia alumina, ceramic aluminum oxide, aluminum oxide, silicon carbide, garnet, emery, crocus, diamond, and chrome oxide.

Grades of Sandpaper

Sandpaper may be graded in one or all of three ways. This grading system can confuse the home workshopper. The information provided in this section will help clarify this system.

The grading of a sheet of sandpaper is found on its back and has either one of two numbering systems or a word description. Table 1 presents a sampling of these systems.

The grits increase in numbers up to 1,200 and higher. Sandpaper that is 1,200 grit is considered ultra-fine. The grits also decrease down. Thirty-six-grit sandpaper is industrial-grade sandpaper.

The 0/0 numbers are called "oughts." This is an old system of rating sandpaper. For example, a fine grade of sandpaper is called eight-ought paper.

Grit Number	Description	0/0 Number
50	very coarse	1
60	very coarse	1/2–0
80	coarse	1/0
100	very coarse	2/0
120	medium	3/0
150	medium	4/0
180	medium	5/0
220	fine	6/0
240	fine	7/0
280	fine	8/0
320	very fine	9/0
400	very fine	10/0

Table 1.

Types of Sandpaper

In addition to the various grit numbers on sandpaper, there are a number of different sandpaper types, as previously mentioned. A general rule of thumb for the various grit types and their common applications is shown in Table 2.

Grit Type	General Application
Flint paper	Softwoods
Garnet paper	Soft to medium hardwoods
Aluminum oxide	Softwoods and hardwoods
Emery paper (wet or dry)	Between finish coats or on soft metals such as aluminum
Emery cloth (wet or dry)	Between finish coats or on soft metals, but mostly on soft metals.

Table 2.

Acrylic Plastics (See Plexiglas®)

Adhesives

Glue, Removing

You've just glued up a small project with white or yellow glue and discovered some seepage on the joints. Try these **shortcuts:** If the glue is fresh, some water-moistened Q-Tips® will clean it up. If the glue has been there for a half hour or so, sharpen the end of a ¼″ dowel to 45 degrees and proceed to clean it up (Illus. 5). Then, use moistened cotton swabs in warm water to wipe up the residue.

For the conventional solvent-based contact cement, there is a contact cement thinner available from LePage. A Q-Tip dipped in this will work well. If you don't have any of the solvent on hand, try nail polish remover, the nonoily type. Be sure to wipe the area clean after use.

Epoxy-type adhesives should be carefully cut away with a utility knife or a well-sharpened scraper.

Next time, before gluing up a project, adhere masking tape to the joint edges (Illus. 6). Any seepage that occurs should run onto the tape and not cause damage to the workpiece. After clamping the workpiece and after the seepage seems to have stopped, remove the tape.

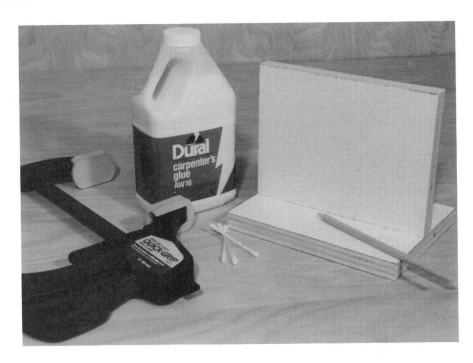

Illus. 5. A sharpened dowel and some moistened Q-Tips® will remove excess glue.

Epoxy, Mixing

The next time you are mixing up a small amount of epoxy, try this **shortcut:** Squeeze out equal amounts of the resin and the hardener into the corner of a plastic sandwich bag (Illus. 7). Mix the two together by kneading the outside of the bag. When they are thoroughly mixed, snip off the corner of the bag and squeeze out the epoxy. When you are done, simply throw out the bag. No muss, no fuss.

Illus. 6. Applying masking tape to a glue joint will prevent the glue from seeping out and staining the wood.

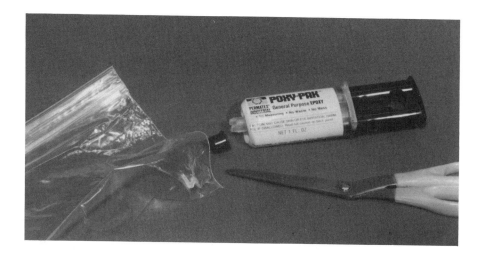

Illus. 7. Mixing epoxy in a plastic sandwich bag and snipping off the corner of the bag allows you to apply the glue without making a mess.

Proper Application of Adhesives

Properly selected and applied wood adhesives (glue) make the joint *stronger than the wood itself*. Ergo, glue-joint failure can only be attributed to improper application or selection of the glue. It is very important to read the adhesive manufacturer's directions *before* applying or, in fact, purchasing the glue.

The most frequent cause for glue-joint failure is neglecting to spread the glue on the *entire* surface of the workpiece. Many woodworkers assume that clamping will thoroughly spread the single line of glue into every nook and cranny. This is not so, and though the joint may last for a couple of years or so, moisture may eventually get into the gaps and weaken the joint to the point where it may break.

The adhesive need not be thickly applied, as this delays the adhesion time and may introduce too much moisture into the joint. Most adhesives require an application that is not much thicker than a coat of paint, as long as it is evenly spread (Illus. 8).

Illus. 8. Evenly spread glue that is the thickness of a coat of paint will ensure a strong joint.

Using the right type of adhesive for your particular work is most important. The obvious mistakes occur when one neglects to use waterproof glue for workpieces that are going to be used outside. The same thing applies if your piece is going to be used in damp areas.

Two other variables that *could* affect the adhesive's bonding strength are whether the product was subjected to freezing before you bought it, or whether the product's shelf life has expired. It's nearly impossible to determine the former, so you have to assume that the product was safely shipped. Purchasing adhesives from a busy, reputable dealer will almost assure you of a fresh product. However, if the product seems unusually thick, check it over carefully, or look for another container.

Adze

I guess the simplest way to describe an adze is that it's similar to an axe, but with the blade running crosswise. There are two types of adze, the carpenter's (Illus. 9) and

Illus. 9. The carpenter's adze.

the shipbuilder's. They both have blades 4″–5″ wide, but the shipbuilder's adze has a bit of flange on the edges. Both blades have an inward curve to make them easier to use. The blades on both are bevelled on the inside only. The adze is a very dangerous tool for the layperson, because it is kept razor-sharp. The user stands on top of the workpiece, usually a log, with his legs astride, and the adze is swung down between them. Hmmm, I wonder if Pegleg Pete built his own boat?

Aluminum, Grinding and Filing

Aluminum can make a mess out of a file or a grinding wheel. These tools are usually used to remove the burr that is left after the aluminum has been cut. The metal is soft and the shavings tend to stick in the crevasses of the files. When a grinding wheel is used, because of the heat build-up when grinding, the aluminum will accumulate and stick to the grinding wheel. When the latter happens, a good wheel dresser is required (Illus. 10). As for the files, a lot of tedious work with a wire brush is required.

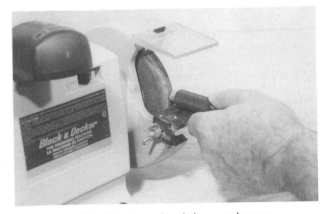

Illus. 10. The Norton wheel dresser in use.

Save your money and your time with this **shortcut:** Your local supermarket sells cans of non-stick cooking spray. A couple of squirts on your grinding wheel and your files before using will help prevent clogging (Illus. 11).

Illus. 11. Spraying your files and grinding wheel with nonstick cooking oil.

Angles, Drawing

The problem: drawing a 22.5 degree line across the face of a 2″ × 12″ board. There are two quick solutions. The first is to use the angle-cutting jigs that I described in my first book (Illus. 12). Their use here is simple. You place the jig against the edge of the workpiece and draw a line. Use a straightedge to complete the line across the full width of the board if the board is wider than the jig.

The second solution is to use your 2′, 3′, or 4′ folding rule. If you lay the rule flat on your workbench and open it scissor style, you can use the table below to determine various angles as you open or close the wedge. The figures are based on the measurement at the inside corners of the blades.

Table 3.

2′ Folding Rule
Angle/Distance

7.5°/1½″
15°/1¹⁵⁄₁₆″
20°/3¾″
22.5°/4¼″
25°/4¾″
30°/5¹¹⁄₁₆″
45°/6⅜″

3′ Folding Rule
Angle/Distance

7.5°/2½″
15°/4¾″
20°/6⅛″
22.5°/7″
25°/7⅞″
30°/9⅜″
45°/13¾″

4′ Folding Rule
Angle/Distance

7.5°/3⅛″
15°/6⅜″
20°/8″
22.5°/9⅛″
25°/10⅜″
30°/12½″
45°/18⅜″

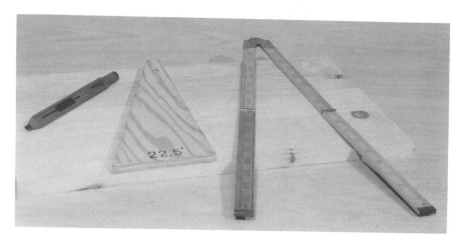

Illus. 12. Drawing a 22.5° angle on a 12″ wide board.

Band Saw

Description of a Band Saw

The band saw is an extremely versatile tool that is a necessity for a well-equipped home workshop. It can be used as a belt sander, scroll saw, and a metal-cutting tool.

There are three basic types of band saw on the market at the time of writing: the two-wheel, the three-wheel, and the tilt-head band saw. The two-wheel band saw is the conventional type that is shaped like the letter G (Illus. 13). This saw is available in either floor- or bench-mounted models. The floor, or fixed, model will have the larger throat sizes, 14″ to 16″ for example, while the bench models will have 8″, 10″, or 12″ throats.

The three-wheel models are also available as bench- or floor-mounted models and, again, the bench types will have a shorter throat depth (Illus. 14). The advantage of the three-wheel band saw is that it is a smaller and lighter machine that can provide a wider cut. The disadvantage is that the blades are more difficult to install and you have one more wheel to consider for alignment.

The tilt-head band saw is relatively new to the market (Illus. 15). The only one that I have seen is made by Sears Craftsman and is called an electronic saw. A small digital panel just below the table reveals the tilt, speed, and tension of the blade. The unique thing about the saw is that, unlike conventional band saws, the table always remains stationary. A hand crank tilts the entire blade assembly to any degree up to 45, in .05 degree increments. Because the table is stationary, a much larger table than normal is supplied. The unit that I have used has a 12″ throat.

The usual options available for band saws are a variable speed motor (to allow for the cutting of nonferrous metals and plastics), a mitre gauge, a rip fence, a work light, and table extensions. There are two cutting capacities to consider when buying a band saw. The throat width or depth is the capacity of the saw to cut a piece of material in that particular length. It is measured from inside the blade to the outer portion of the neck or frame. The most common throat width sizes are 12″ and 14″. The blade-width capacity is another consideration. The norm is ½″–¾″, but the greater the width the better. The reason for this is that the wider the blade, the more accurate the cut when you are resawing.

Selecting Band Saws

If you are planning to purchase a band saw, don't be impulsive. Make sure that the one that the salesman is pushing is, in fact, all that it is touted to be.

A number of features available on the stationary floor models that you should look for are:

Illus. 13. The Delta 14″ band saw.

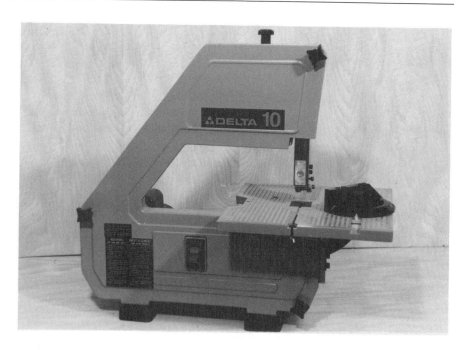

Illus. 14. The Delta three-wheel bench-top band saw.

Illus. 15. The Sears Craftsman 12″ tilting-head electronic band saw.

1. Standard-size mitre slots that the mitre gauges from other power tools will fit into.

2. An accurate table-tilting mechanism that has a positive lock or convenient hand screws.

3. Ball-bearing (sealed) blade guides.

4. Cool blocks that are easily adjustable both vertically and laterally for true blade alignment.

5. Ease of blade changing.

6. A dust-exhaust chute that is adaptable for either a built-in or a shop vacuum.

7. Adaptability either for a rip fence or including a fence, with extension rails, to allow larger pieces of stock to be cut.

8. A table light that can be switched on or off independent of the saw's motor switch.

9. A stand that is *very* sturdy, to compensate for the inherent vibration that occurs in almost all band saws.

10. Variable speed or multi-speed controls. A variable-speed band saw has a rheostat that controls the motor. A multi-speed band saw has a pulley mechanism. Variable-speed band saws are more convenient.

You may not get all of these features in one saw, so choose what you think are the most important ones and ask if the others are available as options.

Angle Jigs for the Band Saw

This **shortcut** will save you a lot of time figuring out angles and having to adjust and readjust your band-saw table when you have to make various mitre cuts. This may

Illus. 16. The angle jig.

Illus. 17. The angle jig in operation.

take a little time to do now, but the later benefits will make it worthwhile.

The jig shown in Illus. 16 and 17 is made at a 45° angle and has a tongue which is screwed and glued to the bottom so that it fits in the mitre gauge slot. It has a solid back and face. The hole is used to facilitate clamps to hold the workpiece. The strip of wood up the edge is for alignment.

Using the jig on the band saw is easy. Set your fence so that the jig just touches the blade. Place your workpiece on the jig and slide both the jig and your clamped workpiece through the blade.

Backtracking

Let's say, for example, that you are going to cut the outside of the letter U. You know that you are going to have trouble making the turn because of the width of the blade that you have in the saw. There are three ways of making the cut: making three straight cuts and then going back and nibbling at the rounded corners; cutting straight down the sides and backtracking out so you can make a straight cut across the bottom, and *then* nibbling at the rounded corners (Illus. 18); the easiest way is making your first cut straight down the side, backtracking about an inch, and slowly starting to nibble away at the rounded corner (Illus. 19). Repeat at the next turn and you have a perfect U

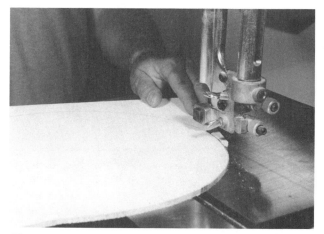

Illus. 18. This way of cutting rounded corners on a band saw is difficult.

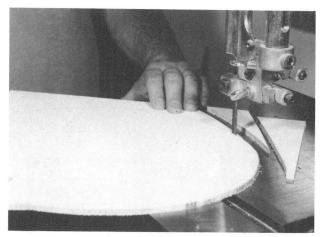

Illus. 19. The easiest and best way to saw rounded corners is to nibble away at each curve.

Backtracking out of a cut can be difficult. What usually happens is that the kerf closes up, binding the blade, and you end up pulling the moving blade out of the guide blocks. You will also move the blade off the crest of the tire and loosen the tension on the blade, probably causing it to come off the wheels altogether and, at worst, breaking the blade. So, it is best to backtrack only when necessary.

Bevel-Cutting with a Band Saw

Whenever you are making any bevel cuts on a band saw, use a fence. It does not matter if you use one that comes with the machine (Illus. 20) or if you make one out of ¾″ plywood. The important thing is that a fence should guarantee a straight and true bevel cut. Needless to say, if you

are bevelling a scroll pattern, the fence will be useless (Illus. 21).

If your tool does not have a fence, the easiest way of making a temporary one is to use a piece of straight-edged plywood clamped to your saw's table at the appropriate position.

Illus. 20. Making a bevelled cut with the fence in place.

Illus. 21. Scrolling an irregular bevelled pattern without the fence.

Rounding Band-Saw Blades

Rounding the back edges of your band-saw blades will help to make the blades cut smoother, reduce the wear on the guide blocks, and extend the life of the blades. This is easy to do. With the machine turned on, carefully apply a sharpening stone to the back edges of the blade in a rounding motion (Illus. 22). With narrower blades, slowly feed a piece of scrap wood into the blade while you are rounding them. This will prevent the blade from twisting.

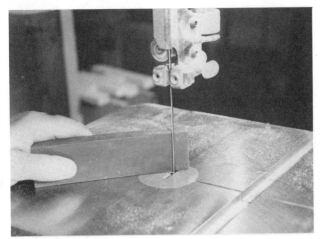

Illus. 22. Using a sharpening stone to round the back edges of a band-saw blade for smoother scrolling cuts.

Selecting Band-Saw Blades

I recently read somewhere (a catalogue, I think) about a revolutionary new type of band-saw blade that cuts circles around the others (pun intended). It's a *bi-metal* blade. A small strip of cobalt steel is welded to the spring steel of a blank band-saw blade. The teeth are then cut from the

Illus. 23. Cutting through oak is like cutting butter with a hot knife when you use a bi-metal band-saw blade.

cobalt. The width of the cobalt material is just enough to go slightly beyond the gullets of the blade.

The main advantage of this type of blade is that, like carbide-tipped circular-saw blades, it will keep its set and sharpness for many times longer than conventional blades. Because it stays sharper longer, it will run cooler and won't tend to bow as easily. Like carbide-tipped circular-saw blades, the bi-metal band-saw blade is more expensive, but is well worth it.

The bi-metal blade will also withstand much more tension than conventional ones, and, of course, more tension means a more accurate cut. If you install one of these blades on your saw, be prepared to really crank it up. I've used a bi-metal blade to easily cut through 2″ oak (Illus. 23).

These bi-metal blades are also available for portable jigsaws and reciprocal saws.

Tensioning Band-Saw Blades

A properly tensioned blade will give a more accurate cut and last longer than an improperly tensioned one. Most band saws have a scale either printed or moulded right by the blade-tensioning screw. In most cases, this scale gives

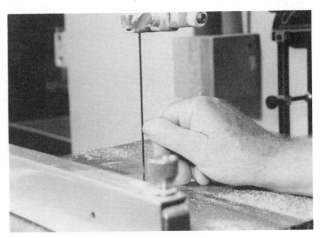

Illus. 24. Plucking the blade to hear its note for proper tensioning.

only a good general indication of the tension of the blade. A good industrial-type blade will usually take considerably much more tension than what the scale indicates.

So, if you want to ensure straight and accurate cuts without the blade wandering or following the wood grain, tighten up your blade. If, for example, you have installed a

¼″ blade, try tightening it up to the ⅜″ mark on the scale. If the blade still wanders, tighten it up a little more. When you are satisfied, pluck the *stationary* blade and listen to it's tone (Illus. 24). If you have any musical inclination, you might even be able to identify the note. If you can, write it down for that size blade and continue testing for other sizes as well.

Circle-Cutting with the Band Saw

When cutting fairly large circles with a band saw, look at your squared piece of stock carefully. If, for example, you are using softwood and there are a lot of knots in it, choose another piece. If the wood is relatively unblemished, make sure that you start your cut on about a 45° angle and into a *cross-grain* area. The reason for this is that the blade may pull slightly if the initial cut is *with* the grain.

More important, don't skimp on the material (Illus. 25). If you want to cut a 12″ diameter circle, your stock should be at least 13″ square. This will allow for a continuous cut, rather than a tight cut that will leave you with flat spots that require a later sanding.

Circle-Cutting Jig

You can make this jig in about 15 minutes, and it's easy to use (Illus. 26). A piece of ½″ or ¾″ plywood that is as wide

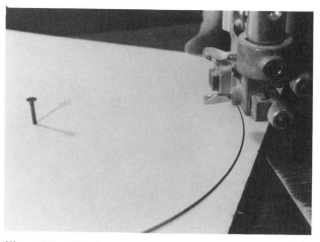

Illus. 25. Don't skimp on the stock when cutting circles on the band saw. The workpiece should be an inch or so wider than the circle diameter.

as your band-saw table is all that is required. The length of the plywood will depend on the diameter of the circle that you want to cut. For general use, I would suggest 12″–24″. This will give you a range of circles up to 4 feet.

The width of the board should be equal to your band-saw table width. Feed the board into the moving band-saw blade, being sure to hold one end flush with the inside edge of the table. Continue feeding, until the two side edges are flush with the table edges. Turn off the saw and back the board out. Using the kerf as a starting point, draw

Illus. 26. This circle-cutting jig is clamped to the band-saw table and can be used to cut a wide variety of circle sizes.

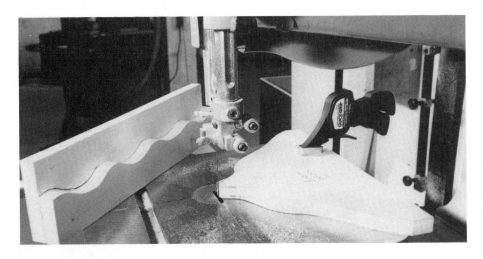

Illus. 27. The band-saw copying jig. Note that the blade just fits in the pocket of the tongue so that the jig can make an accurate duplication.

lines across the width of the board. Do these on 1″ centers. Mark the lines like so: ½, ²⁄₄, ³⁄₆, etc. The first number is the radius, the second the diameter. Draw an intersecting line the full length of the board. This line should start where the saw kerf stops.

Now, cut the circle. Start with a square piece of stock. Find the center with cross lines. These lines will line up with the lines on the jig. Drive a nail through the workpiece and into the jig. Slowly feed the jig and the workpiece into the moving saw blade, along the existing kerf. Turn off the saw. Clamp the jig to the saw's table. Turn on the saw and start to rotate the workpiece.

Cutting Compound Mitres with a Band Saw

You can use Table 4 for doing compound mitre work. For those of you who are unfamiliar with a compound mitre, let's consider the following example. Suppose you want to make a square planter and you want it to slope in from the top to the bottom by 10 degrees. Find the slope angle in the chart, set your table to the correct bevel and adjust your mitre gauge accordingly. In this case, adjust it to 80.25°. The angles will change should you want a six-sided planter, as the chart will show.

A Jig for Copying Parts

The scenario: You just bought a nightstand from a flea market, your mate is complaining that its on your side of the bed and not his/hers, and he/she wants a stand to match. The front edge of the top and the backsplash (a decorative top panel at the rear of the top surface of a cabinet or table) have all kinds of turns.

Well, you have built the carcass, drawers, gables, and the back for the new nightstand, and are now ready to build the backsplash.

The most apparent way of copying these parts is to trace them onto paper or cardboard and then transfer the pattern onto the workpieces. Well, this is fine if you don't plan on making other pieces with the same pattern, because patterns tend to get a little shabby on the edges and, furthermore, they usually end up in a drawer, folded or crumpled.

The **shortcut** solution—and I'm sure you saw this coming—is a jig, a rectangular piece of ¾″ plywood about 6″ wide by the width of the table. Shape it similar to that shown in Illus. 27. Now, make a slotted tongue with a rounded end. The more pointy the end, the more intricate the duplicating. Actually, you can make a number of these jigs with various degrees of roundness. In any event, the tips of the tongues should have a little slot in them that

| SIDES | | | |
| | 4 | 6 | 8 |
Slope	Bevel/Mitre	Bevel/Mitre	Bevel/Mitre
10°	44.25°/80.25°	29.50°/84.25°	22.00°/86.00°
20°	41.75°/71.25°	28.25°/79.00°	21.00°/82.00°
30°	37.75°/63.50°	26.00°/74.00°	19.50°/78.25°
40°	32.50°/57.25°	22.75°/69.75°	17.00°/75.00 °
50°	27.00°/52.50°	19.00°/66.25°	14.50°/72.50°
60°	21.00°/49.00°	14.50°/63.50°	11.00°/70.25°

Table 4.

equals the thickness and the width of the saw blade. The tongue with the slot fits *into* the blade and a pair of clamps holds the entire jig in position. When everything is set up and the saw blade is in its pocket, the fun begins.

Your original piece (the template) should be fastened to the *underside* of new stock, either nailed, hot-glued or taped (with double-face tape); then start your cut. The tongue will follow the template and the result will bee an almost perfect duplicate. For extremely sharp corners, a little cleanup with a sander might be required. Anyway, this is how the professionals do it.

Cutting Accurately with a Band Saw

Like many power tools that you buy, you can't just open the box the band saw comes in, and use it. The band saw is a tool that will give precision cuts if tuned and adjusted properly. Follow the manufacturer's instructions precisely when setting it up. By doing this, you will ensure that accurate cuts can be accomplished without further ado.

The simple procedure of changing a blade could have an effect on the saw's accuracy. So, there are six very important steps that you should perform after every blade change. **The following must be done with the tool unplugged:**

1. With a sharp wood chisel braced on the upper frame, check for roundness of the upper wheel (Illus. 28). Doing this will also remove any sawdust buildup on the wheel's

Illus. 28. Checking for roundness of the tires with a sharp chisel.

tire. Any unevenness may be marked and sanded down with fine sandpaper. Repeat the process for the bottom

(drive) wheel. A light sanding with 180–220-grit sandpaper should remove any sawdust or other adherents.

2. Check the new blade for any defects, especially at the welded joint. If there are any high spots or roughnesses at the weld, grind them down (Illus. 29). This will save wear and tear on the rubber tires and the guide blocks.

Illus. 29. Grinding off the welding flaws at the saw-blade joint.

3. Install the blade and adjust the tension just enough to hold the blade in place. Rotate the upper wheel to be certain that the blade is riding dead center on the tires. Adjust the upper wheel pivot accordingly. Tighten up the tension screw for the blade to the appropriate mark (Illus. 30).

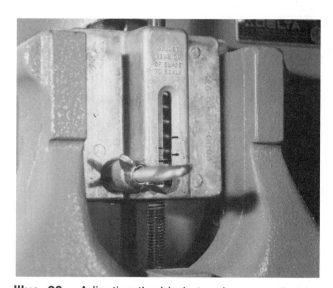

Illus. 30. Adjusting the blade tension according to the tension scale on the saw.

4. Adjust the guide blocks so that they sit *just* behind the gullets of the blade and don't make contact with the teeth (Illus. 31).

Illus. 31. The guide blocks sit *just* behind the gullets of the saw blade.

5. Adjust the bearing wheels so that they *just* touch the back of the saw blade (Illus. 32).

6. Raise the blade guide to its uppermost position. Using a try square, verify the squareness of the blade to the saw table. Adjust the table accordingly and reset the table stop if required (Illus. 33).

Flush Fence for a Band Saw

Band saws, like most other stationary power tools, have rip fences. They are either standard equipment with the tool or can be purchased as an option. Two problems commonly arise with rip fences. The first is making sure that the fence locks *square* to the blade. The second is that thin materials will slip under the fence and thus render it useless.

The first problem is easily dealt with. After you have *set* your fence, use a builder's square to make sure that it is true or square to the table.

The second problem has not been so easy to solve, until now. Cut a piece of ⅛″ thick Plexiglas® to the same size as your rip fence. (You are not restricted to Plexiglas; any *flat* material will do.) Use a fine (180-grit) sandpaper to chamfer (round off) the edges. Go to your local sign painting

Illus. 32. The bearing wheels just touch the back of the saw blade.

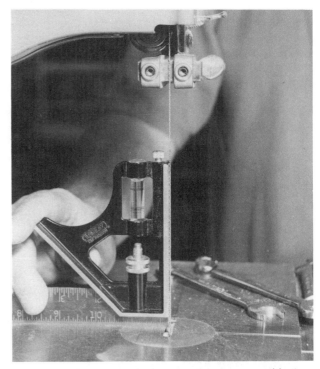

Illus. 33. The saw blade must be square with the saw table. Check this with a try square.

company and ask them for some plastic magnet material. This is the material that is used for all those refrigerator stick-on's. Use double-face tape to adhere the magnet material to the Plexiglas, and then simply let it cling to your rip fence so that it is flush with the tool's tabletop.

This addition will mean you will have to make some adjustments if you are using the rip-fence measuring scale. Use a tape measure to distance the blade to the fence.

Crosscutting Dowels with a Band Saw

The problem with crosscutting dowels on a band saw is that they have a tendency to roll with the downward motion of the saw blade. Because of this, it is hard to get a square crosscut even if you are holding it against the fence. Use the following technique: Make a V block and screw it to a strip of hardwood that will fit snugly into the tool's mitre-gauge groove. Extend the block about 2″ beyond the blade as shown in Illus. 34. I used a piece of thick Plexiglas for the mitre bar, because I had some scrap pieces lying around that just happened to fit. If everything is square, you'll get perfect cuts every time.

Guide Blocks for the Band Saw

The standard guide blocks that are usually supplied with a band saw are generally made of metal and they do show signs of wear in time. Do not throw them out. First do the obvious: Turn them around and use the other ends. When

the other ends show signs of wear, use a bench-top disc or belt sander to re-dress them (Illus. 36).

Another approach is to use Cool Blocks. Cool blocks are made from a graphite-impregnated phenolic resin material. They create a lot less heat than conventional guide blocks, so add to the life of the saw blade. The big advantage is that these blocks can be closed up tighter to the blade, and thus give greater accuracy to the saw cut.

Cool blocks have one other advantage. When you are using a blade narrower than ¼″, the blocks can be adjusted to cover *all* of the blade width without damage to it.

If you happen to live in a coastal area where there are some shipbuilders, boat builders, or shipwrights, make use of these resources to make your own cool blocks. A lot

Illus. 34.   Using the V block to crosscut dowels.

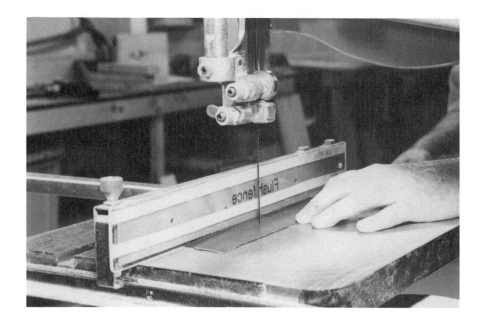

Illus. 35.   This rip-fence addition will prevent thin materials from slipping under it. This shop aid uses plastic magnet material to adhere it to the tool's fence. Note that I purposely put the lettering on the inside of the fence to leave a flush surface on the working side.

Illus. 36. Band-saw guide blocks can be redressed on a bench-top belt sander.

Illus. 37. These Cool Blocks are made from a tropical evergreen wood called lignum vitae, also known as iron wood.

of these trades use what they call "iron wood." Its proper name is ***lignum vitae***. A couple of scrap pieces of this very expensive wood is all that you need to make your own guide blocks (Illus. 37).

There are guide blocks available that are cut on a 45° angle (Illus 38). The advantage of having these on hand is that they can be installed to make cuts wider than the saw's throat. That is, if you install these blocks angled so that the teeth of the saw blade are aimed to the right, they will twist the blade to allow a workpiece to be cut that is longer than the saw throat. Caution, however, is required. Make absolutely sure that the blade guard is in its uppermost position.

Illus. 38. Angled guide blocks are available that will twist the saw blade and allow for wider stock cuts.

Making Long Crosscuts with a Band Saw

Somebody ought to impeach Mr. Murphy and repeal his laws. They always seem to come up in woodworking. For example: You have a band saw with a 14″ throat and, of course, the workpiece that you want to crosscut is 15″ or 16″ long. Well, Mr. Murphy, we have a method of solving this problem. Hold one end of the stock against the support post, line up the back of the cut line with your blade, and pivot the cut through (Illus. 39). Then trim off the waste (Illus. 40).

This shortcut is usually limited to workpieces that are from 3″ to 6″ in width. If the stock is wider, simply turn it over and repeat the procedure. This will save a lot of scrap that would normally be thrown away.

There is another method of making long crosscuts.

Illus. 39. Pivoting the workpiece to clear the band-saw post.

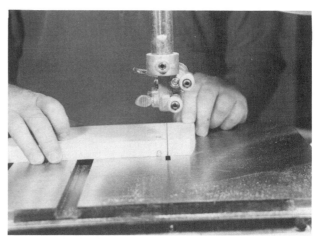

Illus. 40. After the first cut is made, trim off the excess.

Illus. 41. Twisting the work-piece to make a crosscut.

This involves a little more work, however. Raise the blade guard as high as it will go. Relieve some of the tension on the blade. Start the cut. When the blade is fully into the workpiece, back up just a little. Turn off the saw. Place the workpiece kerf into the blade and twist the workpiece so that the blade is cutting off square (to the right) (Illus. 41). The blade should follow the line. The wider the blade, the better. Without question, this method will put extra strain on the blade and the guide blocks, so don't do it too often.

Shop-Made Out-Feed Roller for a Band Saw

Usually, the table on a band saw is not wide enough for cutting or resawing long pieces of stock. Once the stock exceeds the length of the table it starts to drop off the table. Then the problems start. The part that you are feeding starts to lift and you have to control both the lift and the alignment of the cut.

The out-feed roller shown in Illus. 42 was made from an old typewriter. A hex bolt controls the height. The legs are from an old greeting card display that I scrounged from my local drugstore.

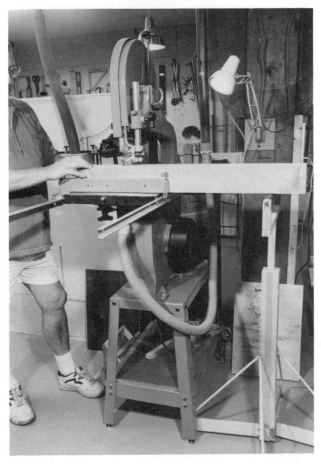

Illus. 42. This band-saw out-feed table was built from scrap hardwood and other recycled parts.

Proper Cutting Techniques with a Band Saw

Preplanning your contour cuts ahead of time should become second nature. You want to eliminate as much backtracking as possible. Backtracking long distances usually means pulling the blade out of its guide blocks at some point in the process. This means that you have to shut off the saw, pull the plug, carefully place the blade back into the blocks, turn the saw back on, and hope it is tracking

properly. The usual result is a very rough cut that requires much more sanding.

Preplanning your cut will also prevent situations in which the workpiece gets jammed between the saw column and the blade—something that happens very often.

Relief Cutting with a Band Saw

Making tight turns when cutting with a band saw is easy to do *if* the right blade is installed. There are times, however, when we get lazy and try to make cuts with a blade that is too wide. For example, you may want to cut an oval (ellipse) and know the blade that is in the saw will easily cut the sides, but will not be able to turn tight enough to cut the tops without binding. This **shortcut** will save some time, irritation, your saw guide blocks, and probably the blade: Before starting to cut the ellipse, make some relief cuts right up to the pattern line at the top and the bottom of the pattern (Illus. 43 and 44). The cuts should be at a slight

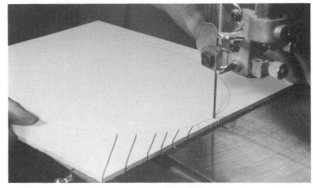

Illus. 43. Making relief cuts prior to cutting an ellipse on the band saw.

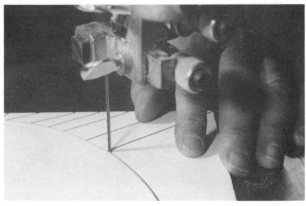

Illus. 44. Relief cuts ease the pressure on the saw and its blade.

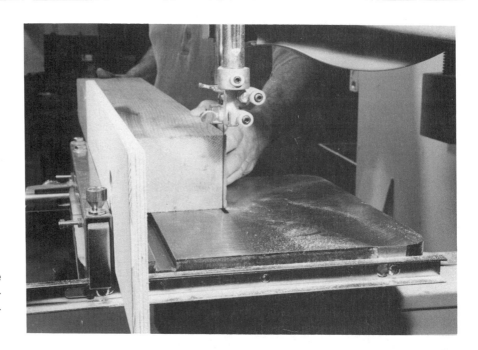

Illus. 45. Resawing a piece of cedar 4″ × 6″ with the auxiliary fence in place for additional stability.

angle to the line. The more cuts that you make, the easier it will be on the blade and the saw. Now, when making those tight turns, the scrap will just break away and ease the tension on the blade.

Resawing with a Band Saw

Resawing in woodworking terms is considered the ability to cut a 2″ × 4″ (nominal measurement) into four 2″ × 2″ pieces. This is done on the band saw. It can also be a precision technique in which woodworkers slice a piece ⅟₃₂″ wide off the surface of a 1″ × 8″ board. Needless to say, to accomplish this, both the table and the blade must be accurate and the widest blade possible for your machine is required. After you have checked the level of the table and the plumb of the blade, the next thing is to make sure that your rip fence is square to the table.

There may be times when you want to resaw a piece that is 4″ high and your rip fence is only 2″ high. This **shortcut** will help: Either use your thickness planer or have your lumberyard mill a piece of elm or maple to precisely ¾″ in thickness. Failing this, a piece of plywood will do. The stock should be 6″ wide and at least twice the length of your saw table. Affix the stock to your existing fence with nuts and recessed bolts (Illus. 45). The reason for using stock ¾″ thick is to ensure its rigidity. If the measurement scale on the rip fence is accurate, subtract the ¾″ from the indicated mark.

Commercial Rip Fence for a Band Saw

Delta makes a dedicated rip fence with rails for its superior 14″ band saw (Illus. 46). My experience with the fence is that it has proven to be extremely accurate, particularly with the fine-adjusting knob. When locked down, the fence stays true.

Illus. 46. The Delta band-saw rip fence. Note the two fence locks (the small knob at the rear top and the large knob at the front). The smaller knob in front on the right is the fine scale adjustment.

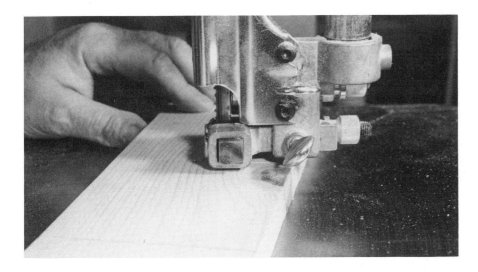

Illus. 47. The upper blade guard should be no more than ¼" above the workpiece. This will increase the accuracy of your cut and will keep your fingers away from the moving blade.

Why am I touting the Delta fence? Well, this fence will probably fit all of the Taiwanese copies of the Delta band saw on the market. A few modifications may be necessary, but it should work.

Safe and Accurate Cutting Techniques

Many woodworkers I know tend to discount the band saw as being a dangerous tool to work with. Do not be too blasé. The band saw can nip off the end of a thumb in a flash. These same woodworkers are probably the ones who have problems cutting a straight line without the blade wandering. Both problems can be solved with this rule of thumb: *Always* place the upper blade no more than ¼" above your workpiece (Illus. 47). This will not only increase the accuracy of your cut, but it will also keep your fingers away from the moving blade.

Scoring for a Straight Line

How often have we taken out the tape measure to make a mark, say 6½" on a 1″ × 4″ piece of stock? Well, we make the mark, find our try square, draw a line, and then proceed to make the cut (Illus. 48). This **shortcut** will save you from having to root around your tool box or going over to your pegboard to find the try square. Simply make your measured pencil mark at the top edge of your workpiece and advance the piece into the moving band-saw blade, just enough to score it (Illus. 49). Now, turn it up so that

Illus. 48. Measuring and marking your workpiece in the conventional way.

the scored line is on top and proceed to follow that line with your cut (Illus. 50). If your saw is properly set up, you will end up with a perfectly square end.

Illus. 49. Scoring the workpiece with the band-saw blade.

Illus. 50. Using the saw cut as a guide line for a square cut.

Bar Clamps, Gripping

The conventional 6″–12″ bar clamps usually have smooth wooden screw handles on them. The manufacturers seem to forget that when someone works with wood, sawdust is created, and that sawdust will absorb the moisture in your hands. Therefore, when you try to tighten the handles, they slip. Here are two methods that will alleviate the problem. Locktite has a product on the market called ColorGuard® (Illus. 51). This is a liquid latex type of material that can be applied by dipping or brushing. It dries in about a half an hour. At least two coats should be applied, according to the manufacturer's instructions. ColorGuard is available in half a dozen opaque colors as well as a clear application and it really works well.

Illus. 51. Color Guard® by Locktite is being applied to bar clamp handles.

The other method of improving the grip is to use an old bicycle or car inner tire tube (Illus. 52). The bicycle tire tube may, in fact, fit tightly over some of the handles without being glued. If not, cut a strip about ½″ wide off the tube. Apply some rubber cement to the handles and then wrap the strip around them.

You might want to look at some of your other wooden-handled tools and apply either one of the above methods to them.

Beam Compass

(See Compass, Beam)

Illus. 52. An old bicycle or car inner tire tube, cut into strips, is being glued to the bar clamp screw handles.

Bench Hook

(See Workbench)

Bench Top Power Tools

The following are descriptions of the more common bench-top power tools that would be found in a well-equipped home workshop, as well as some of their respective features and my recommendations. It should be mentioned here that you can use some of the power tools listed below as stationary tools simply by purchasing a stand. Your woodworking tool dealer will be able to help you select one that is suitable or you may wish to build your own.

Band Saw

The usual type of band saw for bench-top use is the compact three-wheel saw (Illus. 53). These are effective

Illus. 53. A three-wheel tabletop band saw.

tools. The biggest problem with them is changing blades. You have three wheels to put the blade around instead of just two. However, if you use spring clamps, the job will be made easier.

The major advantages of three-wheel band saws are their compactness and the relative size of their throats. These three-wheel saws usually have a 10″–14″ throat, which is as big as the throats on some of the stationary floor tools.

Choose a three-wheel band saw that has all the features of a big band saw, i.e., mitre slot, rip fence, light, etc. A multi-speed or variable-speed control would also be a nice feature. Mounting holes to secure the saw to your bench top is another advantage.

1" Belt/Disc Sander

This is a good tool to have for small sanding and fine-grinding jobs (Illus. 54). The tool is available as either a belt sander only, or for a few dollars more, it has a 4"–6" disc sander attached to it.

Illus. 55. A bench-top 4" belt/6" disc sander.

Illus. 54. A 1" belt sander. A combination belt/disc unit is also available.

When purchasing a belt/disc sander, be sure that both sanding tables are sturdy and infinitely adjustable. The disc sander table should have a standard mitre gauge slot in it. A vacuum port is also a convenience. The belt table should be sturdy and have a sliding adjustment to allow the table to get close to the belt.

4"–6" Belt/Disc Sander

These machines are usually used for heavier removal of stock than the smaller 1" tools (Illus. 55). Because they are bigger, the motor is usually of a higher amperage.

The belt unit on these machines can usually be adjusted from horizontal to vertical. This should be a smooth and easy, but positive, locking operation. The belt-tensioning release should be convenient to use and easy to operate.

Bench Grinder

This is a requisite for any serious home workshop. There are two types to be considered. The usual kind has dual wheels, one with a coarse stone and one with a medium stone (Illus. 56). Fine work is finished on a bench stone. The tool should be equipped with a light connected to the motor switch.

The second type of bench grinder—the wet/dry grinder—is my favorite (Illus. 57). The dry wheel is usually a medium-grit stone, while the wet wheel is very fine. The wet wheel is geared to travel at a slower speed and is partially immersed in water, for fine honing.

Make sure that the fences on both types of grinders are square to the wheels and that they are easily adjustable. Wheel safety shields are also desirable.

Compound Mitre Saw/ Sliding Compound Mitre Saw

The compound mitre saw will cut compound mitres. Wow, what a revelation! Seriously, folks, the compound mitre saw is not unlike the power mitre saw except that the blade and motor housing tilts left or right to at least 45°, with some tilting to 60°. All of those that I have seen have positive stops at 22½° and 45°.

The sliding compound mitre saw is similar to a small radial arm saw, but is made only for crosscutting. This tool, because of its sliding motor feature, will make cross-

Illus. 56. An example of a two-wheel bench grinder.

Illus. 57. The wet/dry bench grinder.

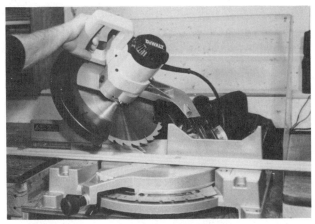

Illus. 58. The compound mitre saw usually has stops at 0°, 22.5°, and 45°. Shown here is the Side-kick, a sliding compound mitre saw by Delta.

cuts in much wider stock than a conventional power mitre saw.

Both of these machines are made for the building contractor trade and should be of sufficient quality to last the home woodworker a lifetime. Delta has a tool called the "Sidekick"® (Illus. 58 and 59). This tool is both a compound mitre saw and a sliding mitre saw.

Drill Press

The bench-top drill press is usually just a compact version of the bigger drill presses. The type of tool to select is the one with the most space between the chuck and the support column. The more speed variations it has, the more versatile the tool will be, so be sure to check this out as

Illus. 59. The Sidekick positioned to cut compound mitres.

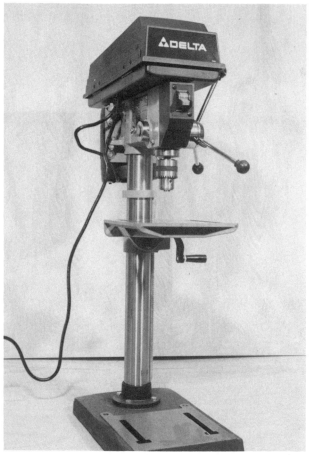

Illus. 60. A tabletop drill press with an elevation handle.

well. A hand crank for the table elevation is almost standard equipment on the newer models (Illus. 60). Some drill presses have interchangeable support columns so that the tool can be upgraded to a floor model when you are ready. The chuck capacity is an important factor. Make sure that the one you select is a chuck at least ½″, although a ⅝″ or ¾″ chuck is preferable.

Lathe

Although this tool is considered a stationary power tool, some manufacturers make compact models that can be mounted on a workbench. However, the lathe bed on these models is generally shorter. Some makers of full-sized lathes sell the machine and the leg set separately (Illus. 61).

Look for a variable-speed model with as large a faceplate-turning capacity as possible. Sturdiness and positive locking mechanisms for the tool rest and the tailstock are requisites.

Router/Shaper Table

This tool will convert your router to a shaper, moulder, and edge planer and generally make the router more versatile (Illus. 62). I suggest, however, that you have a second router to permanently mount on the table, as mounting and dismounting can be a bother. The tool to select should be a "no frills" model, but one that has a high power (amperage) rating.

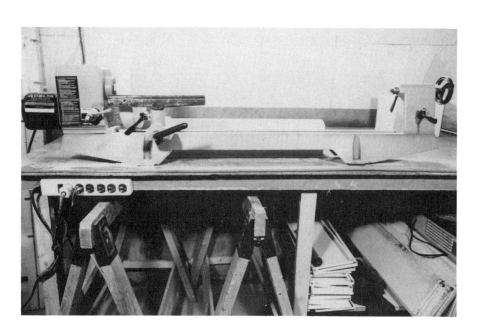

Illus. 61. This full-size lathe is bench-mounted, although a leg base is available.

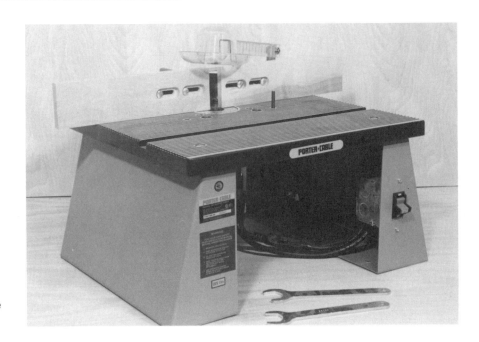

Illus. 62. The Porter-Cable router/shaper table.

The table itself should be sturdy and strong. It should have a mitre gauge or, at least, a slot to accommodate one. The fence should be fully adjustable and have separate in-feed/out-feed adjustments. A vacuum port for this tool is a necessity because the router creates a lot of sawdust and chips.

Scroll Saw

If you are into toy-making or fine detail work, this is the tool to have (Illus. 63). A scroll saw with a 16″, or deeper, throat and blade chucks that accept both the pin-type blades or the flat type would be my choice. A thick (2″ or more) cutting capacity is also desirable as is a variable-speed or, at least, a two-speed motor.

Most bench-top scroll saws have a spring-loaded arm on top. This is helpful because this moveable free arm operates a bellows that will blow your cutting line free of sawdust. A work lamp is also a nice feature. Metal stands are usually sold as an option. Do not make the common mistake that this tool is a toy and that the bargain-basement type tool will do the job. Believe me, it won't. And, it probably won't last nearly as long.

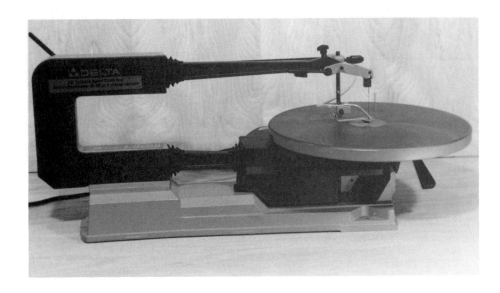

Illus. 63. A Delta variable-speed 20″ scroll saw.

Illus. 64. A typical bench-top 10″ table saw.

Table Saw

There are quite a few bench-top table saws on the market; some are even described as portable.

I would choose a 10″ blade model (Illus. 64) because its cutting capacity is far greater than the smaller 7¼″ models. A good mitre gauge is a must, as well as a positive-locking rip fence. Look for available options such as table extensions that will allow a wider ripping capacity. The mitre cutting adjustment and the height adjustment handles should operate smoothly and accurately. A dust collector port is a nice extra. Stands are an available option, but most may be clamped to a Workmate® or other temporary work surface.

Bench Vise

Normally, one would think of a bench vise as a bulky cast-iron device that is screwed to the corner of a workbench. It is not necessarily so anymore. Vermont American has what they call a Bench Vise® that you can roll out on the surface of your workbench (Illus. 65). It looks like a pad that goes underneath a carpet, and works very well. It is used primarily for holding the workpiece for routing, but it works equally well for sanding, planing and some carving.

Illus. 65. The Bench Vise by Vermont/American will hold most workpieces securely to the workbench.

Blind Riveter

(See Pop Riveter)

Bolts

According to the Random House Dictionary, a bolt is "a

Illus. 66. A selection of the various types of bolts available for the woodworker: 1, Phillips® and slot-recessed flathead bolts; 2, recessed Allen hex-head bolt; 3, eyebolt; 4, stove bolt; 5, carriage bolts with partial and full threads; 6, hex bolts of various sizes and with partial and full threads; and 7, a hex bolt and a T nut.

strong steel (or other material) rod that is usually threaded to receive a nut for fastening." Bolts come in all shapes, sizes, and thread types (Illus. 66). Bolts are used regularly and in various ways as fastening devices in woodworking. There is probably a specific type of bolt available for any application that can be thought of. Most bolts are carriage-, stove-, and hex-head bolts.

Brace

The brace is a tool that you don't often see around a workshop anymore because it is outdated, but surely some of you out there remember it and, hopefully, still use it. Usually referred to as a "brace and bit," it is a marvellous tool. With a sharp bit, extremely clean holes are accomplished. The one shown in Illus. 67, a relatively modern one, has a ratchet and a reverse gear. The ratchet allows you to get the best leverage out of the tool.

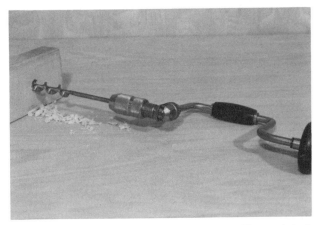

Illus. 67. The brace and bit in use. The ratchet indicates that this tool is a relatively new model.

Builder's Square

(See Steel Square)

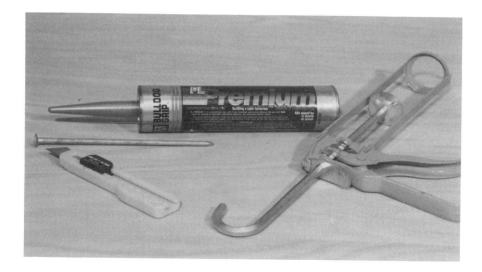

Illus. 68. A spike can be used to seal the end of a caulking tube.

Caulk

Most caulking tubes seem to have more product in them than what you need for a specific job and you end up throwing the rest away. There is a way to prevent this. The next time you are in your local hardware store, pick up a few various-sized spikes (Illus. 68). Use one that fits tightly into the nozzle of the caulk tube and push it in until you think it has gone just beyond the nozzle length. This will ensure a reusable tube the next time that you need it. Simply pull out the spike, set it to one side, and then reinstall it when you are done.

Centers, Drawing

The next time you use a compass to draw a circle on wood or plastics and you don't want to see that hole in the middle that a compass usually makes, this **shortcut** will help.

First, find your approximate center. Next, lay two or three strips of masking tape across the workpiece, to form an X. Measure to find your exact center and use the masking tape to support your compass point (Illus. 69). Because plastics scratch so easily, you may want to put five or six layers of tape down.

Chair and Table Legs, Fitting

Round, dadoed, or tapered legs for tables or chairs often become loose due to the drying of the wood and/or the glue. To repair the loose legs, most of us remove them, clean them off, and reinstall them with new adhesive. Maybe the following is a better method: Run a band-saw cut the length of the dadoed end. The kerf is usually 1/16", so drill a hole at the end of the kerf that is 1/8" in diameter (Illus. 70). The purpose of this is to relieve the kerf and deter the leg from splitting further. Before reinstalling the leg, insert a small wedge into the kerf and trim the edges flush. Leave 1/4"–1/2" sticking out on top. Add the glue and hammer the leg home. The wedge will spread the kerf when the leg is hammered all the way in.

This, by the way, is a good way of installing legs on a *new* project as well.

Chalk Line

Most people think of a chalk line as a tool that should only be in a house builder's tool box (Illus. 71). Not so. The chalk line can be used for a multitude of things in the home

Illus. 69. The several layers of masking tape on the Plexiglas® will protect it when the circles are drawn on it.

Illus. 70. A small hole drilled at the end of a saw kerf will help prevent splitting. The wedge in the kerf will ensure a tight fit.

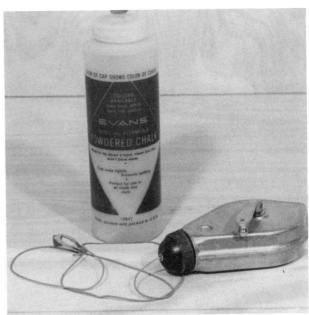

Illus. 71. A typical chalk line and a bottle of powdered chalk.

workshop. For example, the chalk line is a quick and easy way to make a line for ripping a 4′ × 8′ sheet of plywood. It will also make a clear vertical line for nailing in that first and subsequent studs against a foundation wall, and can be used on the end gables of a bookcase to give you a straight line for screwing in shelves. You don't have a plumb bob? The chalk line works just as well. And the list goes on.

Use the chalk line correctly, though. First, make sure that your measurement is accurate, and then set the hook of the line precisely so that the chalked line is on your measurement mark. Use a steel square to true the line and then pull it taut and hold it at the reel end.

Now, grasp the middle of the line and pull *straight up*. Let go and the line will snap down and leave a definitive and straight chalk mark on your workpiece. The important point to remember is to pull the cord straight up or the resulting line will be distorted.

A rainbow of powdered chalk is available so that the line will stand out on a wide range of materials. I prefer blue, as it seems to have an iridescent glow that makes it visible on almost any material. A damp cloth will wipe away any traces of the line.

Chisels, Maintaining

Some of the better manufacturers of wood chisels suggest that you put an additional 2° edge on their chisels before using them because it gives a sharper edge to the blades. Don't stop there. When you are chiselling mortises, it is imperative that all sides are flat and parallel. This can be achieved *only* if the chisel backs are also flat. Verify this by

Illus. 72. A new chisel on the right and a newly honed one on the left.

Illus. 73. As shown on the left, a new chisel may not have a flat surface. The surface on the chisel shown on the right has been honed flat.

laying the chisel blade flat on an oilstone and rubbing it a few times. The high spots will show the grinding marks. If the gaps are serious, the blade will have to be flattened. Start with a coarse stone and work up to a fine stone until all the high spots are removed.

Oh, one thing more. An often neglected area on chisels is the edges. Using the above method, check for high spots and grind them down as well.

Circular Saw

(Also see Portable Power Tools, Radial Arm Saw, and Table Saw)

Circular Saw Blades, Cleaning

Some circular-saw blades have a coating of Teflon® on them to alleviate the buildup of tar and resin. Although this does work well, a buildup still occurs.

The normal blade-cleaning maintenance using either washing soda or an oven spray cleaner is still required. However, because Teflon is involved, special care should be taken. A copper or brass brush is used on regular blades. It should not be used on Teflon. A brush of this sort will quickly remove the coating. An old plastic toothbrush is all that is required here.

Sometimes, the resin gets baked on, especially spruce gum. Do *not* be tempted to use a metal scraper. Instead, put a "blade" on the end of the plastic toothbrush. You can do this by simply using a disc or belt sander (Illus. 74).

Finding an appropriate-sized container in which to clean your circular-saw blades can be difficult. You don't want one that is too deep, and yet it should be deep enough to work with. A pizza pie pan is just the ticket (Illus. 75). Lay the blade in carefully, though; you don't want to damage or dull the teeth. An added benefit will be a clean pizza pan.

Shop-Made Cutting Guide

This shop aid will really save you some time. It will make panel cutting with your portable circular saw more accurate as well.

The cutting guide is made up of two pieces of plywood. One is ¾″ thick, 2″ wide, and 4′ long. The other is ½″ thick

and 4′ long. Its width is 2″ plus the width of the saw's soleplate. To determine this, measure the distance from

Illus. 74. Putting a blade on the end of a plastic toothbrush to scrape a Teflon-coated saw blade.

Illus. 75. A pizza-pie pan makes an ideal tray for circular-saw blades.

the inside edge of the saw blade's widest tooth to the edge of the soleplate (Illus. 76).

Screw and glue the ¾" × 2" piece along the edge of the ½" piece, making sure that it is straight and flush. That's all there is to it. The guide is clamped to your panel and the saw rides on top of the ½" piece (Illus. 77).

You can, if you wish, expand on this by making another guide that is 8′ long. This longer version can be used to rip the panel's full length.

Clamps

Long-Reaching Clamps

A couple of pieces of 2" × 2" × 14" oak or other equally hard wood can convert your pipe clamps into long-reaching C-clamps. Simply drill holes into your pieces the same diameter as the pipe clamp and slip the pieces on the pipe clamp. Glue a couple of pieces of rubber or ¼" plywood to the ends as pads and you're in business. A block of scrap wood at the back of the clamps will help equalize the pressure (Illus. 78).

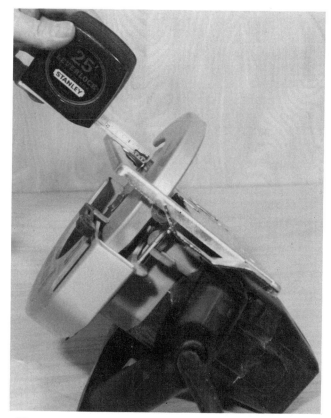

Illus. 76. Measuring the width of the saw's soleplate.

Shop-Made Rubberband Clamps

Got a bicycle that's building up a coat of rust in the back of your garage? I thought so. Remove the tires and pull off the inner tubes. Make two crosscuts, one on either side of the valve stem. Now, with a pair of *sharp* scissors, start to make a continuous cut, about an inch wide. Do this through the entire length of the tubes. You now have a handy clamp (Illus. 79).

When gluing up projects such as chair legs and rungs, wrap the rubberband clamp around the workpiece a couple of times and tie it tight. An added benefit: Take the rubber bands with you next time you go to the lumberyard. They are great for tying material to your car's roof rack.

Shop-Made Mini-Clamps

Wooden hand-screw clamps are expensive and sometimes cumbersome to use. This is especially true when working

smaller projects. Here is a way to save money and a way to make wooden mini-clamps that will work on small jobs.

Get a couple of pieces of 1" × 1" × 10" scrap hardwood. A 1" square piece, rounded on top, will serve as the rocker block. The tightening device is simply a 4" long × ¼" in diameter carriage bolt with a washer and wing nut. Drill a ¼" hole in the bottom piece. The hole should be about 6" from the front. On the top piece, make the hole ⅜" in diameter and, of course, in line with the bottom. The reason for the larger hole on top is that the carriage bolt has to have room so the top jaw will pivot. Sand all parts and slightly chamfer the edges. I made two of the clamps shown in Illus. 80 in less than an hour.

Protecting Your Workpiece from Clamps

Here's a new twist on how to protect your workpiece when gluing it up. If you or your friends are into photography, save the plastic canisters that 35mm film comes in. The plastic caps make great pads for clamps (Illus. 81). There

Illus. 77. Using the saw guide to crosscut a panel.

Illus. 78. The shop-built long-reaching clamp in use.

Illus. 79. The rubber inner tube clamp can be used when gluing up chair legs, etc.

Illus. 80. Mini wood clamps such as these are easy to build from hardwood scrap.

are a number of ways that you can apply the covers to the clamps. The easiest would be to use double-faced tape. Use the thin-foam type.

Compass Cutter

Cutting small circles accurately in veneer has been a difficult task at the best of times, until now. Olfa, a knife manufacturer, has come out with a dandy little tool that makes the job easy. The tool, as seen in Illus. 82, comes equipped with five spare blades. It will cut diameters of approximately ½″ to 6″. A pencil lead may be substituted for the blade to convert the tool to a beam compass.

Illus. 81. The canister covers that 35mm-film comes in make great protectors that prevent clamps from damaging your workpiece.

Illus. 82. This circle cutter makes it easy to cut circles in veneer.

Compasses

Types of Compasses

The compass I'm referring to here is the architect's or draftsman's compass that is used to make circles. Mind you, I've seen people go around in circles using a magnetic one. However, the circle compass has been used and abused for eons now and this astounds me.

The usual type compass will accurately draw a radius of about 3″. This is accomplished with both arms of the compass at about 15° off the vertical. I have seen woodworkers stretch this to 45° and 60° and expect to get a perfect circle. They are really surprised to see that the finish line does not meet the start line.

Some compasses are called "free arm" because they can be opened up until they are almost flat. Other types have a screw mechanism that restricts the opening to allow for an accurate circle. The free-arm types sometimes have "elbows" in them to allow for accurate stretched circles (Illus. 83), while the ones with the screw gears accept extension arms (beams) to stretch their reach (Illus. 84).

To draw an accurate circle, make sure the lead pencil point is sharp and that the pin side of the compass is close to the midpoint of the radius, that is, midpoint between the pencil point and the pin (Illus. 85). This is *very* important. If the pin is not close to vertical, it has more of a chance to slip and also it will make an eccentric circle.

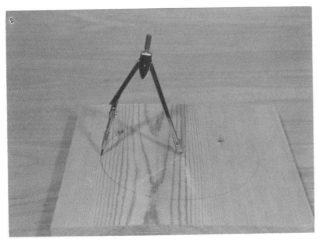

Illus. 83. The free-arm compass with the "elbow" in use.

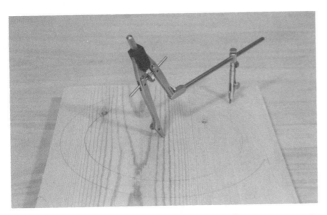

Illus. 84. The more accurate screw-type compass with an extension arm (beam).

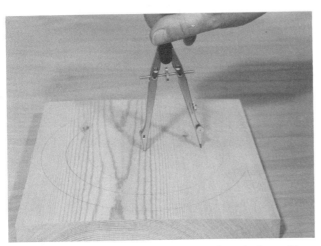

Illus. 85. The correct way of drawing circles with a compass. Note the angle of the arms.

Shop-Made Compasses

If you happen to mislay your compass and you urgently have to draw a circle, try this: Use either a hacksaw blade or a reciprocal saw blade (Illus. 86). A nail through the hole in the blade will hold it on its axis, and the blade teeth should hold your pencil. It works.

Beam Compass, Shop-Made

The shop-made beam compass in Illus. 87 is designed to draw circles from about 4″ to however big you want. The compass is limited by the length of ¼″ dowel or steel rod that you use. The design is very simple. Basically it is made of elm, or oak. The dimensions of mine are 1½″ × 1½″ × 3″. A draftsman's mechanical pencil fits in one end, a Gyproc® screw in the other. Carriage bolts,

Illus. 86. A hacksaw or reciprocal saw blade will work well as an emergency circle compass.

Illus. 87. A shop-made beam compass is perfect for drawing large circles.

washers, and wing nuts serve as the clamps for the beam dowel. The holes for the dowel are ¼″ in diameter or whatever size is best for you.

To store the compass on a pegboard, I just use a 6″ piece of dowel to keep the pieces together.

Coping Saw Jig, Shop-Made

The shop-built coping saw jig shown in Illus. 88 and 89 is easy to make and an indispensable tool if you are doing any fretsaw work.

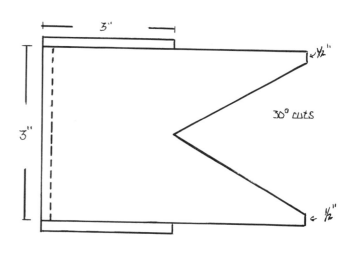

Plan

Illus. 88. The coping saw jig in use.

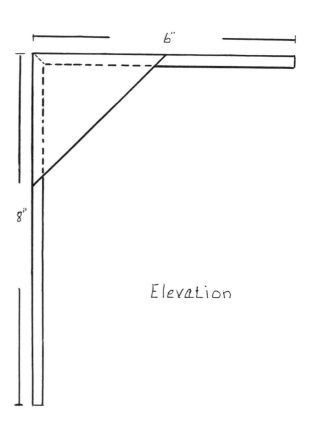

Elevation

Illus. 89. How the coping saw jig is constructed.

Depth Gauge

The depth gauge shown in Illus. 90 is made by Veritas and is available through mail-order houses in the United States and Canada. It's a dandy little tool that is divided into one-eighth of an inch on one side and into one-fourth of an inch on the other. Veritas calls it a "saw setting gauge." The tool can be used for setting the depth of cut on your radial-arm saw, table saw, router, and drill press. It's a real timesaver and is extremely accurate.

Illus. 90. The Veritas Saw-Setting Gauge being used to set the depth of a drill bit.

Illus. 91. Using a steam iron will swell the dented area and make dimples disappear.

Doors, Installing

Installing the striker plate when hanging doors has always been a little difficult, until now. Next time you are hanging doors, be they cabinet or entry doors, try this: After the doors are hung, rub a little lipstick on the latch and close the door. The lipstick mark will transfer onto the frame and indicate *exactly* where to place the striker plate (Illus. 92). In the event that you don't have lipstick, you might try chalk-line powder or tape a piece of pencil carbon paper to the latch. Double-faced tape will work best.

Dimples, Removing

Trust me, this **shortcut** has nothing to do with cosmetics or facials. The type of dimples that I am referring to are the ones that are inadvertently made by the slip of a hammer or the dropping of some heavy object on your workpiece.

There are two methods for removing these dimples. The first is to place a wet rag on top of the dent and let it stay there for a few hours. If that doesn't work, try using a steam iron (Illus. 91). Apply lots of steam and heat, but be careful that you do not scorch the wood.

Both of these methods should work, but they will *raise* the grain on the wood. After the area has dried out, a little sanding with a very fine-grit sandpaper will bring it back.

Illus. 92. A little lipstick on the door latch will tell you where to position the striker plate.

Dowel Joints

The Scandinavians are big exporters of knockdown furniture. As a result, the joint connectors in their furniture have to be easy to assemble and secure. Here is a variation of one of the butt joints that they use, but without the expensive metal hardware. Half-inch dowels are positioned 1" in from the ends on the horizontal members. Two holes are drilled into the vertical pieces. Pilot holes are drilled through and into the dowels. The screws must be long enough to go through the dowel. The end result is a *very* secure wood joint (Illus. 93). For added strength, a little glue will help.

Dowels, Hiding

When using dowels to make right-angle joints, it is sometimes difficult to match the wood of your workpiece. Commercially bought dowels are usually made of birch or some other light-colored hardwood.

Try the following the next time this problem arises: When installing the commercial dowel, set it ¼" to ½" below the surface of your workpiece (Illus. 94). Use a plug cutter of the appropriate size to cut plugs out of your project's scrap wood and carefully install a plug on top of the dowel (Illus. 95). Be sure, though, that the grain is running in the same direction.

Illus. 93. This modified dowel joint is very tight.

Illus. 95. Installing a matching plug cut from scrap.

Illus. 94. Setting a commercially made dowel ¼" below the surface of your workpiece.

Drawer Handle Jigs

Method #1

It's an old story. You are putting handles on that twelve-drawer dresser that you just built and you realize that measuring, drawing lines, and punching starter holes on each and every drawer is a very tedious job. Try this **shortcut**: Cut a piece of polystyrene, available through a plastics wholesaler, to the exact size of your drawer. Measure and place marks on the polystyrene and then drill the

Illus. 96. Using the drawer handle jig to mark the positions of the holes for drilling.

required-size holes in it. Tape this template to the drawer and drill away (Illus. 96).

Method #2

The above drawer handle jig will work if all the drawers are the same size and the handle positions are in the same place on each drawer. If this is not the case, however, try this template: Again using polystyrene, cut a piece that is 12″ wide × the height of your highest drawer. Find the middle of the plastic and draw a line from top to bottom. Now, find the spacings of the drawer handles. If all the handles are going to be 1″ down from the drawer top, for example, drill holes in the plastic accordingly. If some are going to be centered, repeat the above procedure.

I drilled holes on ½″ centers so that the jig can be used on almost any drawer face using the standard 3″ handle spacings (Illus. 97). Now all I have to do is line up the centerline with the drawer, make my mark with an awl, and proceed to drill the holes.

Drill Bits

Sharpening Drill Bits

Here's an easy way to sharpen your high-speed-steel (HSS) bit or almost any drill bit. Use a cone-shaped sharpening stone that is available for the Sears or the Dremmel rotary tool. The stone-tipped bit fits nicely into the drill bit to give it a sharp cutting edge (Illus. 98). The grindstone bit will also fit into the chuck of a portable electric drill or a drill press.

These sharpening stones are available in various sizes to fit most drill bits. Extreme care should be taken to prevent overheating and loss of temper on the bits.

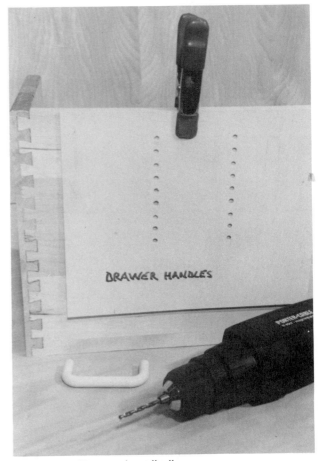

Illus. 97. Drawer handle jig.

Illus. 98. A cone-shaped sharpening stone can be used on a rotary tool, electric drill, or drill press to keep your drill bits sharp.

Truing Drill Bits

The tip of a high-speed-steel drill bit is set at a particular angle for the most efficient cutting. Sometimes after sharpening, whether you do it yourself or have it done professionally, you may want to verify the angle. The following **shortcut** will make it simple:

Go to your parts bins and pick out a couple of hex nuts, place them side by side, and hold them with either a pair of slip-joint pliers or a pair of Vise-grips®. The tip of the bit should fit between the two nuts without any visible air space (Illus. 99).

Illus. 99. This high-speed-steel drill bit is being trued with a couple of hex nuts.

Drilling Techniques

Drilling Around Corners

Nope, this is not a fantasy. Vermont American has a drill bit that can actually drill around corners (Illus. 100). At first glance, it looks like a spade bit. However, its rounded edges actually allow it to be maneuvered in almost any direction while in use. I think this bit would be particularly useful for drilling wiring holes in studs or joists. It's very aggressive, so it works very well in softwoods.

Illus. 100. The Around The Corner drill bit by Vermont/American will twist and bend its way easily through studs and joists.

Drilling Holes in Tight Spots

Trying to get your portable drill into areas that are just too small for a drill to fit into can be a problem. There are actually two solutions to this problem. The first involves using the adjustable chuck on socket wrenches that is similar to the chucks found on electric drills. Fit your drill bit into the chuck and use the wrench to drill the hole (Illus. 101).

The other solution also involves a socket wrench. There are drill bits available that fit into cordless screwdrivers. These drill bits have the standard five-sided shank on them. These five-sided shanks fit nicely into a ¼" socket. The socket wrench can now be used as a drill to get into those tight spots.

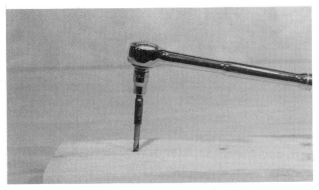

Illus. 101. You can fit a drill bit made for a cordless screwdriver into a ¼" socket to turn your socket wrench into a drill.

Drill Press

Angle Jigs for the Drill Press

Drilling a 30° hole in a small workpiece takes a lot of time, especially when you have an auxiliary table attached to your drill press. A lot of us lazy people look at what's involved and then resort to the portable drill and hope for the best. Here's an easier way: Build yourself a set of ramps, six in all (Illus. 102). Build them at 15°, 20°, 22.5°, 25°, 30°, and 45°. Drill holes in them and hang them up on a pegboard located near your drill press. You'll find that this will be a real timesaver for those angled holes.

Tightening Bits in a Drill Press

After removing a drill bit from your drill press, if you notice some scraping of the bit shank take another look at how you installed the bit. This scraping of the shank is usually caused by a loose chuck; the bit is losing its grip. To prevent this, make it a habit to tighten *all three* holes in the drill chuck (Illus. 103).

Illus. 102. A set of six angled shop-made jigs for use on the drill press and other stationary tools.

Illus. 103. Tightening all three holes in the chuck will prevent scraping and slipping of the drill bit.

Illus. 104. This method will make drilling into spheres easy and accurate.

Drilling into Spheres with a Drill Press

Wooden balls or spheres are used a lot in toy-making and don't usually come predrilled. To drill them precisely through the middle can be very frustrating and wasteful. Here's a **shortcut** that works for me: Let's say you have a 2″ diameter wooden ball that you want to drill through. Clamp a scrap of 2″ thick stock to your drill-press table and, using a Forstner or a spade bit, drill a 1″ hole through the stock. Remove the bit, but do not move the stock or reset the drill press. Now, install the desired size of drill bit into the chuck, place the ball in the hole, and drill. By preventing movement of the scrap piece, you are assured of drilling into the middle of the sphere (Illus. 104).

Drill Press as a Lathe

In my first book, *Ingenious Shop Aids & Jigs*, I described the use of a drill press as a lathe for simpler jobs where an actual lathe was not available. Recently, after reading the book, a friend of mine made these suggestions. Using ½″ × 3″ hardwood stock, cut an L shape with a tail on it. The tail is for firmly clamping the piece to the drill-press table. A wedge is glued and screwed to the upright for stability, and the upright may be used as a tool rest. The base of the L-shaped piece becomes the lathe *tailstock*. Holes are centered on the base to accommodate pointed dowel markers. The headstock is an appropriate-sized Forstner drill bit (Illus. 105).

The three important things to be done here are to make sure that the middle of the stock is turned, the tailstock is regularly oiled, and the drill press is operated at a slow speed. *Extreme care* should be used during this operation and all safety measures should be adhered to.

Setting Angles on a Drill Press Table

The drill press angle jigs described on page 55 can also be used to set the angle of your drill-press table if you prefer.

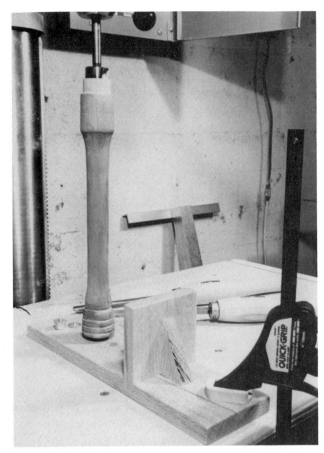

Illus. 105. With this method, a drill press can be used as a lathe for smaller workpieces.

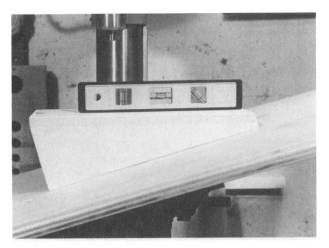

Illus. 106. Adjusting the drill-press table to the desired angle using an angle jig and a level.

The method is simple. Loosen the adjustment screws on the table, set a level on the required angle jig so that it is horizontal, and tighten up the screws (Illus. 106).

Raising the Table on a Drill Press

So many times, I have seen woodworkers struggling with the hand crank to raise the drill-press table to the desired height. The drill press that they own is probably 5–10 years old. I have my doubts that these guys or gals have ever cleaned the rack and pinion. The sawdust just piles up in the gears and the hand crank gets stiffer and stiffer to use.

To prevent this, every so often take a stiff brush and clean out the rack (Illus. 107). Add a little white grease to it and some oil to the hand crank. You will be amazed at the difference.

Illus. 107. Cleaning and lubricating the rack-and-pinion gears on your drill-press table elevator on a regular basis will make it a lot easier to raise the table.

Dust

(Also see Sawdust)

In my first book, I mentioned the hazards of sawdust and the fact that the dust from some species of wood can be toxic. What I did not mention, however, are the other perils. A sawdust-filled workshop can be highly flammable. Dust that is floating in the air can be easily ignited by a spark or a flame. ***Do not*** smoke or allow any open flames in your workshop.

Leaving sawdust on the shop floor is like putting powdered wax on a dance floor. It makes it very slippery. A fall on a dance floor is embarrassing. A fall on your shop floor could be fatal. I vacuum my workshop at least once a week and I recommend you do the same (Illus. 108).

Illus. 108. Cleaning your shop at least once a week will remove hazards like slippery floors and combustible sawdust.

Edging

(See Shelves)

Electric Drill

(See Drill Press and Portable Drill)

Files, Cleaning

Files and rasps tend to accumulate the materials that you have tried to grind away. The materials seem to build up in the crevasses of the tool. The biggest culprit is aluminum. For some reason, aluminum builds up quite readily in a file and soon renders the file useless. Until now.

Laying the file(s) in a warm solution of water and lye will quite quickly melt and eject any traces of aluminum. *Be very careful when using lye. Wear thick rubber gloves, face and eye protection, and follow all safety instructions for use. This is very caustic material.* If you spill any lye, immediately dilute it with water.

After cleaning the file or rasp, rinse it well in cold water, wipe it dry, and then coat the tool with a light oil.

Files and Rasps, Making Handles for

Most files and rasps when purchased do *not* have a wooden handle attached; they come with a pointed tang that is hard to grip. Most woodworkers will turn their own wooden handles on their lathe, and then drill out for the tang and make a slice (kerf) across the end. This is done so that some sort of binding can be wrapped around the end to tightly secure the file on the handle. Ferules can serve as this binding. Ferules can be found at your local plumbing supply store. Ask for copper pipe end caps. These can be drilled and filed to fit the tang and then force-fitted over the end of the turned handle (Illus. 110).

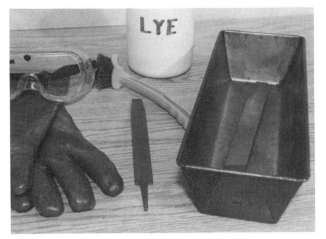

Illus. 109. Soaking your files and rasps in a lye solution will remove aluminum shaving buildup.

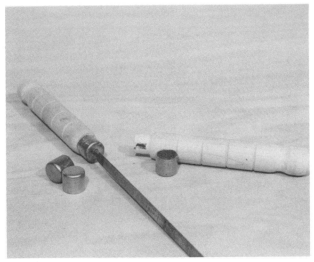

Illus. 110. Copper pipe-end caps make great ferrules for shop-made file or rasp handles.

Filters, Disposable

Don't throw away that paper dust mask just yet; it can be reused. Simply vacuum the outside surface and then use it for filtering paint thinners or other lightweight liquids (Illus. 111). If the dust mask remains clean and the product it was used to filter was clear, the dust mask can be reused as a filter.

Illus. 111. A paper dust mask makes a great filter for paint thinners, etc.

Flooring in the Workshop

The times, they are a-changing. Just when I thought that an epoxy paint was the best way to paint over bare concrete on a shop floor, along comes new technology. Enter an environmentally friendly, water-soluble varathane-(poly-urethane-) type floor paint. Flecto has come out with a "diamond" finish floor paint that is available in many different colors.

Recently, I expanded my workshop to almost three times its original size. I tried the new product for myself, and was impressed (Illus. 112). Not only does it go on easily, but you can walk on it in about an hour.

I particularly liked the fact that this paint can be cleaned up easily with water and does not emit any fumes. Oh, there is an odor, but it is nontoxic and nonintrusive.

Illus. 112. My new expanded workshop with the concrete floor painted with the Flecto Diamond® finish paint.

Foam, Cutting

Cutting the rigid types of foam, such as Truefoam® or Styrofoam® (Illus. 113 and 114), or the types of foams that you find in chair seats, can be done easily. Both types can be easily cut on a band saw. Most types of band-saw blades will work. The exception would be a skip-tooth blade, which will give a rougher cut. The best blades to use are the ones with the most teeth per inch. And, of course, the tighter the scroll pattern, the narrower the blade that is used.

In my first book, I mentioned that freezing the rubbery type of foam overnight will make for a cleaner cut. Another method for cutting foam, although I haven't tried it, is to use an electric carving knife. People have told me that it works just fine on larger radii patterns and straight cuts.

The ideal way of cutting foam is with a hot wire. This is the way the professionals do it, but the setup is specialized.

Illus. 113. Cutting rigid foam on a band saw.

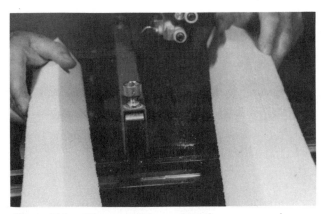

Illus. 114. The result is a smooth, square edge.

Folding Rule, Description

(Also see Angles)

The folding rule is available in 2′, 3′, 4′ and 6′ lengths. Through a combination of hinges, this rule folds up into a very compact and versatile tool. When folded, it fits neatly into your tool pocket or belt. When purchasing a folding rule, make absolutely sure that the blades are true and that the fittings are smooth and tight.

Illus. 115. A 3′ folding rule is extremely useful to have around the home workshop.

There are a number of different types of folding rules available. Some have sliding inserts in them, much like a slide rule, to help in making inside measurements.

The folding rule can be used as a protractor to deter-

mine various angles, as a straightedge for levelling or drawing, and as a very accurate device. No well-equipped workshop should be without one.

Framing Clamps, Shop-Made

Four blocks of hardwood scraps such as elm or oak and some hooks are virtually all that is needed to make the framing clamps shown in Illus. 116. After they are made and the hooks are in place, go out to your car roof rack or into your camping gear and pick out one long or four equal-sized bungee cords. If using four equal-sized pieces of cord, connect each piece to a hook and attach the hook to one of the blocks of hardwood. There you have it.

Illus. 116. The bungee cords from your camping gear can be used to make these framing clamps.

Framing Nailer, Shop-Made

The toughest part of making frames is assembling them. You have to have something solid and secure in which to brace the mitred joints so you can drive in the nails without the pieces moving. The shop-made jig in Illus. 117 will solve this problem.

The back panel of the jig is made of ¾″ plywood and the frame holder is two triangles of the same material.

Illus. 117. This framing jig is shop-made and keeps mitred joints secure for nailing.

These pieces are laminated (glued) together to make one triangle 1½″ thick. The clamp is 1″ thick × 1¼″ wide elm or maple. When the triangles are glued and screwed into position, dado out a 1″ wide slot to hold the clamp. The length of the clamp will depend on the size of the frame holder. A ¾″ × 1″ strip of plywood is glued and screwed to the backside for horizontal clamping. The clamp bar is drilled and held in place with a fully threaded carriage bolt, washer, and wing nut. For additional grip, try adhering a strip of 180-grit sandpaper to the under portion of the clamp.

Framing Square

(See Steel Square)

Framing Vise

(See Vise, Framing)

Fret Saw

(See Coping Saw)

Geometry

(Also see Mathematics)

No, we are not going back to school. This is just a reference for some of the geometry terms that you may have forgotten and that you may find useful while working in your workshop. Illus. 118 shows the various shapes of rectangles. Illus. 119 shows the various shapes of triangles.

Glue

(See Adhesives)

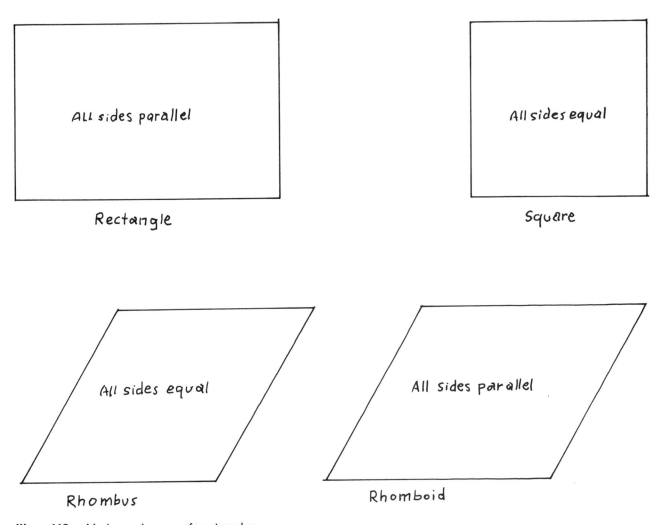

Illus. 118. Various shapes of rectangles.

Handsaw

Shop-Made Handsaw

Often, I have required the use of a small, fine-toothed saw to clean out cuts that are in tight locations. A hacksaw blade would sometimes suffice, but then I thought of using a jigsaw blade. I started with a ¾″ dowel for the handle and cut a slot in the end with the band saw. I then drilled two small holes on the blade like the ones on the tail of the jigsaw blades. I flared the holes with a countersink and put them into the slot. I installed the blade with a couple of ⅝″ #4 wood screws (Illus. 120).

Japanese Handsaw

The Japanese handsaw, usually referred to as a *Dozuki* saw, is much different from the traditional back or tenon saw. In the traditional saws, the teeth are *set* in a crosscut configuration and are meant to cut on the push stroke. Because of the pushing action, the blades must be very rigid, and therefore must be thick.

The Dozuki saw, on the other hand, has teeth that are set to cut on the pull stroke. This results in a more accurate cut. Also, because of the pulling action, thinner steel is required, resulting in a narrower kerf. The finer steel allows for the finer cutting of the teeth. The traditional Dozuki saw has 22 to 26 teeth per inch (tpi).

Olfa, a name usually associated with utility knives, has

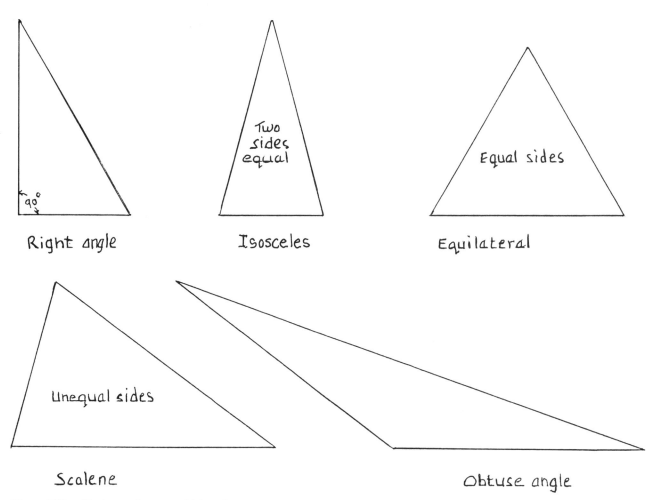

Illus. 119. Various shapes of triangles.

a Dozuki saw that is extremely easy to use and is very well balanced (Illus. 121). The saw comes with a spare blade. The blades are made of tool-quality carbon steel and have 26 tpi.

Although the blades are meant to be thrown away, don't. By themselves, they can be used as scrapers or glue spreaders.

Hand Tools

The following is a list of hand tools that I suggest you acquire for the basic needs of a home workshop. These hand tools, as opposed to portable power tools, require physical force to use. Later on in the book, I list the portable power tools that should be used in a basic home workshop. The tools have been grouped into what I think are logical categories, such as cutting tools, fastening tools, etc.

As I mentioned in the Introduction, you don't have to run right out and spend to the limit on your credit card. Wait for the sales and buy a tool when you need it.

Clamping Tools

You will *never* have enough clamping tools (Illus. 122). There is always a need for that one more clamping device. Keep the following assortment of clamping tools on hand in the workshop: bar clamps (6″, 12″, and 4′); a normal C-clamp; a deep C-clamp; a ½″ pipe clamp; various sizes of spring clamps; clothespins; and spring-type paper clips.

Illus. 120. This shop-made mini handsaw is great for getting into tight spots.

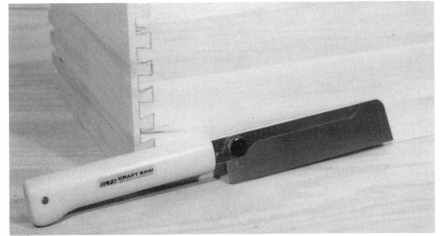

Illus. 121. The Olfa® Dozuki saw makes extremely fine mortise and tenon cuts.

Illus. 122. Some of the clamps that are most useful in the workshop: 1, A 6″ Quick-Grip® bar clamp; 2, a Vise-grip® hand clamp; 3, a mini C-clamp; 4, spring clamps; 5, a bar clamp; 6, a deep C-clamp; 7, a regular C-clamp; 8, a clothespin; 9, a paper clip; 10, a small Quick-Grip clamp; and 11, an Alligator® clamp.

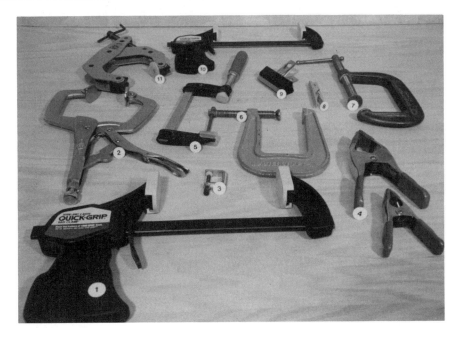

Illus. 123. A set of Stanley wood chisels on the left and a set of steel (cold) chisels on the right.

Illus. 124. A variety of the types of cutting tools that you might consider for your workshop: 1, a keyhole saw; 2, a Dozuki saw; 3, a utility knife; 4, a coping or fretsaw; 5, a hacksaw; 6, a back or mitre saw; 7, a crosscut saw; and 8, a ripsaw.

Chisels

Keep a good set of five wood chisels in sizes of ¼″, ⅜″, ½″, ¾″, and 1″, and two or three steel chisels in the workshop (Illus. 123).

Cutting Tools

Every woodshop has to have cutting tools. These range from a utility knife to a hacksaw. Illus. 124 shows the variety of cutting tools that will be found in a well-stocked workshop.

Fastening Tools

Fastening tools (Illus. 125) that are usually found in a well-equipped home workshop include staple guns for attaching mounts and backs to picture frames, a "Pop" or "Blind" riveter used for fastening a wide variety of thin materials, and powered nail guns that will drive hardened steel nails into concrete, brick, etc.

Filing Tools

Files and rasps are used in the workshop for working with wood, plastic, and metal materials (Illus. 126). The rasp is used to remove greater amounts, while the files are used for finer details (#2 in Illus. 126). Relatively new to the marketplace is a rasp-like tool that fits on a hacksaw. The blades for this tool range from coarse to fine and are flat or curved. They are extremely efficient.

Gripping Tools

There is nothing like Vise-Grips® (Illus. 127) for removing that rusted nut or a stripped screw. I consider them a **must** in the shop.

Hammering Tools

To drive a nail, you usually need a hammer. With the wide variety of nails and other fastening devices available, different types of hammers are required. These hammers are shown in Illus. 128.

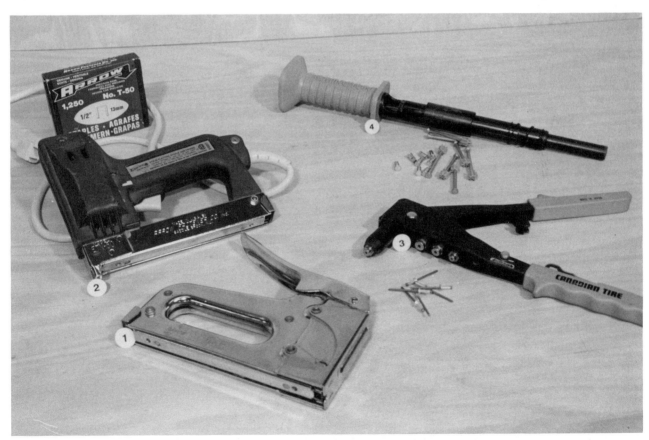

Illus. 125. Some of the fastening tools that will prove useful in the home workshop: 1, a manual staple gun; 2, an electric staple gun; 3, a pop riveter; and 4, a nail gun.

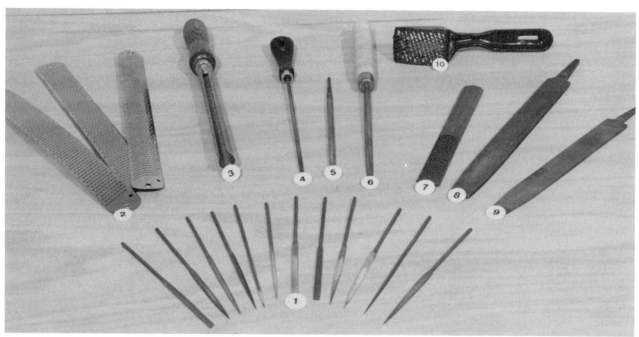

Illus. 126. Some recommended files and rasps: 1, a set of needle files for fine detail work; 2, hacksaw rasps; 3, a round foil rasp; 4, a rat-tail file; 5, a diamond (triangular) file; 6, a coarse rat-tail file; 7, a combination rasp; 8, a fine bastard-cut file; 9, a coarse bastard-cut file; and 10, a softwood shaper.

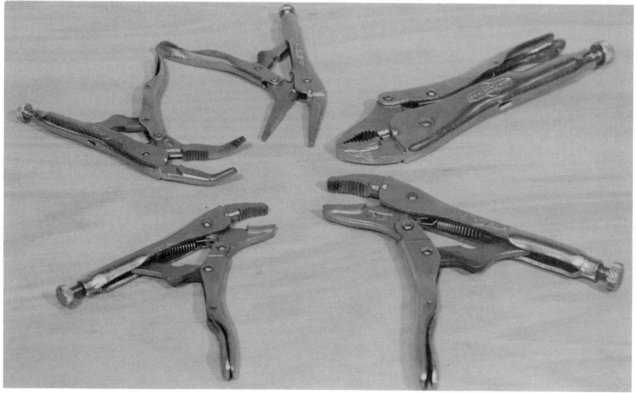

Illus. 127. Various sizes and types of Vise Grips®.

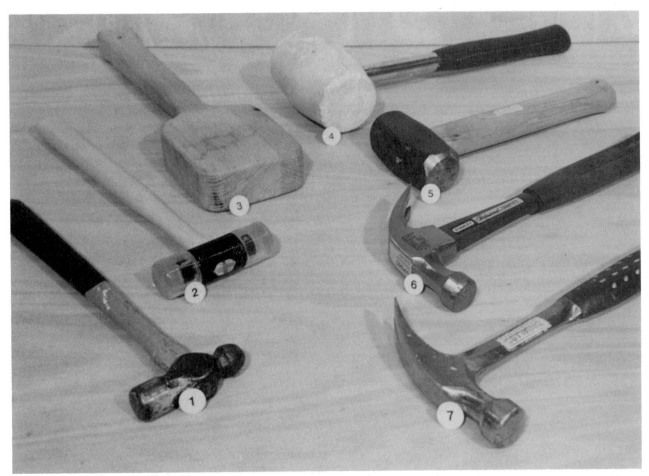

Illus. 128. A variety of hammers that will prove useful in the workshop: 1, a ball-peen hammer; 2, a plastic-head mallet; 3, a shop-made mallet; 4, a rubber mallet; 5, a 2½-pound sledgehammer; 6, a carpenter's nailing hammer; and 7, a framing hammer.

Levelling Tools

Levels (Illus. 129) are used to determine that surfaces are straight, to adjust a saw table, and to make sure that things are plumb (vertical). No home workshop should be without one or two. An electronic digital level is available. This Smartlevel® (#6 in Illus. 129) simulates a bubble, gives degrees of angle, supplies the rise per foot, and will read horizontally, vertically, or upside down.

Marking Tools

A sharp pencil is not the only marking device required in a workshop, because a pencil may not leave a contrasting mark on some materials, for example, plastics. An overhead projection (water-soluble) marker should be used here. On dark woods, a scratch line is probably more desirable. Illus. 130 shows marking tools that will prove helpful in the workshop.

Measuring Tools

Measuring tools are an absolute requirement for any home workshop (Illus. 131). The types may vary, depending on the kinds of work that you are doing.

Pliers

Pliers and tools that function like pliers are indispensable in the workshop. They can be used for pulling, gripping, installing, and for cutting off nails, to name just a few instances.

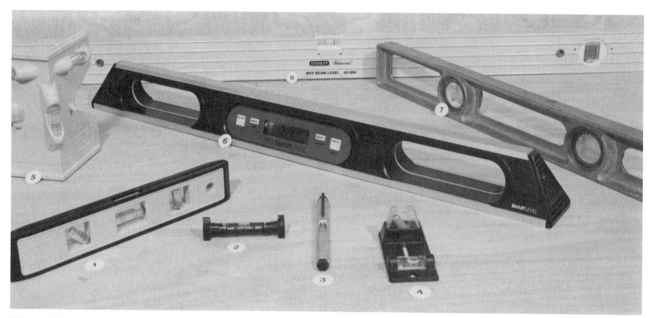

Illus. 129. Some or all of these levels should be in your home workshop: 1, a torpedo level; 2, a line level; 3, a pocket level; 4, a stud finder/level; 5, a fence post and stud level; 6, the electronic Smartlevel®; 7, a 30″ contractor's level; and 8, a 36″ box beam level by Stanley.

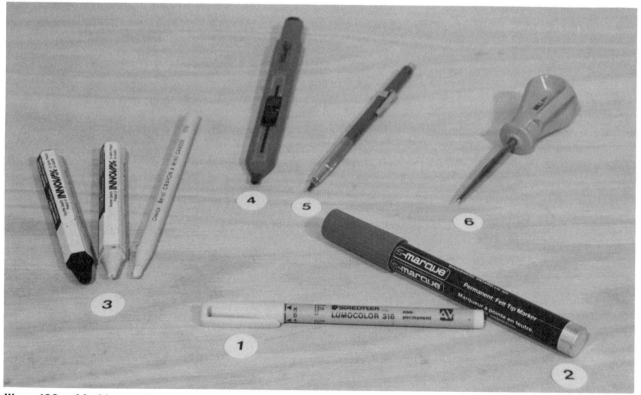

Illus. 130. Marking tools: 1, a water-soluble marker; 2, a felt-tip marker; 3, wax lumber crayons; 4, a retractable carpenter's pencil; 5, a draftsman's pencil; and 6, a scratch awl.

Illus. 131. Some of the measuring devices that are regularly used: 1, the steel square; 2, a sliding bevel; 3, calipers; 4, a try square; 5, marking calipers; 6, a folding rule; 7, a draftsman's protractor; 8, a thickness gauge; 9, an adjustable square; 10, an angle finder; 11, a tape measure; and 12, a yardstick.

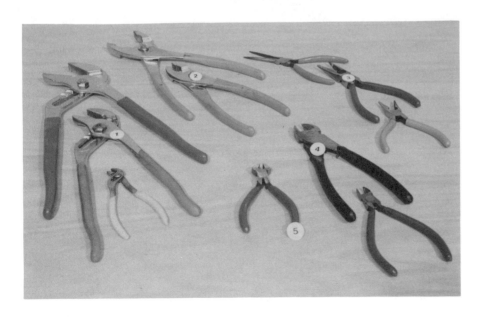

Illus. 132. Plier-type tools that are indispensable around the home workshop: 1, groove-joint pliers; 2, slip-joint pliers; 3, needle-nose pliers; 4, side cutters; and 5, end nippers.

Prying Tools

Prying levers of various types get regular use in the workshop (Illus. 133). They are used for nail removal, to separate paint-encrusted parts, to pull headless screws, etc.

Punches

Punches (Illus. 134) are used for a variety of things around the shop. Some of these include recessing common nails, starting a screw hole, and centering screw holes for hinges.

Scraping Tools

Paint scrapers and spatulas (Illus. 135) are used for finish removal and to apply fillers or putty (thus the name putty knife).

Screwdrivers

Screwdrivers are a necessity in the workshop. The types and sizes selected are your option. The ones shown in Illus. 136 are just suggestions.

Nailsets

Finishing nails are "set" or recessed below the surface of the workpiece. The space is then filled with a matching putty or similar filler-type material. Nailsets are the tools used to set nails (Illus. 137).

Sharpening Tools

Some tool sharpening is best left to the professionals. However, for the honing of gouges, chisels, knives, etc., a

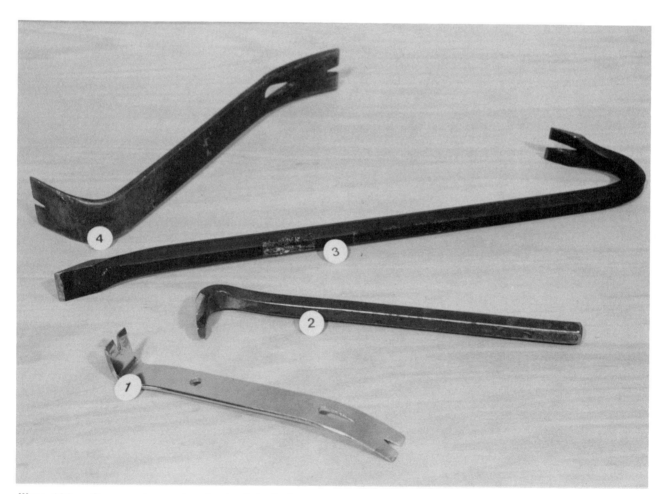

Illus. 133. Commonly used prying tools include: 1, a mini Wonder Bar®; 2, a 10″ nail puller; 3, an 18″ crowbar; and 4, a 10″ Wonder Bar.

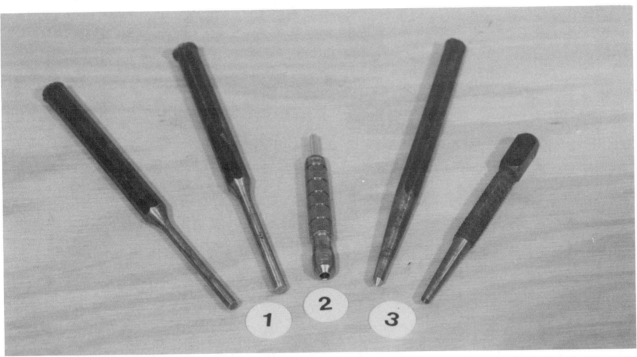

Illus. 134. A variety of punches include: 1, round and flat-end punches; 2, a screw-hole centering punch; and 3, a pointed punch.

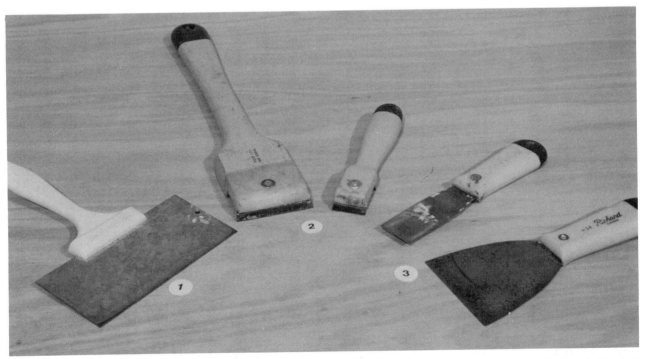

Illus. 135. Various types and sizes of scrapers and spatulas: 1, a shop-made scraper; 2, 2½″ and 1″ paint scrapers; and 3, 1″ and 3″ spatulas.

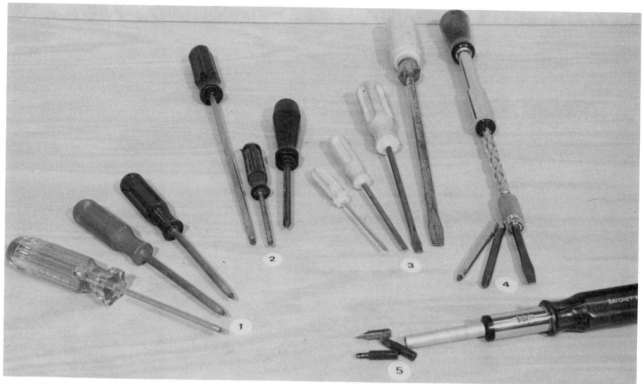

Illus. 136. Some of the many and varied screwdrivers available include: 1, Robertson® (square-head) screwdrivers; 2, Phillips (cross-head) screwdrivers; 3, slot-head screwdrivers; 4, a drill driver with various bits; and 5, a reversible screwdriver that accepts standard ¼″ hex bits.

variety of sharpening stones as shown in Illus. 138 is handy to have.

Smoothing Tools

In these days when power tools have taken over, I'm reluctant to even suggest the use of tools such as hand planes and the like. However, for the purists, hand planes, hand routers, and spokeshaves are a necessary commodity in the tool drawer. Illus. 139 shows an assortment of smoothing tools that will prove useful in the workshop.

Turning Tools

Tools for lathe turning are required only if your stationary power tools include a lathe. If you do have a lathe, chisels, gouges, and parting blades should be among the turning tools. Illus. 140 shows a good starter set. Details of their use is found later in the book.

Wrenches

Wrenches (Illus. 141) are a requirement in the workshop if,

for nothing else, the assembly of those power tool bases that arrive disassembled. Some types of furniture fittings require the use of various types of wrenches as well.

Illus. 137. Some available types of nailsets. From left to right, they are a double-ended nailset, a ¹⁄₁₆″ nailset, and a ¹⁄₃₂″ nailset.

Illus. 138. Sharpening tools are a must in the workshop. Try to have the following ones handy: 1, round-edge slipstones; 2, India and Arkansas file stones; 3, carbide slipstones; 4, an India oilstone; and 5, an Arkansas combination (fine/medium) bench stone.

Illus. 139. Some of the hand smoothing tools that should be considered for the workshop include: 1, a 14″ jack plane; 2, a rabbet plane; 3, a block plane; 4, a bull-nose rabbet plane; 5, a bench or smoothing plane; 6, a spokeshave; 7, a router plane with extra bits; and 8, a side rabbet plane.

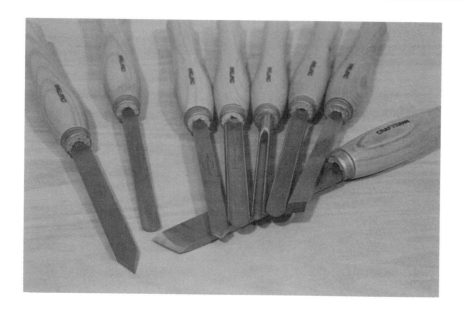

Illus. 140. A Sears Craftsman set of chisels and gouges.

Illus. 141. A variety of wrenches: 1, a ⅜″ socket wrench with regular and long sockets and an extension bar; 2, a ¼″ spanner; 3, a ¼″ socket wrench with an extension bar; 4, a pipe wrench; and 5, an open-end/box-end wrench set.

Hinges, Types of

(Illus. 142)

Backlap Hinge

This is the type of hinge that is seen on the folding tops of antique dining tables. It's called a backlap because it swings back a little more than 90°. It is usually made in solid brass or is brass-plated.

Butt Hinge

The butt hinge is used mostly for entry doors, but is found in some cabinetry. There are a number of styles and finishes available, including brass, brass-plated, steel, chromed-steel, black wrought-iron, hammered black wrought-iron, and Colonial pin hinges.

Concealed Hinges

These are the types of hinges used on some of that modern, imported furniture or some of the more modern kitchen cabinetry. It usually requires the drilling of a large (1¼"–1½") pocket hole in the carcass or the frame to

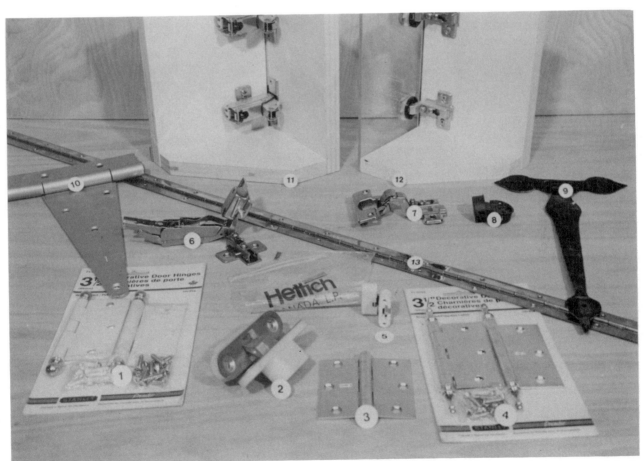

Illus. 142. There are a myriad of specialized and general-purpose hinges available to suit almost any job: 1, painted entry butt hinges; 2, a Soss hinge; 3, a standard brass butt hinge; 4, a Colonial brass butt hinge; 5, a cabinet Soss hinge; 6, a cabinet concealed 170° hinge; 7, a cabinet concealed 110° hinge; 8, a recessed 90° cabinet hinge; 9, an antique hammered strap hinge; 10, a strap/butt gate hinge; 11, a 90° cabinet hinge; 12, a 90° glass-door cabinet hinge; and 13, a brass piano hinge.

accommodate the mechanism and is then screwed to the door. These types of hinges allow for door swings of about 180°. Chromed steel is the usual available finish.

Piano Hinge

A piano hinge is so named because it was first made for the manufacture of pianos. The hinges had to be long and sturdy to facilitate a large, heavy (usually ebony) piano top. The hinges usually come in 2′, 4′, 6′, and 8′ lengths as standard, but they are also available in rolls so that they may be cut to length. The hinge flap is usually available in ⅜″, ½″, ¾″, 1″, 1½″, and 2″ widths. The screw holes are usually placed on 1″ centers. Piano hinges are available in finishes that include brass, brass-plated, chrome, and steel.

Soss® Hinges

These are a unique type of hinge that are totally concealed in the closed position and can open to almost 180°. The hinge is set into a pocket that is drilled into the door edge and the carcass or frame. They range in size; the largest sizes can be used in cabinetry or full-length solid-core entry doors.

Strap Hinges

Strap hinges are usually found on exterior structures such as barn doors and gates. Some, however, are used on cabinetry, usually Colonial-style or knotty pine furniture.

There are two types of strap hinges: the *full* strap hinge and the strap/butt hinge, sometimes called a T hinge. They are available in various sizes and come in black wrought iron, black, hammered wrought iron, in brass or brass-plated, and in galvanized steel or steel.

Hole Saw

Using Hole Saws to Make Rings

There are a number of ways to make various-diameter rings, but the easiest that I have found is to "double stack" a couple of hole saws (Illus. 143 and 144). Say, for example, you want a ½″ thick ring that is 2″ on the outside and 1½″ on the inside. Take your hole saw mandrel and put a 2⅛″ hole saw on it along with a 1½″ saw. The ⅛″ difference is to compensate for the blade thickness. Line them up in

Illus. 143. Setting up the hole saws to make wood rings for toys, etc.

the mandrel, tighten the bolt, and proceed to drill on the drill press. When finished, disassemble the saws and you will have your ring. A number of combinations of hole-saw sizes may be used in this manner as long as the hole saws will fit onto the mandrel and the mandrel nut is secure.

Illus. 144. Cutting the ring.

Releasing Drilled-Out Plugs

It's always a problem when using a hole saw to release the drilled-out plug. These **shortcuts** may ease the problem. For the first method, spray the inside and the outside of the saw with silicone or cooking spray such as Pam® (Illus. 145). Then, drill about three-quarters of the way into the stock or until the pilot bit goes right through the stock. Flip the workpiece over and drill from the other side. You will find that the plug will then drop out of the hole saw quite easily and will not be marred, as would happen if you attempted to pry it out.

Or, try this method if the plug is really stuck in the hole saw: Remove the saw from the drill press, unscrew the mandrel nut, and gently tap the mandrel out. The plug should come out with it (Illus. 146). All that's left to do is "unscrew" the plug off the pilot bit.

For the really tough plugs, here's a third way: Drill a

Illus. 146. Removing the plug by disassembling the bit and mandrel.

Illus. 145. To facilitate easy release of the wheel from a hole saw, spray the inside with silicone or cooking spray.

Illus. 147. Installing screws to force the plug out of the hole saw.

Illus. 148. The self-ejecting hole saw by Vermont American.

Illus. 149. A large V drawn across your workpieces will ensure that they are repositioned properly for later gluing.

couple of holes on either side of the pilot bit. Screw in a couple of screws that are long enough to force out the plug (Illus. 147). Do both sides a little at a time, or you may force the plug into the hole saw.

Vermont American has come up with the ultimate hole saw: one that self-ejects (Illus. 148). The mandrel is threaded into the hole saw itself. You drill the hole and then tilt the saw so that it is tight against the hole walls. Now, put the drill into reverse and out pops the plug.

Honing

(See Sharpening)

Joints, Identifying

Suppose you are working on a butcher-block-type table. The thickness planer has been turned off and you are setting up your pieces for gluing. *Before* you dismantle the setup, get out your pencil. Mark a large V across the setup pieces (Illus. 149). Now, if the phone rings and your youngster decides to play with the blocks while you are talking, reassembly will only take seconds.

Laminating, Safety Techniques for

Plastic laminate such as Arborite® or Formica® is easy to put on surfaces such as tabletops or countertops, but they can create problems later on that are not immediately apparent when you apply them. Changes in temperature and humidity react on both the glue and the plastic laminate, with the result that the plastic laminate causes stress on the substrate (the piece that it is glued to) and causes it to warp, twist, or to lose its bond. The way to prevent this is to purchase a backing sheet when you buy the laminate. A backing sheet is of the same thickness as the top sheet, but has no pattern. Its sole purpose is to equalize the pressures created by the gluing of the top sheet and thus give the countertop a longer life (Illus. 150).

Illus. 150. As this mirror image shows, a properly laminated table or counter top has a backing sheet on its underside.

There are those that say this is not necessary with high-density particleboard or plywood (¾" thick or more), but I'm doubtful. I have seen plastic laminate lift after a couple of years because there was no backing sheet on the underside.

Lathe

Description and Use

The wood lathe is used primarily for wood turning. The length of the stock that can be turned is determined by the distance between the *headstock* (the motor end) and the *tailstock* (the support end). This is called the lathe bed. The diameter or radius of the stock that is being turned is set by the distance from the middle of the headstock to the *bed* of the lathe. For turning bowls and wheels, etc., some lathes have a cutout in the bed to accommodate a larger radius. Some others, such as the Delta lathe shown in Illus. 151–153, have a motor housing that swings 90°.

The stock to be turned is held in position by a *spur center* at the headstock (Illus. 154) and a plain spur at the tailstock (Illus. 155). The tailstock is then tightened to secure the workpiece and further tightened by the adjustable wheel. Be sure to put a drop of oil on the tail end of your workpiece before putting it into the tailstock, because it will prevent the workpiece from burning and the spur from overheating.

The *tool rest* is the T-shaped device that slides along the lathe bed (Illus. 156). It should be placed parallel and close to the workpiece but never come in contact with it.

Illus. 151. This Delta lathe has a bed that will accommodate workpieces up to 36" long.

Illus. 152. Bowls of 12″ in diameter can be turned on this lathe.

Illus. 153. The headstock and motor on this Delta lathe swing 90° for large faceplate turnings.

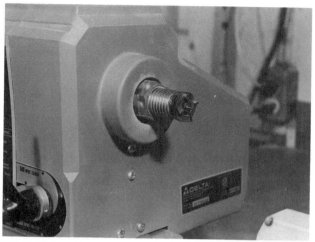

Illus. 154. On the left of the lathe is the spur center of the headstock.

Illus. 155. On the right of the lathe is the plain spur of the tailstock.

Illus. 156. The tool rest can be positioned in almost any way for various types of projects.

Illus. 157. The Craftsman lathe has a pulley drive that can be changed to provide various speeds.

Illus. 158. The Delta lathe has a motor control to provide speeds from 500 rpm to 2,000 rpm.

Two types of motors are used on lathes. Belt-drive motors have a combination of pulleys (Illus. 157). The second type of motor is a variable-speed one (Illus. 158).

A lathe *faceplate* is mounted to the headstock and screwed to the middle of the workpiece for bowl or wheel turning. Some advance planning should be done here, to ensure that your chisels or gouges do not come in contact with the screws. For faceplate turning, the tool rest is turned to face either the edge or the front of the workpiece and locked on the bed (Illus. 159).

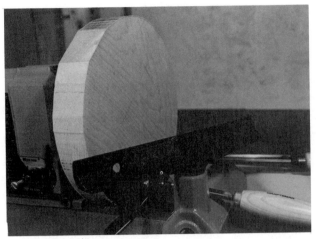

Illus. 159. The lathe faceplate and the tool rest being readied for bowl turning.

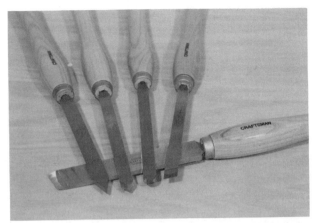

Illus. 161. Long-handled chisels are used for lathe work.

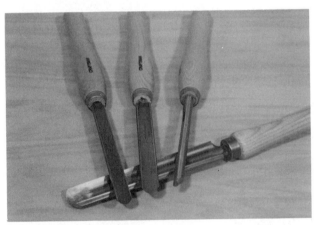

Illus. 160. These are some of the many different sizes and types of gouges available for wood turning.

Illus. 162. A pair of calipers is used to measure and gauge the thickness of the turning project.

Tools for the Lathe

Gouges are tools that look like wood chisels but have longer blades and handles (Illus. 160). Gouges are usually cupped in shape and are used for the first rough cutting in wood turning.

Wood-turning *chisels* are also available in various widths and shapes and are also longer than the conventional wood chisel (Illus. 161). They are used for final close cutting, parting, and shaping.

Callipers are an essential tool for lathe work (Illus. 162). They allow you to accurately measure the various diameters of your workpiece.

A *drill chuck* is another convenient accessory. If the drill chuck is fitted in the headstock, the lathe can be used as a boring tool (Illus. 163). Don't rush out and buy one

Illus. 163. A drill chuck fitted into the headstock of the lathe will turn the machine into a boring tool.

just yet. You may have one and not even know it. Check your drill press. The chuck may fit your lathe.

A *center finder* such as the one from Veritas is an indispensable tool for the wood turner (Illus. 164). It will accurately find the centers of stock for positioning on your lathe.

Lathe Duplicator

The Sears Craftsman® lathe duplicator is fun and easy to use. It allows you to make the same-shaped pieces. Use this little **shortcut**, though, to make your duplicating job easier and a lot less frustrating: *Always* work from the high spots to the low spots first (Illus. 165). Your cuts will be smoother and easier to make.

Prolonging the Life of a Lathe

Most wood turners whom I have seen set up their work-piece right on the lathe. They either tap the piece into the headstock spur or they force it in by screwing in the tailstock. The problem with doing it this way is that it either jolts or puts pressure on the motor bearings. This will, of course, shorten the life of even the best of lathes.

On your next wood-turning project, try this: Remove the spur from the headstock and tap the spur itself into the end of the workpiece with a wooden mallet (Illus. 166). Once your marks are made and the cut is deep enough, put

Illus. 164. The Veritas center finder mounted in a convenient place in the workshop makes it easy to find the centers of stock.

the spur back in the headstock and *then* tighten up the tailstock. You will find that a lot less pressure is put on the motor.

Shop-Made Lathe Safety Guard

Making your own lathe safety guard out of ⅛″ Plexiglas (Illus. 167) is not as difficult as it might seem. With the protective paper on, cut a piece of ⅛″ Plexiglas so that it is 2½ to 3 times the width of your lathe's tool rest. Now, calculate the length of the Plexiglas by using a tape mea-

Illus. 165. Working from the high areas to the low areas makes duplicating parts on a lathe cleaner and easier.

Illus. 166. The proper way to install the headstock spur to prolong the life of the lathe motor.

sure up from the top of the lathe table and then over the lathe bed to about where the tool rest is.

Now for the fun part. Remove the protective paper and, with a heat gun, make a 90° lip on the Plexiglas about 2″ wide. This will form the base of the guard and it will sit parallel to, but behind, the lathe bed. The next bend (in the same direction) will be about 70° and its position will be 6″ or so above the motor housing. The final bend will be about 45°, again in the same direction. This final bend should bring you within 6″ of the end of the workpiece.

Lightly sand the edges with a 180–220-grit open-coat paper and put a slight chamfer on the Plexiglas to remove the sharp edges and corners.

I welded (see Plexiglas Welding) a second piece of Plexiglas to the bottom of the guard to make it twice as thick. With my router, I then made a slot, almost full length. This is a slow operation. Do not attempt to cut the slot with one pass; several are required. The purpose of the slot is to allow the guard to slide left or right. I fastened the guard to a block of wood with a hex bolt, fender washer, and a T nut, and then screwed the whole assembly to the workbench.

Illus. 167. The shop-made Plexiglas lathe guard in position.

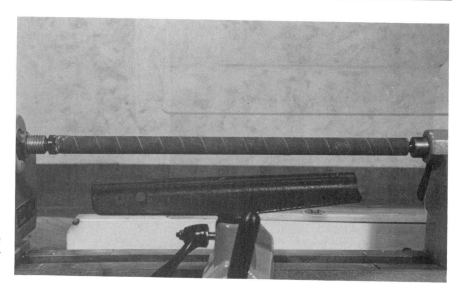

Illus. 168. This shop-made lathe drum sander is handy for sanding concave surfaces.

You may be asking, "What if my lathe table is not metal, it is made of wood?" Then, make the width of the Plexiglas one-half the length of the lathe bed, plus 4″. The base, or lip, will be 4″.

One more thing before the final installation: Wipe the safety guard down with one of those fabric softener sheets. It will eliminate the static that makes sawdust cling.

Shop-Made Sanding Drums for the Lathe

There are two ways that I know of to make a long sanding drum that fits on your lathe. The first is to turn the drum yourself using a piece of hardwood of the desired length (Illus. 168). The diameter of the drum is also optional, but 2″ is a handy size. First, apply a coat of contact cement to the dowel. Then, apply contact cement to the back of a roll of 1″ wide sanding strips; the grit size of the sanding strips is up to you. Start applying the sanding roll to the dowel on an angle (10°–15° is fine). When done, trim off the ends. Be certain to make a mark where the headstock end will be.

In the second method, make or buy a dowel, but divide it in three. Apply a coarse sanding strip to the piece on the left, a medium sanding strip to the piece in the middle, and a fine sanding strip to the piece on the right. Pieces of tape with the various grits written on them will divide the sections. This will improve the drum's versatility and save you the time of changing drums (Illus. 169).

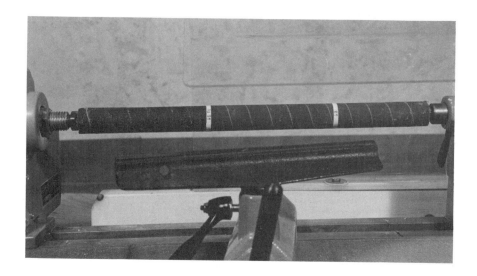

Illus. 169. A long sanding drum that has three different grits of sandpaper is very versatile.

Illus. 170. Durite screen by Norton will last many times longer than regular sandpaper when used for lathe work.

Sanding with the Lathe

After your workpiece has been turned and your gouges and chisels are put away, you reach for the sandpaper. Before you do this, think about the following: There is a product on the market made by Norton that is used by drywall installers that looks like screening. It is, however, impregnated with an abrasive that is 120 or 150 grit. The product is called Durite® screen (Illus. 170).

The beauty of the Durite screen is that it seems to last forever. It will certainly last more than five times as long

as regular sandpaper. When used on a spinning lathe, it doesn't clog up. The sawdust just passes right through it.

Durite screen comes in small sheets 4¼″ × 11″ that are die-cut for a joint sander, but these sheets can be cut with a utility knife or a pair of scissors to the size that you require.

Sanding Tool

Sanding your workpiece on the lathe while it is turning is an efficient way of getting a nice, smooth finish. However, it has its drawbacks. The sandpaper can get pretty hot, sometimes too hot.

Illus. 171 and 172 show a shop-made tool that allows

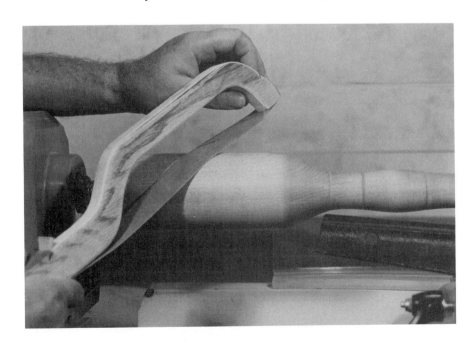

Illus. 171. This shop-made sanding tool is ideal to use to sand a workpiece on the lathe.

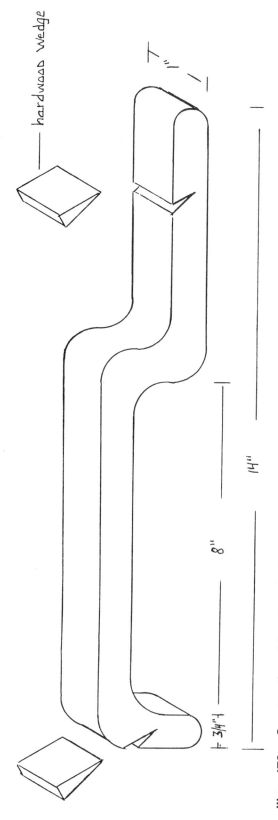

Illus. 172. Construction of the shop-made sanding tool.

hardwood wedge

3/4"

8"

14"

1"

Illus. 173. An adjustable levelling scribe will take the wobble out of tables and chairs.

you to sand a workpiece on the lathe without heating it up. It takes about ½ hour to make, and is made from 4/4 (1″ thick) hardwood or two pieces of ½″ plywood glued together.

The tool uses 1″ wide sanding strips that are sold in rolls of varying lengths and grits. The strips are held in the slots with small wedges. If you plan it right, you can turn the strip end over end to make use of the unused portion. After you have determined the length of the sanding strip and cut it, cut several others of various grits to save time later.

Levelling Scribe

Does anyone remember the dining table that ended up being a coffee table? You know what happens; you keep cutting a piece off one leg to make it level. Well, never again should this happen. Here's a shop aid to eliminate the wobble in tables and chairs (Illus. 173). It takes less than an hour to make. Better yet, you can use up some of that scrap ¾″ plywood that's lying around.

Glue and screw a couple of pieces that are about 3″ square, so they form an L shape. Cut a 3″ diameter wheel. Drill a hole in the middle of the wheel and a corresponding hole in the middle of the vertical part of the L. Drill a counter bore at ¼″ in from the edge of the wheel. Install a Gyproc® screw in this so that about ⅛″ to ¼″ of the screw protrudes. Now, recess a carriage bolt through the center holes and fasten it with a washer and wing nut. Your levelling jig is ready to use.

How do you use this levelling jig? It's simple. Set your table or chair on a level surface. Rotate the wheel until the protruding screw (scribe) is level with the shortest leg. Tighten the wing nut and use the scribe to mark the other legs for cutting. *Voilà*, no more wobble.

Lighting for the Workshop

One of the greatest boons to the lighting industry and now the workshop is the low-voltage halogen lamp (Illus. 174). These little devices will throw off light like you wouldn't believe. And, on top of that, they are economical to run. They come in either individual lamps complete with a transformer or on a track-mounted configuration with one transformer handling six or so lamps. My choice would be the individual units that can be clipped on for task lighting, that is, close lighting for detail work.

The light that these halogen lamps throw off is very white, so it is especially good for woodworking. Next time you go near a lamp store, stop in and check them out.

Illus. 174. One of the many types of low-voltage halogen lamps available.

Mallet, Shop-Made

Here's a **shortcut** for making a wooden mallet that could hit a home run. I'm sure that you have an old wood baseball or softball bat that is either lying around the garage or can pick one up for pennies at a garage sale. Put your hand as high up on the handle as you can and still feel comfortable holding it. Now, cut off the part below your hand and then cut off anything above that you would consider excess for a mallet. Sand and round off the sharp edges and drill a hole through the handle so it can be hung on a pegboard. You now have an ash—or is it hickory?—mallet (Illus. 175).

Illus. 175. Modifying a baseball bat to be used as a mallet.

Marking Gauge

The marking gauge is a very accurate instrument used to scribe thicknesses and widths for planing, cutting, or sanding. However, it often becomes a discarded tool in that it is put back into the tool chest never to see the light of day again. The reason it's tossed back in the tool chest is because the woodworker probably did not know how to use it properly. Most people who use the tool incorrectly are heavy-handed and want to scribe a deep line and, therefore, put the pressure on the scribe pin. This is wrong. The pressure should be on the adjustable head, to make sure it stays in contact with the surface of the workpiece (Illus. 176). With this in mind, rotate the shaft only slightly so that the scribe just scratches the surface. Now, do it again to reinforce the line.

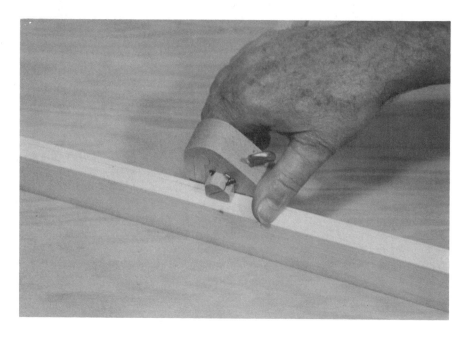

Illus. 176. The correct way to use a marking gauge.

Mathematic and Geometric Formulas for the Woodworker

I guess mathematical formulas are like a second language; if you don't use them on a fairly regular basis, you tend to forget a lot of them. Here's a little refresher course.

Arc

The length (circumference) of an arc in a given circle is easy to determine. Since a circle is 360 degrees, through the use of the protractor you can determine the arc to be 60°. The circumference of the given circle is 10 feet. Here's the formula: 360° ÷ 60 = 6. Therefore, the circumference of the arc is one-sixth of 10 feet, which equals 1.66 feet.

Cube Area

To find the area of a cube, multiply one side × the other side × the depth; for example, $4' \times 4' \times 4'' = 64$ cubic feet.

Circle Area

There are two ways that I know to determine the area of a circle. The old standby that I learned in grade school is the diameter × 3.1416. The other is just as simple if you remember the formula. Multiply the squared *diameter* by .7854. Both will give the same answer.

A circle is divided into 360 degrees, but the degrees are also divided. If you have any experience in sea navigation, I'm sure you would know the divisions. For you landlubbers, here it is: Sixty seconds (60″) equals one minute (1′), 60 minutes (60″) equals 1 degree (1°), 360 degrees (360°) equals 1 circle. Therefore, 22½ degrees would be expressed as twenty-two degrees, thirty minutes and written 22°30; 22½ and 22.5 are also acceptable.

Circle Circumference

To get the circumference of a circle, multiply the diameter by 3.142. The circumference of a 10′ diameter circle, for example, is 31.42′.

Parallelogram Area

To find the area of a parallelogram, multiply its height by the length of the base. For example, a parallelogram with a base 5′ long and a height of 4′ would have an area of 20 square feet ($5' \times 4' = 20'$).

Polygon Areas

Use the following formula to determine the area of regular polygons. Square the length of one of its sides and do the following: Multiply by .433 if it has 3 sides, by 1 if it has 4 sides, by 1.721 if it has 5 sides, by 2.598 if it has 6 sides, by 3.634 if it has 7 sides, by 4.828 if it has 8 sides, by 6.181 if it has 9 sides, by 7.694 if it has 10 sides, by 9.366 if it has 11 sides, and by 11.196 if it has 12 sides.

For example, let's calculate the area of a seven-sided polygon (septagon) with sides that measure 5′. Multiply this by the square of one side: $3.634 \times 25 = 90.85$ square feet.

Rectangle Area

The area of a rectangle is determined by multiplying the base or length by the height. For example, a rectangle with a base of 6′ and a height of 5′ would have an area of 30 square feet ($6' \times 5' = 30'$).

Square Area

To find the area of a square, multiply one dimension by itself; for example, $4' \times 4' = 16$ square feet.

Trapezoid Area

The trapezoid is basically two triangles, so if you draw a straight line from one corner to the other, determine its length (as a base line), multiply this number by the height, do the same thing with the other half, and add the two totals you will get the area.

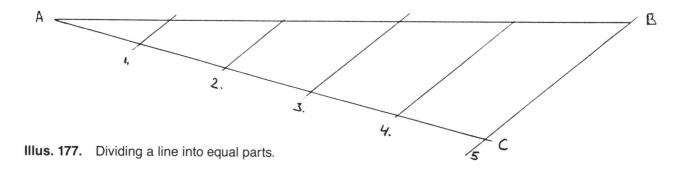

Illus. 177. Dividing a line into equal parts.

Triangle Area

For the area of a triangle, multiply the length of the base by the height and divide by 2. If the base is 4′ and the height is 6′ the triangle has an area of 12 square feet (4 × 6 ÷ 2 = 12).

Dividing a Line into Equal Parts

To divide a given line into equal parts, this is what you do: Let's assume that the given line is 6½″ long (A–B in Illus. 177) and you want to divide it into five equal parts. Draw a line at an angle (about 15°) from point A. The length of this line (A–C) should be easily divisible by 5, in this case, 5″. Now, draw a line from C to B. While maintaining that angle, draw lines from the 4″ mark, 3″ mark, etc.

Making an Equilateral Triangle

To make an **equilateral triangle** with a given base, use a compass as shown in Illus. 178. Let's use as an example a triangle with a base of 4″. With your compass point at A, draw a 4″ radius arc at C. Repeat this with the point at B. Where the two arcs intersect (C) is the apex. Now, draw lines A–C and B–C.

Making a Pentagon Within a Circle

A pentagon is a five-sided figure. To make a **pentagon** within a circle, do the following: Draw the circle to the

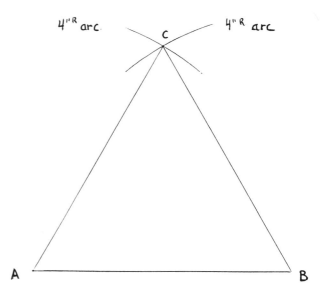

Illus. 178. Making an equilateral triangle with a given base.

desired size. Make two intersecting lines (A–C and B–D in Illus. 179). Bisect the radius at A–O (one-half the distance) and place your compass point at E. Set it so that it joins at B. Now, it is important that you do not change the compass setting. Intersect O–C at F and, at a point near the top of B–D, connect F; then draw G.

Go back to the horizontal line and bisect O–C, repeating the above but on the upper left quadrant on the circle to make intersection H. Set your compass point at H and intersect at K; do the same with G and I. Join your lines to form the pentagon.

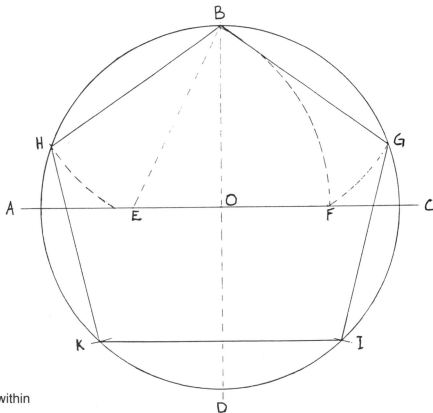

Illus. 179. Making a pentagon within a circle.

Making a Hexagon Within a Circle

To make a **hexagon** within a circle, do the following: With a compass, draw a circle of the desired diameter. Without changing your compass setting, place the point of the instrument at A as shown in Illus. 180, and intersect at B. Place the point of the compass at B to intersect at C, etc. Draw a straight line through all of the intersections.

Making Octagons

To make an **octagon** from a *given base line*, do the following: Let's assume that the given base line is 2″. Draw this base line (A–B in Illus. 181) 2″ long and then make a perpendicular (vertical) line from both A and B. From point A, draw a 45° line exactly 2″ long. Do the same from point B. From points C and D, make a vertical line, again 2″ long, to points E and F. Continue with a 45° angle to G and H, which should equally intersect with the two vertical lines drawn from A and B. Join G and H and your octagon is done.

To make an **octagon** *within a square*, do the following: First, draw your square and then make 45° angles from points A–D and B–C as shown in Illus. 182. This will give you your center, where the two lines intersect. With your compass point placed at A and your drawing point in the middle of the square, draw an arc. Without changing your compass setting, do the same from B, C, and D. Now join arcs 1 and 2, and then 3 and 4, etc., until the octagon is completed as shown.

To make an **octagon** *within a circle*, do the following: Draw a circle of the desired diameter and intersect it as in point A–B and C–D as shown in Illus. 183. A 45° angle will join A to C, C to B, B to D, and D to A. Again, using a 45° angle, intersect the center and make marks at 1–4 and 2–3. Join A to 1, 1 to C, etc., around the perimeter until the octagon is complete.

Making an Ellipse

To make an **ellipse**, do the following: Draw the desired major (A–B in Illus. 184) and the minor (C–D) axis lengths. At an equal distance from A and B on the major

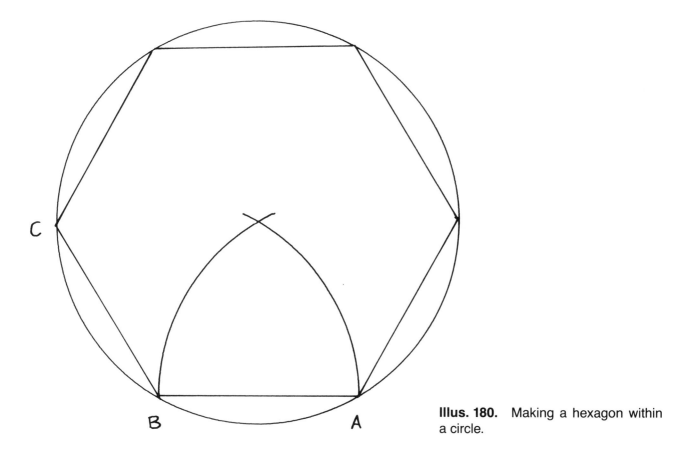

Illus. 180. Making a hexagon within a circle.

axis, place a couple of push pins (at 1–2 in Illus. 168). Take a length of string or thread and tie the ends to the pins. The thread, when pulled in the middle, should reach the end of the minor axis C–D, and when moved left or right should reach either end of the major axis.

With a pencil point, pull the thread tight up to C and, while keeping it tight, draw a line to B and then to A. Reverse the procedure for the other half of the ellipse.

Measuring Techniques

(Also see Radial Arm Saw)

Setting the depth, width, and even the length of a cut can be extremely easy. A set of three shop-made wooden blocks called one-two-three blocks can be used alone or in various combinations to give accurate measurements from 1″ to 9″ (Illus. 185). The blocks, usually made of a kiln-dried hardwood, are made precisely 1″ thick × 2″ wide × 3″ long. They *must be square* all around and their dimensions must be *precise*.

One-two-three blocks have been used for years in the machining industry. These blocks are precision-cut and made out of steel.

When you use one-two-three blocks with the fractional plywood blocks (see Radial Arm Saw: Depth setting), you have an almost infinite number of measuring possibilities without even touching your tape measure. Also, they are high enough to include any out-set teeth on a table-saw, radial-arm-saw, or band-saw blade and thus will give an accurate measurement every time. One other benefit is that if your blocks are truly square, you can use them to determine the accuracy of your saw blades.

Drill a hole in the blocks and hang them up close to your stationary power tools.

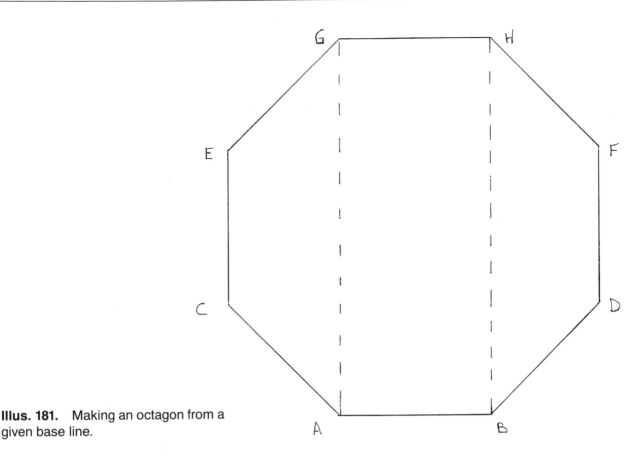

Illus. 181. Making an octagon from a given base line.

Mitre Gauge

Extending a Mitre Gauge

The mitre gauge is a tremendous help for making square or angled cuts with tools that are equipped with slots to handle the mitre gauges. Mitre gauges do have drawbacks, however. They are usually too narrow to handle smaller pieces. The shop-made jig shown in Illus. 186 will solve this problem, however. This L-shaped mitre gauge extension will handle the small pieces as well as those round dowel-type pieces that keep slipping all over the place. It is made of ¾" plywood that is glued and screwed together. The screws should be installed in a position on the extension that will *not* come into contact with the saw blade. An angle (about 30°–45°) is cut on the surface of the plywood close to the joint. This is done to support dowels and other round workpieces to prevent them from slipping.

The extension shown in Illus. 186 is made for my band saw, and one end is angled at 45°. If you are going to make one for your *table saw*, make it so that it actually extends beyond the blade. The blade of the table saw should be raised only enough to cut through the workpiece.

If made high and deep enough, this jig can be used for cutting mitres on odd-shaped workpieces such as crown mouldings, ogees, etc.

The mitre extension can be mounted to your mitre gauge in one of two ways. You can use double-faced tape or directly screw it on.

Fitting a Mitre Gauge

Occasionally, the mitre gauge on your stationary power tools should be checked for snugness in the table slot. If

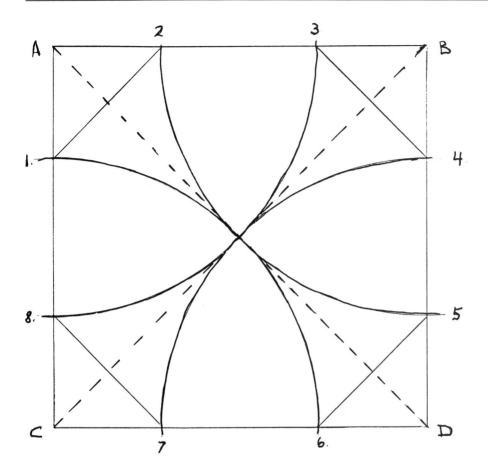

Illus. 182. Making an octagon within a square.

you find that the gauge is loose, try the following: With the bar of the mitre gauge on its side, place it in a steel vise or on a block of scrap hardwood. Take a pointed metal punch and peen the bar (Illus. 187). Peening makes the steel of the bar expand and will therefore make the gauge fit tighter. It's best to tap the punch lightly at first and do it to *both* sides of the bar.

While we are on the subject of mitre gauges, you may have noticed that the slots on your table saw or band saw are a little lower than the thickness of the bar. This sometimes makes the gauge "catch" on the edge when it is used with larger pieces of wood. Preventing this is easy: Simply grind or file a 45° angle on the edge of the metal saw table (Illus. 188). This will ease the mitre gauge up to the table level without disturbing your workpiece.

Mitres, Hand-Cutting

Tight-fitting mitres for picture frames are usually in a mitre box. The problem with a lot of the inexpensive mitre boxes is that their sides wear out, which affects the accuracy and the tight fit of the mitres.

Don't throw the mitre box out just yet. Make your cuts in it. Remove the pieces and clamp them to a builder's square (Illus. 189). Using a backsaw, carefully saw through the joint and stop just before touching the square (Illus. 190). Remove the builder's square and saw the rest of the joint.

Be sure to mark the corners on the pieces, because your handsaw cut may not have been truly perpendicular and that joint may not fit in another position. This may seem like a lot of trouble to go through, but the end result will be a mitre joint without any gaps.

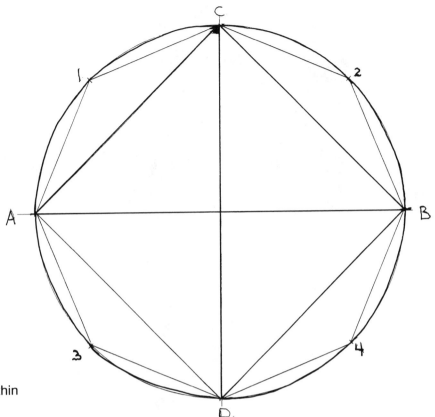

Illus. 183. Making an octagon within a circle.

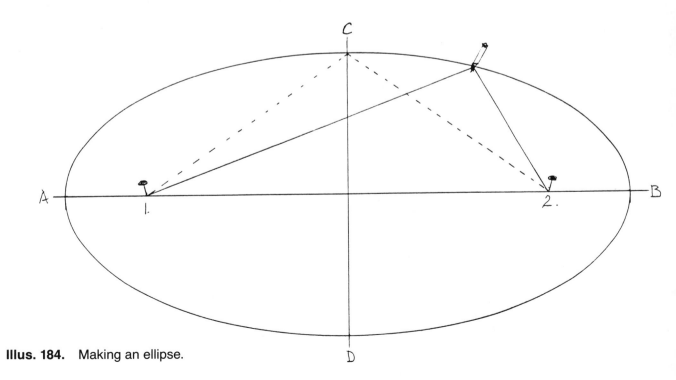

Illus. 184. Making an ellipse.

Illus. 185. A set of 1–2–3 blocks will quickly help in measuring the depth, width, and length of a cut.

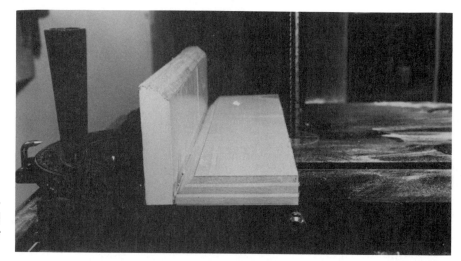

Illus. 186. A mitre-gauge extension jig allows for safer and more accurate cuts of smaller and odd-shaped workpieces.

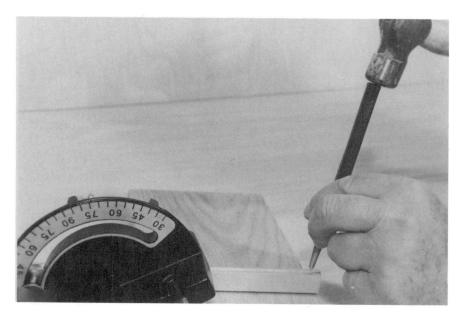

Illus. 187. Peening the bar of a mitre gauge makes it fit tighter in the saw table slot.

Illus. 188. Grinding the saw's table edge to 45° prevents the mitre gauge from catching on the edge.

Illus. 189. To cut accurate mitres by hand, clamp the two pieces together with a steel square under them.

Illus. 190. With a backsaw, saw through the joint. Be careful; don't saw into the steel square.

Murphy's Laws of Woodworking

Occasionally throughout this and my previous book I've made reference to Murphy and his blankety-blank laws and how they affect us woodworkers. I thought it would be fun to add a few here. After all, we can use a little chuckle now and then. Who knows, you might even recognize yourself or someone close to you.

The Law of the Clamps

You never have as many clamps as you need for the project that you are working on. The clamps that you do have are too big, too small, or the wrong type.

The Ladder Law

You are on the top step of the stepladder straining to reach into that tight corner with your staple gun. Murphy's law says that the staple gun will be empty.

You are near the top of a 40′ extension ladder applying caulk to the soffit or the eave. You have 2′ left to do. Murphy emptied the caulking tube.

You're up the ladder installing that first ceiling tile. You have it all lined up, reach into your nail pouch . . . yup, no nails. Murphy took 'em.

You are up the ladder and about to install that last shingle on the roof. You've already had to go down the ladder once because you ran out of nails. Now you are all ready. Right? Wrong. You reach into your tool belt for your hammer and. . . .

The Screw Law

Your project requires 1½″ #7 screws. You check your cabinet and find that all you have are 1¾″ screws. You have to make a trip to the hardware store to buy those screws and find that they come in plastic packs of 20, exactly the amount that the project calls for. You guessed it: when you get home, you open the pack and find only 19. On top of that, Murphy switched the drive type. They are square and you don't have a Robertson screwdriver.

The Law of the Nail

There is only one more finishing nail to hammer in. Sure enough, the nail hits a knot and it bends. Murphy made sure it's in a spot the hammer claw can't get at.

Nailing Techniques

Nailing Close to the Edges

You have to drive a nail through a board and you are only ½″ or so away from the edge. You know that the board is

Illus. 191. Flattening the tip of a nail helps prevent splitting when you are nailing close to the edge of a workpiece.

going to split. As a matter of fact, you can probably sense it before you even put the hammer to it. I'm not guaranteeing this shortcut will work all the time, but it's worth the risk: Before driving the nail(s), flatten the point with a hammer and then place the nail with the flattened end *across* the wood grain (Illus. 191). The same rule applies when nailing into the *end* grain of a piece of wood such as a 2 × 4.

Nailing in Close Quarters

That last nail is always the most troublesome one to nail in. It usually has to be located in some tight spot. And, of course, it's hard to get the hammer in there.

Here is an effective shortcut involving using either a C-clamp or slip-joint pliers (Illus. 192): Put a small piece of double-faced-tape on one surface to hold the nail and then tighten up the clamp. For smaller nails, try using slip-joint pliers. Be sure, however, to put some padding on the jaws to protect your project.

Nailing Guards

Illus. 193 shows a helpful little nailing guard that you can make in a couple of minutes. It will safely prevent inadvertent dings in your workpiece and help you to keep your nails straight.

Cut a piece of ⅛″ thick Plexiglas or Lexan 2″ wide by

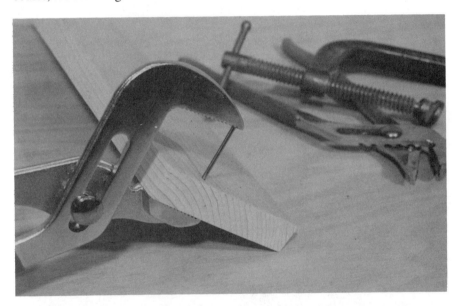

Illus. 192. A C-clamp or slip-joint pliers can be used to squeeze a nail that is in a tight position.

Illus. 193. A shop-made Plexiglas nail guard will protect the surface of the workpiece from hammer marks.

about 8″ long. Sand the edges and slightly round off the corners. Make a slot about halfway up the middle of the guard with your band saw. That's all there is to it. Place your nail in the slot, line it up on your workpiece, and hammer it in. *Do not* hammer it all the way in; keep the head just above the Plexiglas to allow you to remove it. Continue nailing with a nailset.

There is another method of protecting your workpiece. Do not throw those scrap pieces of pegboard into the kindling bin just yet, especially if you are doing some finish-nailing. Pegboard strips are ideal makeshift nailing protectors (Illus. 194). Simply start your nail, hang the pegboard strip on it, and then drive it home. The remaining ¼″ should be driven in with a nailset. Don't try this with common nails unless you can fit the nail head through the pegboard hole.

Toenailing Technique

Toenailing a 2 × 4 stud into the soleplate usually makes the stud slip out of position a little. The reason for this is that it takes a few hits with the hammer for the nail to bite.

Here's a trick of the trade I learned while visiting a jobsite: If you turn the nail upside down and hit it on its head, the result will be a "pocket." Now, turn the nail the right way and drive it home (Illus. 179).

Nailing the Correct Way

To obtain a tight nail joint, there is a correct way of driving nails. Let's assume that you want to join a 2 × 4 to the end of another 2 × 4, to make a right angle. First, select a nail that is a length three times the thickness of the board, in this case, a 3″ finishing nail. A 4″ wide board should take three nails, equally spaced. The first nail to be driven in will be the middle one. Drive the nail until it *just* protrudes from the underside, making sure that the nail is perpendicular to the work. Now, line up the two boards and finish driving in the nail. The remaining two nails should be driven in on opposing angles of about 15°. The result will be a secure joint (Illus. 180). Of course, a little glue before nailing is added security.

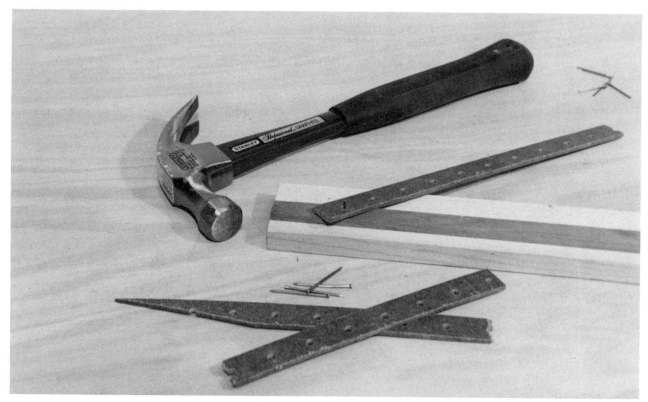

Illus. 194.   Pegboard strips will protect your workpiece when you are nailing it.

Illus. 195. The nail head will make a pocket that makes toe-nailing easier.

Illus. 196. The correct way of nailing two boards for a secure joint.

Nails

Past Cost of Nails

I'm a bit of a trivia buff and this *is* trivial. I was thumbing through an old (circa 1920) hardware catalogue and came up with these little tidbits: In 1920, the cost of a *keg* of 10d (3″) nails was 20 cents; the price for a keg of 2d (1″) finishing nails (brads) was the incredible price of $1.25. Oh my, how inflation has set in. But, there is more. If you wanted the 10d nails blued, it would cost a whopping 25 cents extra per 100 pounds. Special heads or points would cost another 25 cents per 100 pounds. Wouldn't it be nice to see those prices today?

Common Nails

Table 5 indicates the length and quantity per pound for different sizes of nails. *Note:* A 10-pennyweight nail is referred to as ten-penny nail and is written 10d. The quantity/pound figures in the chart are approximations. There is no pennyweight reference after 60. In most areas, common nails 6 inches and longer are referred to as spikes.

PENNYWEIGHT (SIZE)	LENGTH	QUANTITY/ POUND
2	1 inch	850
3	1¼ inches	540
4	1½ inches	290
5	1¾ inches	250
6	2 inches	165
7	2¼ inches	150
8	2½ inches	100
9	2¾ inches	90
10	3 inches	65
12	3¼ inches	60
16	3½ inches	45
20	4 inches	30
30	4½ inches	20
40	5 inches	17
50	5½ inches	13
60	6 inches	10
	7 inches	7
	8 inches	5
	9 inches	4
	10 inches	3
	12 inches	3
	14 inches	2

Table 5.

Penny System

Have you ever wondered where the penny system in sizing nails comes from? I have, and I've done a little research. Now, though, I think I'm more confused than ever.

My first thought was that the penny system has its origins in pennyweight. The *Random House Dictionary* says that a pennyweight is equal to ⅟20th of a troy ounce. There are 12 troy ounces to a pound. Ergo, a 2d (d is the symbol used for penny) finishing nail (1″) would weigh 2 pennyweight, there would be 10 of these to an ounce and

160 to a pound. This does not calculate; there are 1,050 pennyweight to a pound. Back to the library.

The 1923 *Audel's Carpenters and Builders Guide* speculates that the penny system originated in England and that two possibilities for its origin exist. One theory is that 100 six-penny nails cost sixpence, 100 four-penny nails cost fourpence, etc. This seems somewhat logical.

The other theory is that the penny system is based on the fact that 1,000 ten-penny nails weighed 10 pounds. The historic and modern abbreviation for penny is d, after the Roman coin *denarius*, which was probably equal to a penny. The same abbreviation was used in early England for a pound in weight. Penny has been with us ever since. Today, though, only the purists use the term. I would bet a penny that if you walked into a new hardware store and asked for a pound of six-penny finishing nails, the clerk would react with a puzzled expression on his face.

Oil Stain

(See Stains, Wiping and Applying)

Paint

(See also Painting and Spray-Painting)

Paint for Shop Floors

In my previous book, I expounded on the merits of an epoxy-type paint for painting wood or concrete floors in the workshop. Well, times sure do change quickly. A new product has emerged on the market that is probably a direct result of the impending toxic substance laws from the environmental protection agencies (Illus. 197). It is produced by Flecto and is a water-soluble polyurethane (varathane). It is called Diamond Colours™. The beauty of it is that it is as hard as or harder than the traditional plastic-type finishes, but is virtually odor-free. Another

Illus. 197. The Flecto Diamond Colours® floor paint is harder and more durable than the traditional floor paints.

major advantage is its drying time. I recently painted my concrete shop floor, which measures 48′ × 50′. I used a roller and by the time I had painted it, I could walk on the first half. A coat of Diamond Colours takes two hours to dry, and becomes totally hard in three hours. It is available not only in the traditional grey, but in a good variety of other colors as well.

Mixing Small Amounts of Paint

Before recycling those plastic soda pop bottles, cut the tops off them and put the remaining section on your paint shelf. These small "bowls" will make great disposable

Illus. 198. Use small, plastic soda-pop bottles for mixing smaller amounts of paint.

containers for mixing small amounts of touch-up paints and finishes (Illus. 198). If you drill a couple of small holes up near the top of the bottle, a bent coat hanger will hook it onto a ladder. Oh, save the top section. It makes a handy funnel.

Paintbrushes, Cleaning

Method #1

There are several methods of easily and effectively cleaning your paintbrush. In the first method, cut an X in the plastic top of a coffee can. Force the paintbrush handle through the cut. Half fill the empty coffee can with the appropriate brush cleaner or solvent and then put the cover back on (Illus. 199). Now, the brush will stay suspended and you can swish the brush back and forth without worrying about splashing.

Illus. 199. Cut an X in the top of the plastic top of a coffee can and fit your brush through this cut. This will suspend your brush in the cleaner in the can.

Method #2

The second method involves an economical way of cleaning your paintbrush after the paint has hardened. Usually, cleaning paintbrushes after the paint has hardened on them means using a fair quantity of brush cleaner. You pour the cleaner into an old coffee can or similar-sized container. Then you let the brush soak overnight. The next day you end up disposing of the used cleaner.

This more economical way of doing it consists of using old, small oval-shaped glue bottles (Illus. 200). They are usually just big enough for most paintbrushes to fit into. Cut the top off just below the shoulder. Now, set the brush

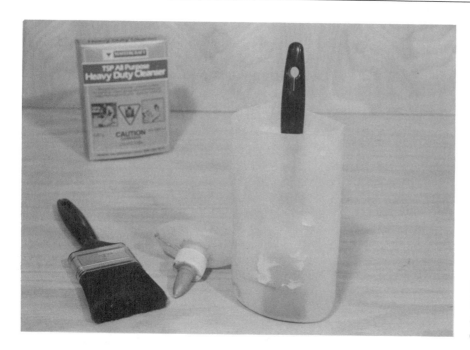

Illus. 200. An old plastic glue bottle with its top cut off makes an ideal paintbrush cleaning container.

in the container and *then* pour in your brush cleaner until it covers the bristles. A lot less cleaner is required.

Most paintbrushes have a hole in the lower part of the handle for supporting the brush so that the bristles don't touch the bottom of the container. If yours doesn't, drill one. A ¼" hole will do nicely. A small dowel or a piece of coat hanger will support the brush. By doing this, you will double or even triple the amount of brushes that can be cleaned with a standard container of brush cleaner.

Method #3

Don't go out to a hardware store and buy any of those expensive paintbrush cleaners that promise to restore your brushes and make them look like new. Instead, purchase a pound or so of trisodium phosphate (TSP) at the same hardware store.

A solution of 1 pound of TSP mixed in a gallon of water will melt any caked-on paint and soften the brush bristles (Illus. 201). For easy reference, here are the rough solutions: 1 pound TSP and 1 gallon of water; 12 ounces TSP and 6 pints of water; 6 ounces TSP and 3 pints of water; 3 ounces TSP and 1½ pints of water; 1½ ounces TSP and 1 pint of water. A little more or less is not crucial. Warm water will work best. The brushes should be left to soak in the solution and should be checked from time to time. The

amount of time will depend on just how saturated the brushes are. A second cleaning may be necessary.

Removing Paint Inexpensively

Here's a quick tip: Trisodium phosphate mixed with water (1 pound to 1 gallon) will remove a coat or two of old paint on furniture (Illus. 202). Brush a generous amount of the solution on and allow it to soften. A scraper or dull putty knife will remove the softened paint quite readily. Rinse the cleaned surface immediately afterwards with water and then wipe it dry. A stronger solution may be required for areas with more paint. Rubber gloves and safety *goggles* should, of course, be worn when working with these materials.

Paint Rollers, Cleaning

Cleaning paint rollers can be a pain. Here are a couple of methods that will make this chore less painful.

After you have removed the excess paint from the tray, use your stir stick to scrape down the roller. This will act like a squeegee. Do this in the paint tray, and then pour the remains back into the can. Roll the paint roller over a couple of layers of newspaper to remove any further excess.

Illus. 201. Trisodium phosphate (TSP) mixed with water is a less-expensive way of cleaning old paintbrushes.

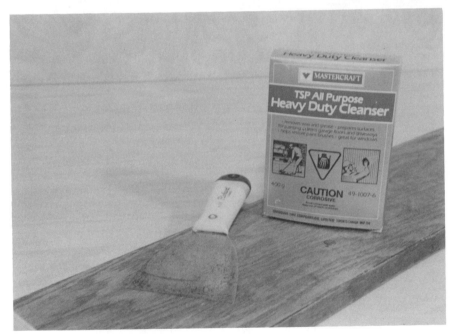

Illus. 202. Trisodium phosphate (TSP) is an inexpensive substitute for commercial paint removers.

Now, get a clean or at least dry roller tray and put paint thinner in it (water, if you are using latex paint). Roll the roller back and forth several times until it seems to be coming clean.

In the second method, use the commercial paintbrush/roller spinner shown in Illus. 203. Install the roller on the tool and then pump the handle. Centrifugal force takes over and spins out the paint residue. Doing it inside a plastic shopping bag will no doubt save the walls and yourself from being splattered. Most paint stores have them available.

I have used the same roller five or six times, so the tool has more than paid for itself. Oh, the spinner has a grip for paintbrushes as well.

Illus. 203. This paintbrush/roller spinner will make your paint rollers and brushes reusable many times over.

Paint Roller Trays, Cleaning

Most of a painter's time is spent in preparing the surfaces for paint and then cleaning up the tools afterwards. This **shortcut** will save time and money when cleaning up the tools: Plastic roller tray inserts are fairly expensive. A pack of three is about the same price as a new tray.

Your dry cleaner has the answer. The plastic bags that they wrap suits and dresses in make ideal tray covers (Illus. 204). Slip the tray halfway into the bag, set it on the floor, and pour in the paint. When you are finished, pour

Illus. 204. A plastic dry-cleaning bag makes an ideal paint-tray liner with which to clean up paint easily.

any excess carefully back into the can, roll up the plastic inside-out, and toss it away or recycle it.

Estimating the Amount of Paint

It's spring and you and your spouse have decided to repaint the living room. Don't go blindly to your neighborhood paint store and ask for a couple of gallons. You know that if you do, one of two things is going to happen: You will either end up with too much or you will end up with too little. The former is not so bad; it's the latter that will end up being a problem, especially if you have a custom color mix. One little drop of the color tint could make a *big* difference.

To properly estimate the paint requirement, do the following: Multiply the length of each wall by the height of the wall in feet (Illus. 205). Ignore the doors and windows. Add up the totals. This will give you the total number of square feet for the room. Add 10% to the figure. This will take into account those little touch-ups and leave a little left over.

Now, it's time to go to the paint store. You have the information that they require and they will tell you the quantity needed of the type of paint that you want. Be sure to tell them what the wall texture or material is as well.

After the painting is done, pour the leftover paint into

Illus. 205. When you're buying paint, make sure that you are armed with the dimensions of the room that you plan to paint.

an airtight container that will *just* hold what's left. Mark it with the paint mix number and the room that it was used on.

Paint Thinner, Recycling

Pour your used paint thinner into clear-plastic containers such as soda pop bottles. Label the containers and cap them.

After awhile, you will find that the paint or other materials will have settled to the bottom of the bottle and that the rest of the bottle is now clear (Illus. 206). Carefully pour this paint thinner into another clearly marked container. This paint thinner can be used again.

Some words of caution: Don't mix these fluids together and, if you have kids around, lock these chemicals up.

Illus. 206. Note the used paint thinner in the clear-plastic container. The paint and the other materials will settle to the bottom, allowing you to reuse the paint thinner.

Patterns, Transferring

Woodworking book patterns are fun to use because they are usually tried and tested *before* they are put into pattern books. Therefore, you can be assured that the whirligig or other project will turn out as expected.

However, transferring the patterns from the pattern book to your workpiece can be a tedious operation. The usual method consists of dividing the pattern into, for example, ½″ squares and then doing the same on your stock. To double the pattern size, you use 1″ squares on the stock.

Now there is an easier way: photocopying. You simply make a high-contrast photocopy of the pattern, reducing or enlarging as required. Most libraries, post offices, and drugstores have coin-operated machines available.

Once the photocopy is done, place it upside-down on the workpiece and, using an iron that is *not* too hot, press it onto the wood (Illus. 207). Voilà, your pattern is transferred. Testing on scrap wood beforehand is always a good rule.

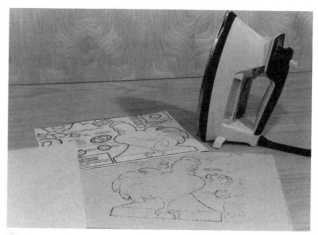

Illus. 207. A warm iron applied to the back of a photocopied pattern will transfer the pattern onto your workpiece.

going to lose about 1½″ of hanging space every 16″, more or less, depending on the stud placement. And, you *know* that Murphy's law will prevail.

Now for the accessories. Regular hooks, straight, an-

Pegboard

Placement and Installation of Pegboard

One of the wisest investments a home woodworker can make is the purchase of a few sheets of ⅛″ thick pegboard. Pegboard is one of the most useful materials in the workshop.

I try to mount at least a piece of pegboard right near all of my stationary tools. It's a great place for hanging sanding belts, band-saw blades, and shop aids and jigs. Before hanging it, I usually frame the back of it with 1 × 2s and then add a vertical strip down the middle, depending on the width of the panel. The 1 × 2s are screwed on edge to the board so that the board sticks out from the wall and allows plenty of room for inserting the metal pegs. You can mount the pegboard directly onto the wall studs but I wouldn't recommend this because you are

Illus. 208. Some of the Rubbermaid accessories available for pegboard storage.

gled, or cupped, and specialty hooks for screwdrivers, hammers, etc., can be purchased at most hardware stores. However, Rubbermaid has a whole system that fits beautifully onto a pegboard (Illus. 208). Rubbermaid's system is composed of a series of various-sized opened and closed containers, brackets for hammers and screwdrivers, and myriad other special tools. It's worth looking into.

Uses of Pegboard

Pegboard is mighty useful to have around the shop. I make sure that I have at least a partial sheet on hand all the time. In addition to the obvious use on the wall for tool storage, there are many more uses. Here's one. Most stationary power tools come equipped with an open sheet-metal stand. Try covering one, two, or three sides of the stand with pegboard (Illus. 209). It also makes a great place to

hang saw blades, mitre gauges, and other accessories. Don't stop there. Make a shelf out of pegboard that will fit on the stretchers that support the base (Illus. 210). The pegboard's holes will let most of the sawdust run through, and the shelf will come in handy.

Illus. 210. Making a shelf out of pegboard will help reduce dust accumulation.

Securing Hooks on Pegboard

One of the most annoying things about pegboard is the way that the hooks keep falling off when you remove a tool. A number of companies that make the hooks also make clips that go around the hooks and fasten into the holes. The problem is, I can never seem to find them in the store.

Here's an easy and inexpensive way to solve the problem: Plug in your glue gun. When it's hot, squirt a little hot glue in the hole where you intend to put the hook (Illus. 211). While the glue is still hot, install the hook. For

Illus. 209. Attaching pegboard to sheet-metal tool stands will keep the tools' accessories in a convenient place.

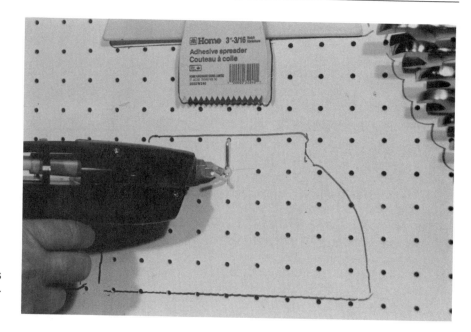

Illus. 211. To keep the hooks on pegboard secure, apply a little dab of hot-melt glue.

longer hooks, repeat the above but also place some glue into a lower hole. Be sure that the glue goes into the hole *and* around the shaft of the hook.

Pencils, How to Use

So many times I have walked into a woodshop and seen a

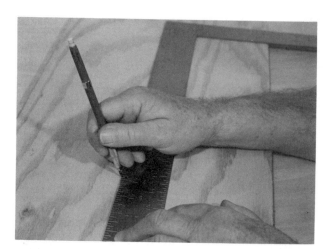

Illus. 212. Keeping your pens/pencils in a near vertical position makes a more accurate line for cutting.

variety of pencils being used to mark lines. The material is cut on a band or jigsaw and then looked at. Sure enough, out comes the plane or the belt sander.

Save yourself some time with these **shortcuts**: Use what is called a mechanical or draftsman's pencil instead of a carpenter's pencil that is big, usually dull-tipped, and has an uneven point. Then make sure you draw the line properly. Always hold the pencil in a near-vertical position and draw the line without altering the rotation of the pencil (Illus. 212). By practising this, you will see that your lines don't waver and, therefore, you will end up with a much more accurate line and, subsequently, a more accurate cut.

Planes

Description and Use of Planes

When researching planes, I was astonished at the versatility of these tools. I can just imagine, back in the days before all of today's new power tools, a cabinetmaker's shop having a hundred or more variations of the hand plane. Back then, the plane was not only used for levelling and squaring, it also did the work of a router, table saw, and jointer. And it was all done by hand.

Following is a brief description of some of the planes available in the past and today (Illus. 213). If you are a collector, a lot of the routing and dadoing planes can be found at flea markets and antique stores.

Bench Plane

This is a levelling or smoothing plane that is 8"–10" in length and is used as a finishing plane.

Block Plane

The smallest of all the planes, block planes are used for squaring off end grain. Generally, the block plane does not have an iron (the piece that sits on top of the blade and has a curve near the bottom to facilitate shaving removal), because the end grain does not give off long shavings as such.

Chamfer Plane

This tool has a V-shaped sole for producing a desired chamfer on a workpiece.

Compass Plane

A compass plane has an adjustable spring-steel soleplate that will take various radii that allow this tool to smooth inside curves.

Fillister Plane (See *Rabbet Plane*)

Fore Plane

A shorter, less-heavy version of the jointer or trying plane, the fore plane is used for levelling the stock after the jack plane is used. The fore plane is about 18" long.

Grooving or Trenching Plane

This plane is used for cutting grooves *across* the grain and has a stepped soleplate.

Jack Plane

A hefty levelling plane used for rough lumber. It is 14"–16" long.

Jointer Plane

As its name implies, this 22"–32" plane is used for truing up joints.

Moulding Plane

This tool was used in the same way that we would use a router today, but without the noise and the dust and with considerable amount of effort and time. A well-equipped woodworking shop would have at least as many moulding planes as there are router bits. The moulding plane is a dedicated tool that will produce only the shape of the sole or base, because it and the blade are identical in shape.

Nosing Plane

Concave in shape, this tool is used primarily for shaping the front of stair treads.

Rabbet Plane

This tool generally had an adjustable side plate to vary the depth of the rabbet, and the blade rides flush with the edge of the surface sole. Some, however, did not have the adjustable side plates. The ones that did were sometimes called *fillister planes*.

Router Plane

Similar to a grooving plane, the router plane has a small blade that bends forward in the tool and is shaped like an L. The blades are available in various widths.

Illus. 213. Some of the various types of planes still available: 1, side rabbet plane; 2, spokeshave; 3, smooth or bench plane; 4, rabbet plane; 5, bullnose rabbet plane; 6, block plane; 7, 14" jack plane; and 8, router plane.

Smooth Plane

This is a short plane, about 6″ long. Because of its short length, it is able to smooth out those small, uneven areas.

Spokeshave

This has also been called a draw knife. The tool has most of the mechanisms of a conventional plane, but the blade is drawn towards you.

Trying Plane

A trying plane, like the jointer plane, is used for jointing. It is shorter than the jointer plane, about 24″ long.

Smoothing the Edges of Boards with Planes

Smoothing the edges of a board or the full surface of a narrow board with a bench plane is a precise operation. It is, at the best of times, difficult to keep the plane square. This **shortcut** should prove helpful: Use small carriage bolts, washers, and nuts to hold a scrap piece of ¾″ hardwood or other stock securely to the side of your hand plane. This will act as a fence to keep the plane level and perpendicular to the edge surface of the board. The hand-plane blade is set in from the edge by about ¼″, so a rabbet made in the jig will ensure full blade contact with the edges (Illus. 214).

Plastics

(Also see Plexiglas)

Bending Plastics

Bending acrylics or styrenes can be accomplished in many ways. Here are three. In the first method, using a propane blowtorch with a pencil-thin flame aimed at the desired crease will soften ⅛″ or ¼″ acrylic or styrene enough to make a bend in the material (Illus. 215). Do not concentrate the flame in one spot, but wave it back and forth across the workpiece and do both sides. The workpiece should be hanging over a straight edge at the bending point.

The heat gun or hair dryer is another method to use for bending, but it will take longer to bend acrylics or styrenes of any thickness over ⅛″.

The third method involves baking (that's right, baking)

Illus. 214. A piece of scrap hardwood rabbeted and clamped to the side of a hand plane will ensure squared surfaces and edges on a workpiece.

the plastic. Use a clean cookie sheet. Lay the workpiece on it, turn up the oven to about 200 degrees, leave the oven door ajar, and turn on the exhaust fan. The workpiece will soften into a rubbery state that should be placed into a precut mould. Oven mitts are a *must* in this operation.

Cutting Plastics

In my first book, I described how to score and cut plastics such as acrylic. Here are a couple more ideas. For large sheets or pieces, assuming that you have scored them, put the piece on the floor with the scored side down (Illus. 216). Place a piece of scrap wood with a straightedge or a square across the material and snug to the score line. Stand on the wood and pull up on the workpiece. It should readily snap clean.

Laying your scored material over the top of a dowel or tube and applying equal pressure to both sides of your workpiece is equally effective.

History of Plastics

The year: 1863. The place: New York. The man: John Wesley Hyatt. John Hyatt was trying to make a substitute for ivory and win an award that was offered by a billiard-ball manufacturer. The prize was $10,000, a substantial amount of money back then. John may have not won the prize, but he did invent Celluloid®, the forerunner of all the forms of plastic that we know today.

Plastics in the 1950s and '60s were known as inferior substitutes for natural material. Now, of course, plastics do a tremendous variety of jobs better than any natural materials.

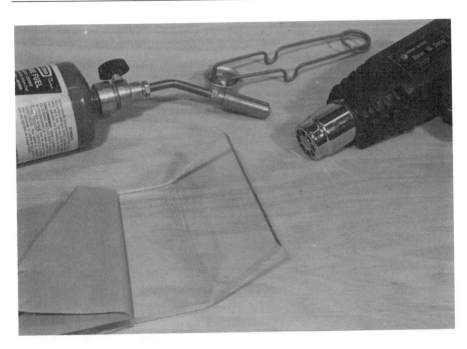

Illus. 215. A blowtorch, a heat gun, and oven-baking are three ways you can use to bend Plexiglas.

Plastics, in the form of resins, are used to bond the plies in plywood. Nylon, a derivative, replaces metals in such things as gears and cams. Plexiglas, an acrylic trade name, has replaced glass in a multitude of applications. General Electric has carried it further by developing a polycarbonate that it calls Lexan, an almost indestructible material that is as clear as glass. Lexan is the material that is used as windows for armored cars, bank teller's cages, etc.

What is even more amazing is the complete turnaround that the plastics industry has taken since the 1950s and '60s. The industry now produces polymer-based oils that are so slick they outlast conventional motor oils ten to one or better and that they sell *back* to the oil companies. And I'm sure I read somewhere that there is now a plastic substitute for dimensional lumber. I do know that joists, rafters, and trusses are now being pre-formed with plastic-

Illus. 216. Snapping Plexiglas by using a straightedge and pulling the Plexiglas up to break it on the scored line.

or resin-reenforced plywood or wood particles. It won't be long now before we see dimensioned hardwoods that are plastic-based. I do hope I'm wrong.

Safety Techniques

Working with plastics poses the same safety hazards as working with wood. When sawing you must use a dust mask because the dust is extremely fine and is an irritant to the mucous membranes, and some forms of plastic could be toxic (Illus. 217). ***Do not smoke or allow sparks or an open flame anywhere near your work.***

Types of Plastics

ABS
ABS is a tough, rigid plastic primarily used for sewer and water pipes.

Acrylic
More commonly known as Plexiglas, a trade name, acrylic is available in sheets, tubes, rods, and blocks. It is used in a multitude of products such as windows, tabletops, etc.

Epoxy
A chemical-resistant material used in adhesives.

Melamine
Melamine is usually available in sheets as a surface veneer that is resistant to scratching and heat, and has been more recently available as a paint-on material for kitchen counters and concrete floors. It has been successfully used to refinish rusted bathtubs and sinks.

Nylon
Aside from its obvious use in panty hose, nylon is also used for gears, cams, and other small parts. It is extremely durable and self-lubricating. Wire tie wraps are made of a type of nylon that makes them extremely strong.

Polycarbonate
This clear, Plexiglas-like material, which is available through the common trade name of Lexan, is extremely tough and sometimes considered bullet-proof in its thicker dimensions. Polycarbonate is available in sheets, rods, and tubes. However, like Plexiglas, it is easily scratched.

Polyethylene
Polyethylene is most commonly used in paper-thin sheets as a vapor barrier or in the making of garbage bags.

Polystyrene
Polystyrene is similar to acrylic in that it is clear and is available in sheets, rods, and tubes. It is very brittle and is not resistant to ultraviolet rays. Exposed to the sunlight, it will discolor and crack.

Polyurethane
Polyurethane is a tough material that is resistant to chemicals but is highly flammable and gives off *toxic* fumes when burning. It is used as insulation and foam in products such as moulded chairs.

Polyvinyl Acetate
This material is a major component in paints, adhesives, and wood fillers.

PVC
PVC (polyvinyl chloride) is most commonly found in the manufacture of piping.

Silicone
Silicone is a very elastic material that can be found more readily in caulk and adhesives.

Illus. 217. Some of the safety gear that should be used whenever plastics are being worked with.

Plexiglas, Welding

Hold on! Don't put a match to that acetylene torch just yet. The Plexiglas, a trade name for acrylic, will be cold-welded; that is, a liquid acrylic solvent is used to bond the pieces together and the solvent is applied with a hypodermic syringe (Illus. 218). *Extreme* care should be taken when doing this operation because the needle is very sharp. The pieces to be "welded" should be clamped or taped together and *must* be close-fitting. Any gaps will weaken the joint.

Inject the solvent into the joint only until you see it fill the seam, because any surplus will leak out and permanently damage the surrounding area. Once it is done, let the workpiece sit for an hour or so before removing the clamps or tape. When the job is completed, store the solvent and the hypodermic needle in a safe place, preferably under lock and key.

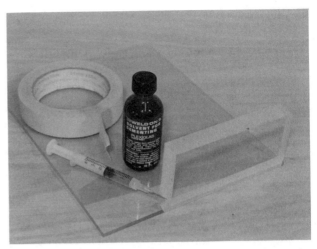

Illus. 218. Welding Plexiglas with a hypodermic needle filled with acrylic solvent. Note the use of masking tape to maintain the position of the joining pieces. When you have finished welding the Plexiglas, store the solvent and the needle in a safe place, preferably under lock and key.

Plywood, Preventing Tear-Out in

Crosscutting plywood with anything less than an 80-tooth, carbide-tipped saw blade will invariably cause tear-out (rough edges), but not all of us have or can afford an 80-tooth, carbide-tipped blade. Here is a **shortcut** that will save you both time *and* money the next time that you are crosscutting a piece of plywood. Run a strip of masking tape across the width of the workpiece, where your cut will be (Illus. 219). Make your line *on* the masking tape and then make your cut, also cutting the masking tape. The result will be a nice, clean cut.

The downside of this technique is that you will probably have to clean your saw blade more often, but if you are making a lot of these crosscuts, it's worth it. You won't have to run out and spend $50–$75 or more for a new blade. You won't have to spend time filling in the chipped areas with plastic wood, either.

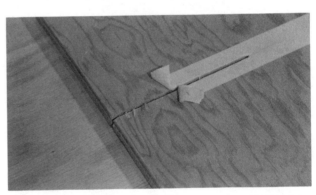

Illus. 219. Applying masking tape to plywood to ensure a tear-out-free crosscut.

Polygons

By definition, a polygon is a geometric figure having three or more equal sides (Illus. 220). Most of these shapes have names. Here they are:

Triangle: 3 sides
Square: 4 sides
Pentagon: 5 sides

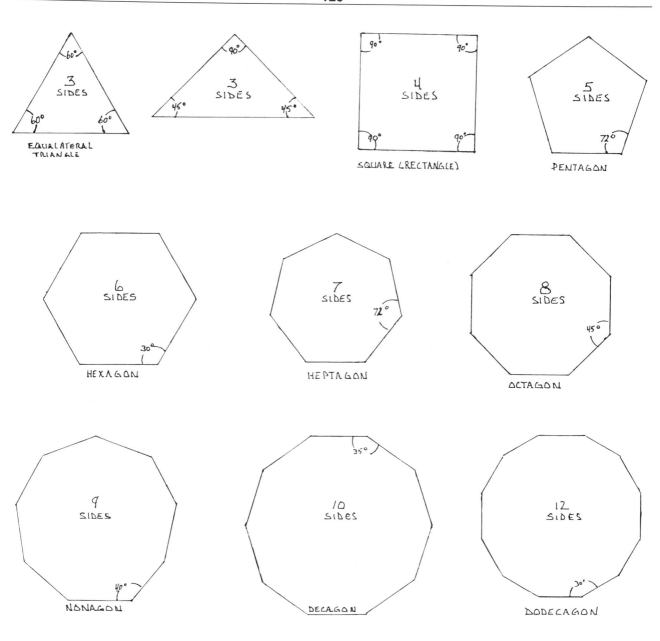

Illus. 220. Polygons.

Hexagon:	6 sides
Heptagon:	7 sides
Octagon:	8 sides
Nonagon:	9 sides
Decagon:	10 sides
Undecagon:	11 sides
Dodecagon:	12 sides

Veritas sells a handy little jig for setting up the proper angles for 4- , 5- , 6- , 8- , and 12-sided polygons. It's called a Poly-Gauge® (Illus. 221).

Illus. 221. The Veritas Poly-Gauge being used to set the angle on a radial arm saw.

Pop or Blind Riveter, Description and Uses

The pop riveter is one of the handiest tools that I have used. If you don't have one, get one. Basically, the tool, also called a blind riveter, installs a rivet type of fastener that will secure plastics, sheet metal, aluminum, and other thin material (Illus. 222). The rivet itself is made of aluminum and has a pin, or nail, running through it. The tool pulls on the nail, which compresses the rivet on the underside of the workpiece. The nail breaks off and you are left with a riveted top surface and a bumpy piece of compressed aluminum underneath. As when using any type of rivet, you must drill an appropriate-sized hole first. Washers are available to place on the underside for securing soft, flexible materials.

Get the type of riveter that has three or four accessory tips that screw in. These allow you to use just about all of the different assortment of rivets available. The rivets themselves are available in an assortment of lengths and diameters.

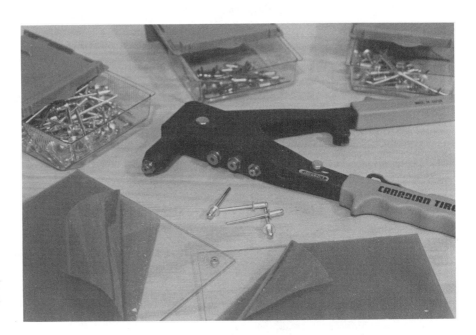

Illus. 222. The pop riveter will join a variety of materials securely.

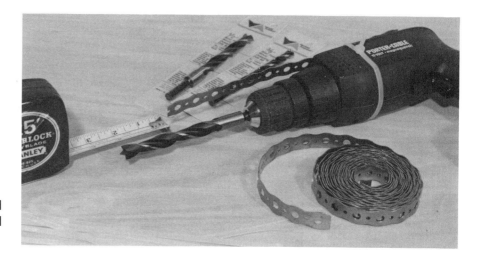

Illus. 223. Perforated steel strapping makes an ideal drill depth stop.

One other point: If Murphy's law messes you up, simply drill out the rivet. Use the same size of bit that you used to drill the original hole. Because it's made of aluminum, it's easy to drill through.

Portable Drill

Shop-Made Depth Stop

Most portable ½″ electric drills are equipped with a side handle that just screws into position. Some ⅜″ drills have them as well, or at least the holes are there to accommodate one. If you are hand-drilling holes where the depth of the hole is critical, the depth stop shown in Illus. 223 might work for you. Simply cut a length of perforated steel strapping and install it between the side handle and the drill housing. Measure the strapping for the depth of cut with the appropriate bit in the chuck and cut it off with tin snips. If your drill does not. have a threaded hole for a handle, use a nylon tie wrap, cord, or piece of elastic to secure the strapping.

Drilling Perpendicular Holes with a Portable Drill

The electric drill was probably the first portable power tool invented. I am not sure when this tool was first put on the

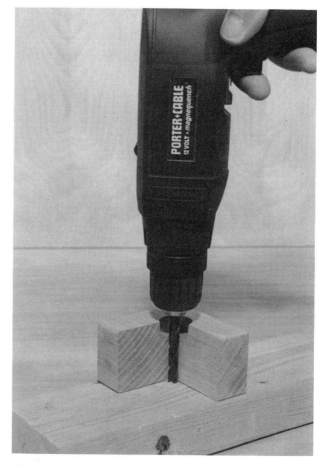

Illus. 224. This V block is an inexpensive way to ensure perpendicular holes when using your portable drill.

market, but it still has major drawbacks that have not been improved on. It is difficult to drill a truly perpendicular hole in a workpiece with a portable drill. Oh, so many manufacturers have come up with myriad ideas that would "guarantee" perpendicular holes everytime, but most of these ideas have meant either dismantling the drill chuck or attaching (with straps, screws, nuts, and bolts) some elaborate gizmo or some sort of flimsy drill-press type of attachment.

Here's a **shortcut** that won't take long, costs very little, and does not require any elaborate installation (Illus. 224). It's a V block. The block is made from a piece of scrap hardwood and can be clamped to your workpiece. All you have to do is make sure that the drill bit is kept snug in the wedge.

Making Repeat Holes with a Portable Drill

Making a series of equally spaced holes in, say, shelf gables is a snap with this **shortcut** (Illus. 225). Let's assume that the required holes are ¼″ in diameter and spaced 3″ apart. Take a piece of scrap ½″ thick plywood and cut it 1″ wide × 4″ long. Make a mark ½″ in from either end and ½″ across. This will give you 3″ centers. Drill a ¼″ hole at these marks. A Forstner bit works best because it produces very clean cuts. Insert a ¼″ dowel in one of the holes. The length of the dowel should be about ¾″. You may have to glue it in position on the scrap.

Determine where your first hole is going to be and drill it. Place a straightedge on the gable and clamp it. Place the dowel of the jig in the hole and tight against the straightedge and drill the second hole through the hole in the jig. Repeat as necessary.

Portable Power Tools

Portable Power Tools for the Workshop

The following is a list of my recommendations for the types of portable power tools that a well-equipped home woodworking shop should have on hand. This, however, does not mean that you have to run right out and buy them all. Most woodworkers buy them only when needed or if they are on sale at bargain prices. Black & Decker, for example, has factory outlets that sell reconditioned power tools at big discounts. They carry the full warranty. To ensure a good-quality product, stick to the brand names.

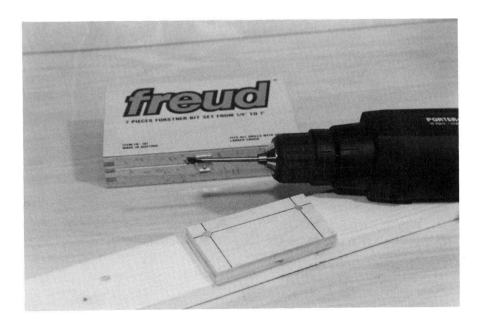

Illus. 225. A series of equally spaced holes are easy to make with this jig.

Illus. 226. Some types of belt sanders: 1, a Black & Decker variable-speed model that can be used inverted; 2, a Black & Decker Professional 3″ × 21″ belt sander; and 3, a Black & Decker 16″ × 2½″ belt sander.

Belt Sander

The type of belt sander (Illus. 226) that I would select will have a variable-speed, high-torque motor. It should have a belt at least 3″ × 21″ and a vacuum port and/or a dust bag option. Another nice feature to have is the ability to mount the sander upside down on your workbench.

Biscuit Joiner

This is a handy tool to have if you are into a lot of cabinetry work (Illus. 227). Basically, it's a router or a mini circular saw that will rout the slot for a glue biscuit.

Circular Saw

The 7¼″ portable circular saw is a must for a home workshop (Illus. 228). My choice is one with a heavy-duty ball-bearing motor and high amperage. The saw should also be equipped with a quick-stop break for safety and a

Illus. 228. A Black & Decker circular saw.

Illus. 227. This biscuit joiner by DeWalt is one of the many makes of biscuit joiners on the market.

lock button for ease in changing blades. Check also for accuracy in the mitre-setting gauge and the depth stop.

Drill

You should have these drills on hand: a ⅜″ variable-speed, reversible (VSR) drill; a ½″ variable-speed drill with two ranges of speed and a hammer setting; and a ⅜″ variable-speed, reversible cordless drill with a torque control (Illus. 229). My reasoning for having three electric drills on hand is that the first one, the ⅜″ variable-speed reversible drill, is fairly lightweight and is useful for getting into cramped quarters, such as inside a bookcase or a stereo cabinet. The ½″ drill is a more wieldy tool that generally has a lot of torque that can easily do those heavy-duty jobs such as boring into the end of a 4″ × 4″ post. The hammer setting vibrates the drill bit in a hammering motion. This

Illus. 229. Three types of drills that are handy to have around the shop: 1, a Black & Decker ⅜″ drill; 2, a Porter-Cable ½″ cordless drill with a keyless chuck and torque control; and 3, a Black & Decker ½″ variable-speed, reversible drill with a hammering feature.

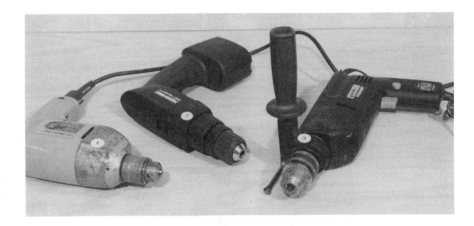

makes drilling into concrete a lot easier. These drills are usually equipped with a depth stop as well.

The third drill, the cordless one, is for those types of projects that are too far away from a plug. The torque control is a handy feature for installing drywall, as an example. The drill will stop before the screw goes all the way through.

Electric Staple Gun

A really handy tool to have around the shop, the electric staple gun makes it easy to drive ½″ or ⅝″ staples (Illus. 230). The types to buy are the ones that have optional attachments for stapling wires (great for installing that phone extension or television cable) or riveting. Some staplers have a nearly flush front face. This is a real advantage for getting in close.

Engraving Tool

This inexpensive little tool (Illus. 231) could save you hundreds of dollars if you put it to use. Use it to engrave

Illus. 231. With the engraving tool, you can etch your name on all your tools to prevent theft or your neighbor from borrowing the tool permanently.

your name or some other identifying mark on *all* of your tools as an aid in the event of theft. It's also great for spotting that long-lost screwdriver that your neighbor borrowed last year.

Glue Gun

A glue gun (Illus. 232) is a necessity around the shop. The heavy-duty one works best in that it takes less time for the gun to heat up. Glue guns will accept a variety of glue and hot caulking sticks. Both the glue and the caulk sticks are available in a range of colors. The gun is also a great tool for "tacking" or caulking.

The mini glue gun is good for those hard-to-reach areas.

Illus. 230. The Arrow electric staple gun.

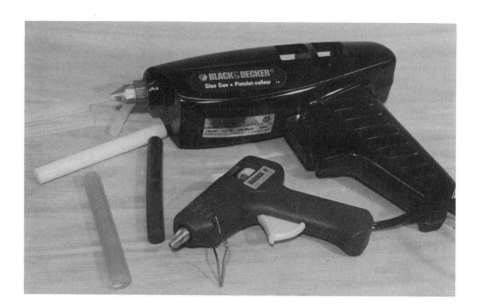

Illus. 232. The standard-size glue gun and a variety of glue and caulking stocks.

Heat Gun

Surprisingly, the heat gun (Illus. 233) is a very handy tool to have around the workshop. Not only will it soften and remove old paint, but it will do myriad other chores as well. The heat gun may be used (cautiously) to force-dry some adhesives, soften some plastics for bending, heat "heat-shrink" tubing, and soften up the glue under veneer that has lifted, to name but a few applications.

Jigsaw

This versatile tool (Illus. 234) is great for cutting irregular shapes, pipe or other soft metals, and plastics, etc. A jigsaw with a variable-speed feature would be my choice.

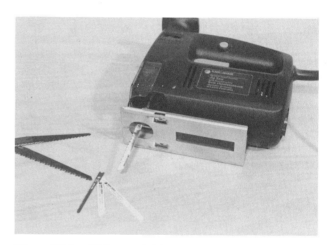

Illus. 234. This variable-speed jigsaw has two blade positions, a scrolling feature, and a vacuum port.

Illus. 233. The newest-model heat gun from Black & Decker (left) and an older model (right) from the same company.

Other features to look for would be a scrolling switch that allows the blade housing to turn freely, a dual-blade housing, and a fully adjustable soleplate.

Mitre Saw

There could be some debate as to whether or not the mitre saw (Illus. 235) is a portable power tool. Basically, it was designed to be one. It was designed primarily for building contractors who wanted a tool that cut precise 90°, 45°, and other mitred cuts and was light enough to carry from job to job. This tool fits the bill. However, most home woodworkers fix it to a recessed table in their workshop.

Illus. 235. The mitre saw mounted level with the workbench to facilitate cutting longer stock.

Make sure you select a mitre saw with a heavy-duty motor with ball-bearing construction, a directional exhaust chute, and a quick-stop blade brake.

Orbital Sander

Here is where it is *really* worthwhile to invest in a professional-quality tool. The orbital sander (Illus. 236) is used often and is often abused in that most people tend to apply a lot of pressure on it. Believe me, this is not necessary. The tool is designed to do the job all by itself. Applying pressure will do no more than shorten the tool's

Illus. 236. A professional-quality Porter-Cable orbital sander that turns at 10,000 OPM (orbits per minute).

life expectancy. Select a ½-sheet-type sander that turns at at least 10,000 OPM (orbits per minute).

Palm Sander

The palm sander (Illus. 237) usually takes a ¼-sheet of sandpaper, so, as the name implies, it is small enough to get into cramped quarters. Palm sanders are *finishing* sanders. They are not designed to remove a lot of the surface.

My choice of palm sander would be one that turns at at least 12,000 OPM, is quiet, and has a longer than normal electrical cord on it. Sandpaper with a grit of 180 is the coarsest type of sandpaper that you should use on this machine. Coarser sandpaper (with a lower number) will make the machine work too hard.

Planer

A portable power planer (Illus. 238) will make hand-planing seem like unusual and cruel punishment. This tool will make short work of the toughest planing jobs.

Some planers have a shallow groove cut into the length of the soleplate. The purpose of this groove is to make chamfering easier. The tool you should select should have carbide-tipped blades, operate at a high RPM, and have an exhaust port adaptable to a shop vacuum.

Random Orbital Sander

The random orbital sander (Illus. 239) is one of the newest tools to enter the market. Random orbital sanders are great in that they rarely leave any swirls. The smaller ones are designed for finishing. The larger ones are usually right-

Illus. 237. Two types of orbital palm sanders. The palm sander is used for finishing with very fine sandpaper.

Illus. 238. The power planer makes it easy to smooth the edges of wood.

Illus. 239. Two types of random orbital sanders from Porter-Cable. The one on the left is meant for finishing work, and the one on the right for heavy-duty work. This one may also be used as a grinder and a polisher.

angle tools that can grind, sand, and polish. The latter is my choice, but I would pick one with a variable-speed motor.

Reciprocating Saw

There are a number of different names for this tool, but the term reciprocating saw seems to be the standard. The saw (Illus. 240) is useful for cutting wood, metal, and plastics, and will get into really tight corners such as cutting 2 × 4s that are tight against the floor and flush to the walls. The blades for these saws can range in length anywhere from 6″ to 12″ or more and will "bend" to get into tight spots.

The type of saw to look for is one with at least two speed ranges or a variable-speed range. It is also an advantage to select a saw that will allow you to change the blade position because in some circumstances it may be advantageous to have the blade of the saw facing up instead of the normal down position.

Illus. 240. This reciprocating saw has two speeds and a reversible blade chuck.

Router

One tool that I regard very highly is the router (Illus. 241). This versatile machine can cut dadoes, mould, dovetails, etc. My preference is for an electronic model, in that it maintains a constant speed within its settings. The settings are entered by type of wood (hard, soft) and the thickness of the stock (¼″, ½″, ¾″).

Another nice feature is a plunge mechanism. This allows you to set the depth of your cut with the router bit above the soleplate. You then place the router in position, push it down into the work, and press the plunge lever. The bit plunges into the workpiece to the exact depth that you want.

When selecting a router, look for one that has a built-in light within the housing and one that is rated commercial or professional. The extra cost will be a good investment.

Illus. 241. The router on the left is a plunge router with an edge guide attached. The router on the right is an electronic Sears Craftsman router. Both have built-in work lights.

Selecting Portable Power Tools

The basic rule "You get what you pay for" certainly applies here. Be very wary when purchasing portable power tools. Select brand-name products from a reputable dealer. A knowledgeable salesperson is an asset.

A number of manufacturers of power tools grade their tools; for example, light-duty for serious do-it-yourselfers, heavy-duty, for professionals (Illus. 242). Be sure to select the right tool for your purposes. There is no doubt that the heavy-duty or professional tool will last longer and take more abuse. It will, of course, be more expensive.

When buying portable power tools, there is *one* very important thing to look for in the quality of the tool: ball bearings. A motorized tool with sealed ball bearings will last at least three times as long as a sleeve-bearing motor.

Another important factor in the selection is the tool's amperage or power. The higher the amperage rating, the stronger the motor and, usually, the higher the torque. Torque can be compared to a car's motor. A four-cylinder engine may have trouble climbing a given hill without down-shifting. An eight-cylinder engine will have no trouble at all.

As a safety factor, make sure that the tool is properly grounded. This warning should be given in the instruction manual under the specifications. If the tool has a three-prong plug, **never** remove the round ground plug. It's there for your safety.

Illus. 242. Portable power tools rated Professional will last many times longer than other types of portable power tools.

Pulleys, Sizing

This has always been a trial-and-error situation for most woodworkers. The math grads probably find it a snap. For the rest of us, this may help. Let's suppose you want to build your own bench grinder. You have an electric motor and the speed is marked on it in rpm (for example, 1,725). The grinder has a 2½″ pulley already on its shaft. You want to increase the speed of the grinding wheel to around 4,000 rpm. What size should the pulley be on the motor shaft?

The formula is easy with a calculator. Multiply 4,000 by 2½ and then divide by 1,725. You end up with a calculation of 5.797. This is the diameter of the pulley required to attain the desired speed. A 6″ pulley will do just fine.

Illus. 243. As described in the text, it is easy to calculate the right-size pulley to use for a given speed.

Radial Arm Saw

Checking a Radial Arm Saw for Square

At least once a month or more, depending on use, check the accuracy of the saw, particularly in the crosscut position. It's easy to do and only takes a few minutes.

First, with the *power plug removed and the saw switched off*, as in all operations like this, remove the blade. Now, remove the inside washer (the first came off with the blade and nut). Check the washer's surfaces for flatness. If there are any little bumps, grind them off on a *flat* oilstone. A small bump or flaw will make the blade wobble. Check the sharpness of the blade and then reinstall it, but do not overtighten the nut.

Now, for the squaring. First, butt the tail of a steel square against the fence and line its body along the kerf (Illus. 244). Pull the carriage (*with the motor off, the key out, and the saw unplugged*) towards you. Use one tooth of the blade as a guide; the tooth should just touch the square equally on the full pull of the crosscut. If you can do this, the saw is cutting at 90° horizontal. If you have to adjust the saw, loosen the Allen bolts on the rear post.

With the blade guard off, lift the body of the square about 30° so that the square rests against the full surface of the saw blade and is not touching any teeth or the arbor. If the square is flat against the saw blade and the tail of the square is tight against the fence, the saw is cutting at 90° vertical (Illus. 245). To make an adjustment you will have to loosen the bevel screws.

Illus. 244. Checking the horizontal plane of the radial arm saw blade with a steel square held firmly against the fence.

Illus. 245. Checking the vertical plane of the saw. Be sure to keep the steel square in the gullets of the saw blade.

Adjusting the Depth of Cut on a Radial Arm Saw

Method #1
Okay, so you want to make a ⅜″ cut into a ¾″ piece of stock. You get out your tape measure and try to figure

where the bottommost saw tooth is and take your measurement from there. Wrong!

Veritas has a saw-setting gauge that can be used to determine the depth of cut (Illus. 246). This extremely accurate tool has ⅛″ gradations on one end and ¼″ graduations on the other. This tool can also be used for adjusting *table saw* blade heights and widths, router bit depths, drill press depths, etc.

Illus. 246. The Veritas saw-setting gauge being used to set the depth of cut on a radial arm saw.

Method #2
Specifically marked 2 × 4 pieces of ⅛″, ¼″, ⅜″, ½″, ⅝″, ¾″, and ⅞″ plywood can be used to set the height of your radial-arm-saw blade (Illus. 247). They can be used alone or in any combination to give you the desired depth of cut.

Illus. 247. You can use this set of shop-made blocks alone or in various configurations to adjust the height of your saw blade.

These jigs can be used for setting the height of your table saw blade, the depth of your router and drill press, and to set the cut for myriad other tools. The one-two-three blocks used in combination with these will give you the whole numbers with fractions as well.

Drill ¼″ holes in the top center of these jigs and hang them on a pegboard near your saw.

Extension Table for the Radial Arm Saw

Well, I've expanded my workshop and now I finally have enough room there to be able to move around. I can now remove the wheels from the stationary power tools, and the workbench can now be used solely for what it was intended.

A problem still exists, however. When I moved my radial arm saw, I moved the out-feed table with it but then realized that a fixed in-feed table would also be desirable. The in-feed table (assuming that ripping is done from left to right) should be 6′–8′ long to handle 8′, 10′, and 12′ stock. This, of course, would take up a lot of space in the shop and would probably alter the work flow.

The solution was to split the hinged in-feed table in two, as shown in Illus. 248. Half of it drops down out of the way. The fixed portion will handle 8′ stock quite easily. I raise the other half for longer stock and for sheets of plywood.

The fixed portion has a slot in it to allow for a longer fence, but the table itself is as wide as the saw's table. The table can now rip a 4′ × 8′ sheet with ease.

With some modifications, this extension table can be adapted to your **table saw** as well.

Mitre Cuts

Making accurate mitre cuts, whether on a table saw or on a radial arm saw, is usually difficult. The workpiece tends to wander away from the saw blade when the blade is tilted for the cut.

Mitre jigs are the answer (Illus. 249). Cut six pieces of ½″ plywood. The first one will be 12″ square. The second will be 11″ × 12″, the third will be 10″ × 12″, etc. Now, cut triangles, two for each piece. The triangles for the first piece will be 45°, for the second piece 30°, and for the third 25°. The rest will be at 22.5°, 20°, and 15°. Glue and screw the triangles to the tops. The piece with the 45° triangle will be the widest. Make certain that the bases of all the triangular pieces are plumb to the tops.

When completed, all six pieces should nest within each other. Cut ½″ or so off the bottom slope, and drill holes near the tops for hanging. And there you have it, a set of six angle jigs.

The beauty of these angle jigs is that they can be used on your band saw, drill press, table saw, and radial arm saw with equal efficiency. This little **shortcut** may take a little time now, but it will save a lot of time later.

Illus. 248. The in-feed table is hinged to take up less shop space when not in use.

Illus. 249. The mitre jig being used with a radial arm saw.

Mortise-and-Tenon Jig

The mortise-and-tenon jig shown in Illus. 250 and 251 is a timesaver that can be used to make repeat, large mortise-and-tenon joints as found on some tables, chairs, and other joinery. This jig can also be adapted for dovetail mortises and tenons as well.

This jig consists of a higher-than-normal hardwood or plywood fence to which a platform is glued and screwed. The platform should be about 2″ high, 12″–14″ deep, and about 12″ wide. The rear fence will sit in the saw's fence slot and rise above the jig platform by an inch or so. I used a couple of T nuts and ¼″ bolts to secure a top clamp for holding the workpieces in place.

The operation is simple. Swing the saw bevel so that the blade is horizontal. Raise or lower the blade as required for

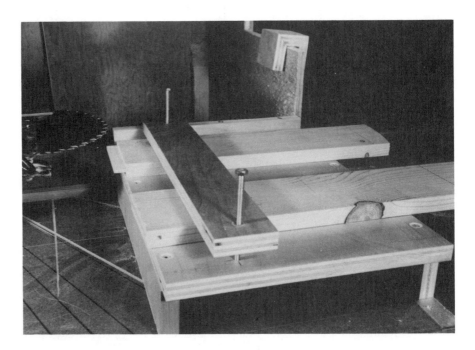

Illus. 250. Using the mortise-and-tenon jig.

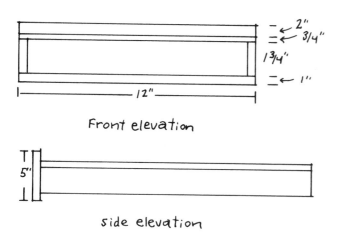

Front elevation

side elevation

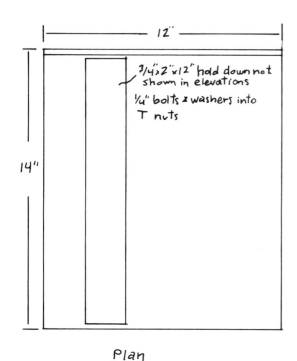

3/4"x2"x12" hold down not shown in elevations
1/4" bolts & washers into T nuts

Plan

Illus. 251. Construction of mortise-and-tenon jig.

Illus. 252. A typical dovetailed mortise-and-tenon joint made with the jig.

the tenon thickness. Tilting the blade will give you dovetail tenons (Illus. 252).

Setting Up the Radial Arm Saw

Although I try to be safety-conscious, I sometimes forget to set the prawls on the saw when it is in the rip position.

As a result, pieces of stock can come flying out at bullet speed. I know I learned my lesson when a thin strip of wood came loose and smashed through the front of one of my parts cabinets. So now I clamp a piece of scrap to the saw table before ripping small pieces (Illus. 253).

Be extremely cautious when using the radial arm saw. *Always* stand to one side when ripping and make sure that there is nothing breakable in the path of the blade. Better yet, *remember* to set your prawls when ripping material.

Stop Block

In *Ingenious Shop Aids & Jigs*, my previous book, I described how to make and use the stop block shown in Illus. 254. However, I recently thought of an idea that, when modified, will double the usefulness of this jig.

Rather than putting the T nut in the middle of the block, install it closer to the bottom. By making this simple modification, the stop block can be raised, tightened, and used as a hold-down for ripping or for mitred cuts.

Swinging Fence for the Radial Arm Saw

The swing fence shown in Illus. 255 will save you a lot of time and frustration when making angled cuts. The fence itself is a little higher than normal and it is split and hinged to the left of the saw blade. A small cabinet or butt hinge will do, but be sure, though, that the pivot of the hinge does not extend beyond the front surface of the fence. Also, be sure that the hinge screws do not come in close contact with the saw blade.

To make the jig, I drilled two holes on a 15° angle into a

Illus. 253. Clamp a piece of scrap to your table to deflect any projectiles in the event that you forget to set your prawls or they slip.

Illus. 254. This modified stop block can now be used as a hold-down for ripping or mitring. A T nut and a hex bolt secure it to the saw's fence.

Illus. 255. The swinging fence in place on the radial arm saw, to cut a 20° angle. Note that it is longer and higher than a normal fence. A common nail locks the fence in position.

piece of wood, and put a couple of nails into the holes. This locks the swing arm for regular 90° crosscutting.

To use the swinging arm, check the angle required with a sliding bevel and then transfer it to the arm. You may want to scribe the commonly used angles right on your saw's auxiliary tabletop surface. I drilled a vertical hole at the end of the arm and then drilled corresponding holes at the most commonly used angles. A common nail fits through the holes tightly and keeps the fence locked in position.

True Crosscutting with the Radial Arm Saw

You are down to that *last* piece of oak and you want to make a small true and square crosscut. But the piece that you have does not have a square corner on it. What to do?

Try this little **shortcut**: First, roughly measure out the piece that you need to cut and make the appropriate pencil lines. Nail, spot-glue, or use double-faced tape to attach this workpiece to a piece of *squared* scrap wood (Illus. 256). If you are nailing, be sure that the nails are on the cutoff piece and well clear of the saw cut. Now, hold the pieces firmly against the radial-arm-saw fence and make your first cut. Remove the under piece, place the straight cut side of the oak against the fence, and make your second cut. You now have two sides squared. Do the same to the other two sides.

Not only will this give you a squared piece of stock, but it will save you a lot of money. Most woodworkers would throw that piece of oak into the scrap bin.

Rasp, Shop-Made

Don't throw away those old hacksaw blades. As a matter of fact, if you can scrounge some from your local friendly plumber, do so. A pile of them about 1½″ high will suffice. Make a stack and alternate the tooth direction of each blade. Install a nut and a bolt through the holes at each end and you have a really efficient rasp (Illus. 257).

Refinishing, Methods

Your spouse has just come back from a flea market with an "antique" table in the back of the station wagon. It has 10

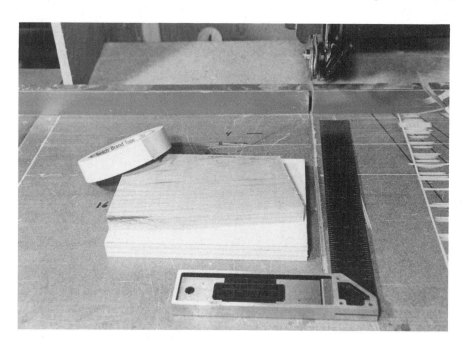

Illus. 256. Using double-faced tape and a squared piece of scrap to cut a straight edge on a workpiece.

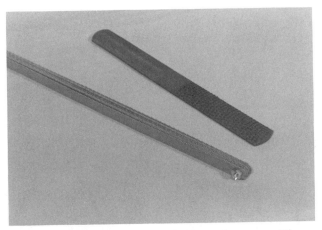

Illus. 257. This efficient shop-made rasp utilizes old hacksaw blades. Also shown is a Stanley 4 in 1 rasp.

or 12 coats of paint and varnish on it, so you know what he/she has in mind. Off you go to the workshop.

The first thing to do is get a scrap piece of plywood or panelling that is two feet larger all around than the table. Set the table on it and move all your refinishing paraphernalia so that it's close at hand. With conventional strippers, the area should be well ventilated. 3M's new product Safest Stripper® does not require such a high degree of ventilation, though some is needed. This product cleans up with water, has high penetration strength, and gives off little odor or toxic fumes (Illus. 258). The area temperature, though, should be around 21° Celsius or 72° Fahrenheit for the most effective penetration of this or almost any stripper.

Rubber or latex gloves are mandatory when you are restripping furniture, as are safety glasses. If conventional strippers are used, I recommend the use of an approved respirator. *Proper ventilation is also required.*

Let's assume that you are using the Safe Stripper product. The materials required (Illus. 259) are as follows: old clothes; a selection of 3M's or Norton's finish removal pads (coarse, medium, and fine); a bucket of clean water or easy access to a laundry tub and faucet; a couple of rolls of paper towels; some pieces of scrap foam rubber; a wide putty knife; a copper wire brush; an old toothbrush; mineral spirits (varsol or paint thinner); screwdrivers; a small pry bar; a utility knife; and an old plastic pail.

Before starting, I suggest you take a couple of photos with a Polaroid® camera of the piece for both later comparison (it's nice to get a pat on the back once in a while) and to know where all those little pieces of hardware go (Illus. 260). Remove *all* of the hardware pieces and set them

in the plastic pail. The Mini-Wonder Bar® by Stanley can be used here to carefully remove those parts that are glued on with paint. Use the utility knife to carefully score around some parts to break the paint seal. Pour a little Safest Stripper over the parts in the bucket and put them aside.

Now, go to work. Follow the manufacturer's directions to the letter when applying the stripper. Use the removal pads and rinse them often in clean water. The putty knife, wire brush, and toothbrush are used for getting into those tight corners and the intricate details or carvings. The paper towels are for the final cleanup.

When applying the stripper, try this **shortcut**: Place a used plastic ice-cream container under each leg (Illus. 261). The stripper that doesn't adhere will collect in the containers and can be reused.

When brushing on the stripper, do it in one direction only and do not go over the preceding strokes. Going over will weaken the penetration.

To determine if all the old finish and oils are removed

Illus. 258. A refinishing project ready for stripping and sitting on a scrap piece of plywood.

Illus. 259. Some of the items that you should have ready before starting your refinishing project.

Illus. 260. Taking a couple of photographs of a project before you refinish it will allow you to compare it before and after the job and help you to replace the hardware in their exact positions.

Illus. 261. Placing plastic containers under the legs of your refinishing project will allow you to collect the stripper drippings and reuse them.

Illus. 262. Household bleach will usually remove dark rings and some burn marks.

when you are done, go over the entire piece with mineral spirits and clean paper towels. If there is any trace of the old finish on the paper towel, try one more application of stripper.

The tedious part is removing the paint from all of those little hardware parts. The copper brush should speed things up for you.

When you have finished stripping the project, you can see what it looked like when it was originally built. *However*, there are some unusual dark-stained rings on the top as well as what looks like a cigarette burn. Don't fret. Go into the laundry room and get a bottle of laundry bleach. Apply some to the spots (Illus. 262). Usually, the rings will disappear, but the burns may only lighten up. But, as the antique dealers say, this will give it character.

Now the fun begins. You are getting close to realizing what a bargain you got at that flea market. It's time to start the final finish.

Determine the type of wood that the table is made of. If you don't know or can't identify it, take a sample to either a lumberyard, cabinetmaker, or antique dealer. If you don't particularly like the natural color, then stain is the answer. My choice is the Diamond Finish® stains by Flecto (Illus. 263). These are water-soluble and easily cleaned up with a damp cloth.

Before applying the stain, however, try this: Moisten the end of your finger and press it on the top of the wood. The moistened area will be close to what the unstained

Illus. 263. Some of the Flecto water-soluble stains that are available.

color will be with an oil finish. If you are still convinced that the piece needs stain, start applying it. The easiest way that I know of applying stain is to use a scrap piece of foam rubber. Here's another **shortcut**: To increase the brown shades, use dark walnut. To increase the yellow shades, use oak. To increase the orange shades, use maple. To increase the red shades, use mahogany or cherry.

Apply your stain lightly and then use a clean soft cloth and wipe *diagonally* across the wood grain to help fill in the areas that are missed. Add more coats until the desired density is achieved. A light buffing with a synthetic sanding pad between coats will ensure a smooth finish.

If the natural wood is to your liking, then all that's left to do is apply a protective finish. Let's deal with this now. There are a number of options that you have. You can use the methods of the old-school wood finishers and start with fillers, conditioners, etc., or you could use the new methods, which I prefer. Whichever you choose, do the insides, edges, and underneath parts as well. This will help prevent the wood from expanding or contracting, which will cause warping and splitting later.

Using a high-speed palm sander and 240-grit or finer sandpaper, sand the entire piece (Illus. 264). Vacuum the dust off it; *all of it*. Then use a tack cloth to wipe up any remaining dust. Apply water-soluble polyurethane (varathane) with a fine brush or a piece of scrap foam rubber. Use a synthetic (plastic) finishing pad between coats. *Note: Never use steel wool with these products. They are either water-based or have water in them. Any residue from the steel wool may leave rust spots.*

After the third and final coat, I like to use boiled linseed oil rubbed in with a very fine finishing pad. I let it stand

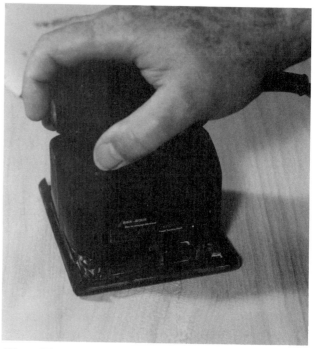

Illus. 264. Sanding the stripped piece with a high speed palm sander and very fine sandpaper.

overnight and then wipe it off with a soft cloth dampened with mineral spirits.

One important point: Water-soluble polyurethane will lighten the finished product and will *not* darken the grain of the wood. The polyurethane product will tend to yellow the workpiece, but *will* enhance the grain. Staining the project will compensate for the color differentials.

Illus. 265. Some of the finishing products that are readily available.

Should you want to change the natural color of the piece before finishing, you could select from some of Minwax's pastel shades of stain that look like milk paint. Minwax Polyshades are another option. These are polyurethane-based finishes with stains built in them. Flecto has similar products that are water-soluble and very easy to clean up (Illus. 265).

If you are going to use an oil-based stain, the final finish should be a varnish, lacquer, or polyurethane. A water-based stain should be followed by a water-soluble polyurethane. Read the instructions on the labels.

A very important note: Do not just throw your old saturated rags away in a pile. They will probably self-combust. Put them outside or lay them flat over a clothesline until they are absolutely dry.

Rotary Tools

Sears Craftsman Rotary Tools

The Sears Craftsman rotary tool is one of the most versatile tools in the power-tool cabinet. This tool will grind, saw, polish, buff, rout, drill, carve, and do lots more.

There are over a hundred different types of bits and attachments available for the tool. I use the metal cutoff discs for cutting piano hinge to size and the mini sanding discs for sanding in those tight corners. The rotary tool shown in Illus. 266 has a variable-speed motor, which is a necessity for the various types of bits available.

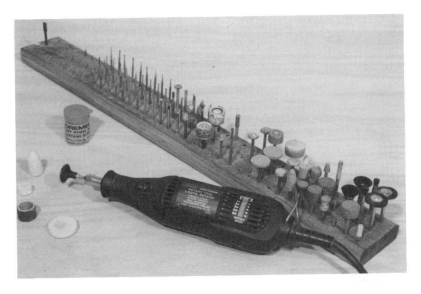

Illus. 266. The Sears Craftsman rotary tool and some of the many accessory bits available.

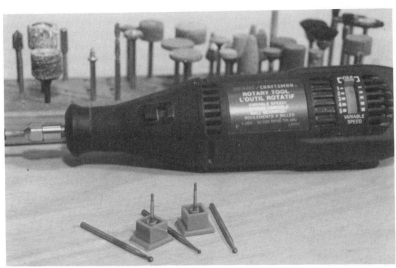

Illus. 267. These are just a sample of some of the dental bits that will fit into a rotary tool.

Rotary Tool Bits

If woodcarving is something you like to do, the motor tool is right up your alley. The purists will shun the tool, but I like it because it allows me to get clean and intricate cuts.

The next time you go to see your dentist, ask him/her to save the used (sterilized) dental drill bits for you (Illus. 267). They may be too dull for teeth, but they still have a lot of life left in them for woodcarving. The beauty of them is their size. They are very small by comparison to the normal motor tool bits, so they are great for carving those very fine details. The shafts are usually smaller than the regular bits, so you may have to purchase a smaller collet or chuck. This is not, however, a major expense.

Router

Shop-Made Cross-Grain Jig

This jig (Illus. 268) will prevent tear-out when you are using your router for making dadoes across the grain for such things as bookcase gables. Using ¾" plywood, cut four pieces 18" long × 3" wide. Rout a slot through each of the four pieces. Glue and screw two pieces together to form an L shape. Repeat this for the remaining two pieces. Referring to Illus. 268, assemble the two L-shaped pieces with carriage bolts, washers, and wing nuts. Obviously, all corners of the jig must be square when you are assembling it.

To use the jig, simply fit it over your workpiece, set your router in it, and tighten up the wing nuts (Illus. 269).

Trimming Laminates with the Router

When edge-trimming veneer or plastic-laminated tops, think twice about using a ball-bearing-type pilot bit. The glue from the surfaces can heat up and possibly drip onto the bit and the bearings. This could cause the bearings to burn out.

Next time you are trimming, this **shortcut** may save the cost of a new bit: Dab some Vaseline® along the edge of your workpiece and use a router bit with a *fixed* pilot (Illus. 270). The petroleum jelly can be easily cleaned up with paint thinner afterwards, but leaving the Vaseline on the bit will help prevent rusting.

Rust, Preventing

Graham's law: Tools will rust. Unused tools will rust faster. Well, it's not really *my* law; Mother Nature has followed it long before me.

There are a number of ways to sidestep this law. Here are two.

Get friendly with your neighborhood electronics dealers, the ones who sell televisions and stereos. Ask them to save the little packs of "silica gel" that are usually packed with the new equipment that they get. Throw a couple of these in each of your tool chest drawers (Illus. 271). They will absorb a lot of the moisture that causes your tools to rust.

Another way to prevent your tools from rusting is to spray silicone on the drawer bottoms of your tool chest

Illus. 268. The cross-grain router jig helps to prevent tear-out.

Illus. 269. The cross-grain router jig in operation.

Illus. 270. A router bit with a fixed pilot works best when you are edge-trimming plastic laminate and veneers.

(Illus. 272). Do not do this with the tools in place. Spraying the tools will also prevent rust, but it will also make the handles and grips *very* slippery. Make sure that the silicone has dried before placing the tools back in the drawers. Before using the tools, check the handles to make sure that there are no traces of the silicone on them. Any residue may be removed with mineral spirits.

Sanders, Safety Guard

One of the handiest little sanding machines that I have seen

Illus. 271. Silica gel packs placed in your tool drawers will absorb moisture and help prevent rust.

Illus. 272. Spraying your tool drawers with silicone will help prevent the tools from rusting.

Illus. 273. The shop-made Plexiglas guard will deflect sanding debris on this Delta 1″ belt sander.

is the one shown in Illus. 273. It's made by Delta and has a 1″ wide belt. The table tilts for angle sanding and sharpening. I have found, however, that because of the opening at the top wheel, some debris will come flying out. There is a vacuum port that will pick up most of the dust, but there is still a risk.

I solved this problem by making a small curved Plexiglas flap that I simply taped on with fibreglass tape. The flap directs the debris down towards the table. Should I want to use this upper portion of the sander for rounding off, I simply flip the guard up and out of the way.

Sanding Discs

Refurbishing Sanding Discs

When you remove PSA (Pressure Sensitive Adhesive) sanding discs—the sticky-back discs—from the pad, the slippery backing sheet will no longer stick to them properly. Later, when you want to reuse the disc, you find that it is full of dust and other accumulated crud. Norton has a product available called Universal Adhesive Solvent &

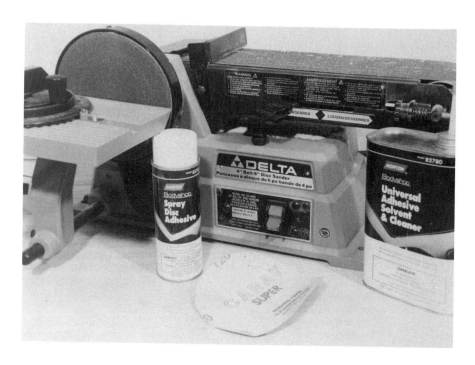

Illus. 274. Cleaner and spray adhesive will refurbish adhesive-backed discs.

Cleaner (Illus. 274). This solvent will remove the adhesive and other stuff from the discs. It will also remove any adhesive residue on the sanding pad.

Okay, so here I am, left with a sanding disc that won't stick anymore. Norton has the answer to that problem as well: a product called Spray Disc Adhesive. Simply spray a coat of adhesive on the back of the disc and you're in business.

Both of these products are available at automotive supply stores.

Removing Sanding Discs

Those pressure-sensitive-adhesive-backed sanding discs that I referred to above go onto the sander quite easily but are tough to remove. No matter how careful you are, they always seem to tear and leave little bits stuck to the surface.

Try one of these **shortcuts** next time you have to replace one of these sanding discs: In the first method, turn your machine on and sand a couple of scraps of wood. This will heat up the disc. Turn the machine off and unplug it. Now, peel off the disc. You will find it a much easier and neater task when the adhesive is warm (Illus. 275). Another way to warm up the adhesive is to use a heat gun.

Before placing a new disc on the wheel, use a little solvent to clean the wheel first. Make sure that the wheel is metal and not a plastic substance. Otherwise, the solvent may eat or melt the plastic.

Sawdust, Removing

The most efficient way to remove sawdust is in the area where it is being produced, and the best way to do this is to install a commercial dust-collection system. However, these can be very expensive. If you are a pack rat like I am, you probably have most of the parts necessary to make your own. I used a 45-gallon plastic drum and installed a vacuum power head (motor) to the top of it (Illus. 276). I then drilled a hole to accept a 2″ hose and connected the hose to some PVC vacuum piping (Illus. 277). I connected the pipes in a series of T, L, and Y shapes to my stationary power tools.

The next thing I made was the gates. Gates serve the purpose of closing the sections of pipe that are not being used so that the vacuum suction is more efficient on the tool that you are running (Illus. 278 and 279). The gates should be conveniently close to each tool.

To make the gates, I made a cut halfway into the pipe with my radial arm saw. I then made a U-shaped piece out of 1/8″ Plexiglas. Using a connector, I first cut partway into it, and then sliced about 40% off it. Now, when the gate is out, I rotate the connector over the open slot to prevent any air loss.

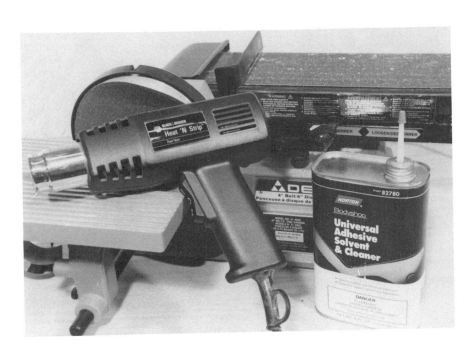

Illus. 275. Adhesive-backed sanding discs can be removed more easily and cleanly when the adhesive is warm.

Illus. 276. A dust-collection system made out of an old 45-gallon plastic drum that I modified. The motor is from an old commercial vacuum. Note the flexible 2″ pipe connected to the rigid PVC vacuum pipe. This allows me to remove the top more easily.

Illus. 277. The rigid PVC pipe mounted on the ceiling.

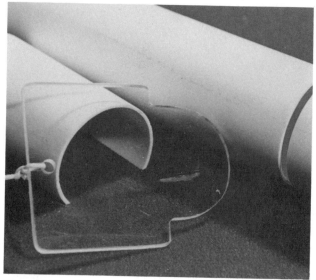

Illus. 278. The components of the shop-made gate.

There are, of course, commercially available gates or valves, as they are called (Illus. 281). These work very well and they allow you to run *flexible* vacuum hose from the machines to the pipes. These are my preference because they allow for any movements by the machines.

A word of caution that I learned the hard way: Make sure that at least *one* gate is open at all times when the vacuum is turned on. It will be a lot easier on the motor. My motor is quite strong, so when this happened it collapsed the plastic drum. To prevent this from repeating, I made a plywood ring to fit inside the drum.

I had an electrician friend of mine install a power switch for the vacuum. It's in a central location in my shop, for convenience. When I turn it on, I make sure that the

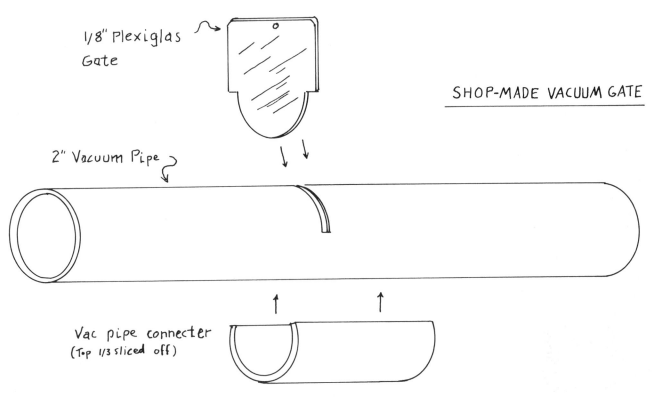

Illus. 279. Construction of the shop-made vacuum gate.

only gate that is open is the one for the tool that I am using. This prevents loss of suction.

Screwdrivers, Reusing

Never throw old screwdrivers away unless they are really bent out of shape. They can be reground to become a very useful tool (Illus. 282). For example, grinding them to a point will turn them into a useful scratch awl. Grinding an old flat-bladed screwdriver to give it a razor-sharp blade will turn it into a chisel. Cut a thin V slot in the blade and then bend it. You now have a brad or staple remover. Other uses include a punch, a nailset, etc.

Screws

Countersinking Screws

Some of us don't have as complete a workshop as we would like to have. More than likely, a set of screw countersinks are among the missing items in our tool drawer. Well, don't rush right out and buy them now. You probably have some and don't know it.

A Phillips®-head screw bit, the short hexagonal type that fits into your ratchet or cordless screwdriver, will do for a starter. Simply install the bit into your cordless screwdriver or electric drill and use it as a countersink (Illus. 283).

Another way of countersinking screws is to just use a drill that is the size of the screw head. Both approaches work as temporary methods.

Illus. 280. This gate, made of wood, is on the dust box behind my radial arm saw. The flexible hose allows for any movement.

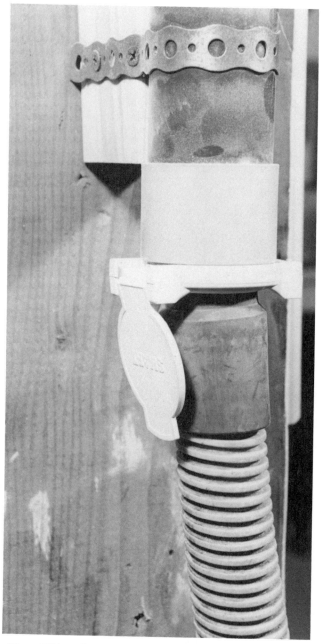

Illus. 281. A commercially made available gate or valve is spring-loaded so that it closes when you remove your vacuum hose.

Driving Screws into Hardwood

Driving screws into hardwood can be difficult at the best of times, even with a pilot hole drilled. This little **shortcut** will make things a little easier for you: Keep either a wax candle, some beeswax, or a block of paraffin wax right close to your screw cabinet. After you have drilled your pilot hole, apply either of the above to the screw threads and proceed to drive the screw (Illus. 284). You will find a big difference in the effort required.

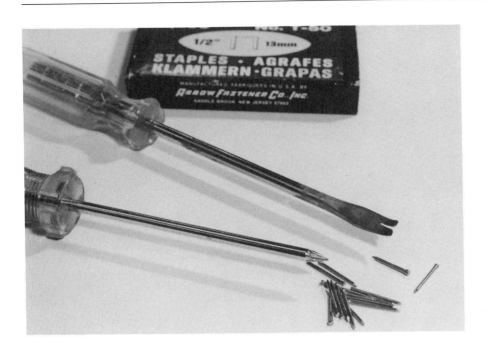

Illus. 282. These "new" tools were made from old screwdrivers that would normally be thrown out.

Illus. 283. A Phillips head screw bit or a drill bit the size of the screw head work well as temporary countersinks.

Driving Screws into Wood in Tight Spots

Those short five-sided bits that come with cordless screwdrivers will fit nicely into a ¼″ socket (Illus. 285). A socket wrench is just the thing then, if you are working in tight corners or where the height is restricted. Drill pilot holes from underneath, or, if this can't be done, use drywall screws.

Measuring Screws

When is a 2″ screw *not* a 2″ screw? When it's a panhead screw.

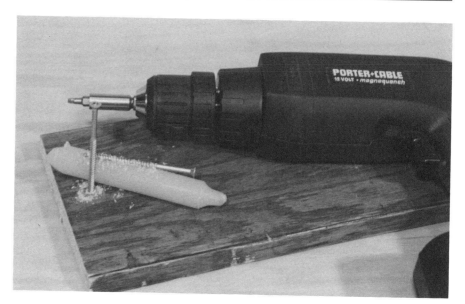

Illus. 284. Applying wax to a screw makes the installation easier in hardwood.

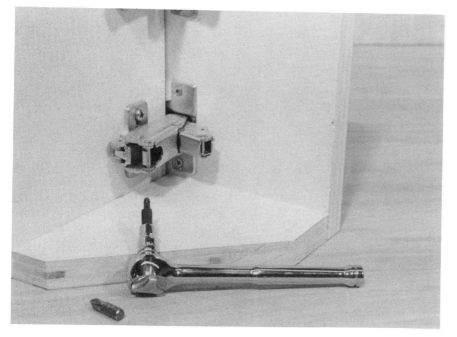

Illus. 285. A socket wrench with a ¼″ socket will hold a screwdriver bit for placing screws in a restricted area.

Care should be taken when using a tape measure to verify the length of screws because the measurements vary with the type of screw being measured (Illus. 286). As an example, a roundhead screw is measured from the under portion of the head, while a flathead screw is measured from the top surface of the head.

Wood-Screw Pilot Holes

The following table will tell you what size drill bit to use for making pilot holes for wood screws. The chart shows different diameters for hardwoods and softwoods. The reason for this differential is because the screws in softwoods require a bigger *bite* to secure the wood.

Screw Gauge	Shank Diameter	Pilot Hole Diameter	
		Hardwood	Softwood
2	0.086″	3/64″	
3	0.099″	1/16″	
4	0.112″	1/16″	
5	0.125″ (1/8″)	5/64″	1/16″
6	0.138″	5/64″	1/16″
7	0.151″	3/32″	1/16″
8	0.164″	3/32″	5/64″
10	0.177″	7/64″	3/32″
12	0.216″	1/8″	7/64″
14	0.242″	9/64″	7/64″
16	0.268″	5/32″	9/64″
18	0.294″	3/16″	9/64″
20	0.320″	13/64″	11/64″
24	0.372″	7/32″	3/16″

Table 7.

Selecting Screws

When building projects out of oak and some other hardwoods, do not use the common steel screw. Over a period of time, the metal will react with the natural acids of the wood and black rings will appear around the screw holes. Select stainless steel or brass screws when working with oak (Illus. 287). They are more expensive, but they are worth it.

Illus. 286. Note the difference in the length of these screws. Both are called 1¾″ screws. The pan-head screw, the one on top, is measured from the under part of its head.

Scroll Saw, Sanding with a

No, this is not a misprint. You *can* do sanding with a scroll saw, and it works quite well. Why, you ask, would you want to sand with the scroll saw? For the same reason that you want to cut with the scroll saw. To smooth out the inside of the intricate detail cuts that are left a little rough.

Here's how to sand with a scroll saw: Remove the saw blade. Cut a couple of narrow strips of cloth-backed sandpaper that is the length of the blade (Illus. 288). Glue the strips to an old blade or glue the strips back to back. Lock the sandpaper strip into the blade chucks just as you would

Illus. 287. Use brass or stainless steel screws when working with oak.

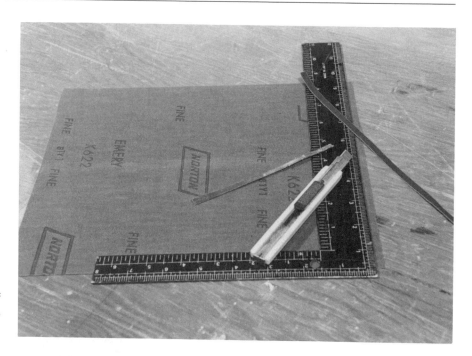

Illus. 288. Cut thin strips of cloth-backed sandpaper for use in your scroll saw.

Illus. 289. Sanding inside cuts is easy when you use sandpaper in your scroll saw.

do with a new blade. Adjust the blade tension and turn on the saw. Now, you can smooth out those rough cuts (Illus. 289). The sanding surfaces will be on the side, but the scroll saw still does an effective job. The strips can be cut as narrow as required.

Occasionally use a crepe rubber block to clean off the surfaces. This will prolong the life of the sanding strip.

While you are cutting the sandpaper and have its dimensions, cut a few more and keep them with your spare saw blades.

Seat, Shop-Built

Standing on a hard wooden or cement floor for long periods of time is eventually going to take its toll on your back. Precisely for that reason, I designed and built the high stool shown in Illus. 290 and 291. The stool is made of scrap pieces of spruce and other softwoods. The footrest is from an old broom handle. The stool works well, although I find that the seat (made from glued-up plywood) is a little hard. Someday, I'll put some foam on and maybe cover it with a vinyl or cloth material.

I made the stool high enough so that I can sit comfortably at the workbench or the scroll saw to do carving and other relaxing things. The footrest brings my knees up and makes for a more comfortable sitting position. The stool is an important tool around my shop.

Sharpening

Aids for Sharpening

Two of the finest sharpening aids that I have come across are shown in Illus. 292. The Multi-Oilstone that is made by Norton is three grades of sharpening stone (fine, medium, and coarse) mounted on an axle that has positive

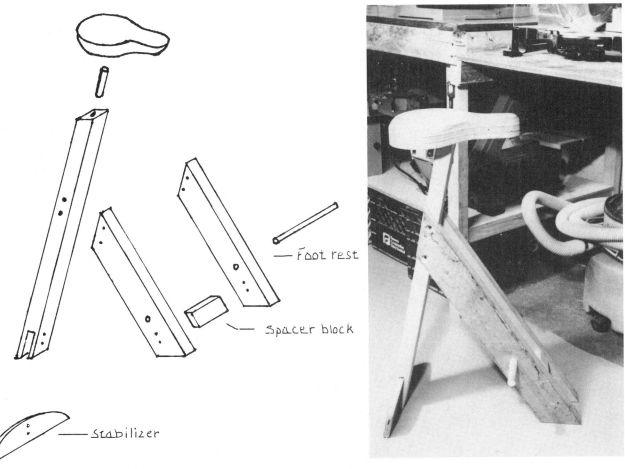

Illus. 290 and 291. This shop-made stool is great for relieving the strain of standing on a hard floor.

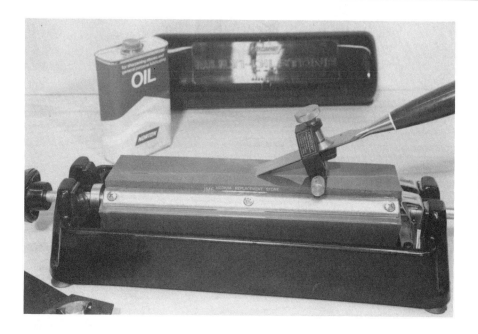

Illus. 292. The Multi-Oilstone by Norton and the Honing Guide by Veritas make accurate tool sharpening easy.

stops. The unit contains Norton honing oil. As you rotate for the next grade of stone, the stone picks up a generous coating of oil and the previous stone drops off any metal residue. The residue sinks to the bottom, so you always have clean oil on the stone.

The other tool is a honing guide that is made by Veritas and is sold by Lee Valley Tools and other mail-order tool houses. The honing guide takes all the guesswork out of blade sharpening. The tool holds your blade at the precise required angle. A cam adjustment raises the angle for final honing.

Both of these tools are indispensable around my shop.

Illus. 293. A combination Crystalon® bench stone is ideal as a general-purpose sharpening tool.

How to Sharpen Tools

Maybe I've bitten off more than I can chew on this very important subject. I'm sure that volumes have been written about it. I am going to try to condense the important material into a few paragraphs.

First and foremost, if a blade isn't sharp, it won't cut. It may appear to, but it is probably cutting with friction and heat. The first sign of a dull blade (powered or otherwise) is that more effort is required by either the tool's motor or by you. The other sign is frayed edges. If you can see any reflected light off the edge of the blade, it's time to get out the sharpening gear. Believe me, there is a lot of gear. I don't want to scare you off, but there are specially shaped sharpening stones for just about every type of blade in existence.

Let's start with the sharpening stones needed to meet the basic requirements. You will need a combination India® or Crystalon® bench stone that is medium on one side and fine on the other (Illus. 293). These bench stones are usually about 3″ wide by 6″ long. They are oilstones, which means that a very light oil should be used when using them to sharpen tools. The oil prevents a buildup of metal particles in the pores of the stone. A larger stone is preferable, but a 3″ × 6″ stone is a good and inexpensive starter for sharpening chisels, plane blades, scrapers, and knives.

Other special stones are slip stones and files. Slips are specially shaped (usually one-half round, oval, or round) stones that are used for curved blades. A lathe gouge is one example. Files are similar in shape, but are more often square, rectangular, or triangular. A stone file would be used in sharpening the cutting edge of an auger bit.

Now, we get into the fun part—the actual sharpening. Let's use a 1″ wood chisel as an example. First, look at the blade. If it is badly damaged, set it into a bench vise and carefully file down the *angled* side with a bastard-cut steel file. Be sure to maintain the same angle, usually 25°. Remove the chisel from the vise and get out your bench stone and the oil can. Wet the stone with oil on the medium side. Grasp the blade of the chisel with both hands and hold the blade at its 25° angle (Illus. 294). Use long, firm strokes the length of the stone. Check the blade often to make sure that the angle is correct. If not, it will be obvious by a deviation on the surface area. Continue this until all file markings are eliminated and the blade edge is getting sharp. Remember, though, keep the stone wet with oil.

Now, repeat the process on the fine side of the bench stone. This should give you a razor-sharp edge, but you are not done yet. Raise the blade just a little and continue sharpening. This angle should be 27½° (Illus. 295). The angle change will show up on the blade as a straight or slightly arced line across it. The change should be about ⅛″ in width across the blade. The purpose of this is to remove any burr that may be on the blade and to give it a truly razor-sharp edge. If there is any burr left, slide the blade along a piece of hardwood to remove it.

Illus. 294. The correct way of holding a chisel blade for sharpening on a bench stone.

The above process can be repeated for bench plane blades, knives, and other similar flat-bladed tools. Be absolutely certain to follow the blade's original angle.

Illus. 295. This close-up shows the angle change for a razor-sharp edge.

Maintaining Your Temper

Sorry for the pun, but as you know, most tempered metals will lose their temper if heated and not suddenly cooled. One way to prevent this is to keep a container of water handy to your bench grinder. But that creates a problem. The container keeps moving due to the vibration of the grinder.

Try this: Use an old coffee can, but don't discard the plastic lid that comes with it. Screw the lid upside down to a convenient spot on your bench close to the grinder. Now, set the bottom of the coffee can into the lid (Illus. 296).

Shelf Brackets, Making

Making fancy scrolled shelf brackets is easy if you are just making one. Unfortunately, most shelves require at least two.

There might be the occasion when you want to make a set of shelves all with the same style brackets. Here's how it's done. Use a thick piece of stock. The thickness is determined by the thickness of each bracket × the number

Illus. 296. A coffee-can lid will prevent water spills near your grinder.

Illus. 297. Making several shelf brackets by resawing thick stock on the band saw.

of brackets required. Draw your pattern on the surface and cut it out on your band saw. Now, set the fence on your band saw to the desired thickness of the brackets and proceed to resaw (Illus. 297).

Here is another tip. It's pretty difficult to find wood stock that is 6″ or 8″ thick. The answer is to laminate (glue and clamp) several pieces together. When resawing, though, make sure that the glue joints are somewhere near the middle of the brackets.

Shelves

Making Shelves

The next time you are making shelves for that bookcase that your spouse wants, this **shortcut** will save you time,

energy, and clamps. Let's say the shelves are made of pine and you want to have a ½″ solid walnut nosing on them. Try this: Cut your solid nosing stock 1⅛″ wide × whatever thickness your shelves are. Lay your shelves flat, face to face. Place the solid stock between the front edges of the shelves and glue and clamp them together (Illus. 298).

When the glue has set, gear up your radial arm saw or your table saw to rip down the *middle* of the solid stock (Illus. 299). That extra ⅛″ protects the saw's kerf.

Normally, you would use two bar or pipe clamps on each shelf. Now, two clamps are used for two shelves.

Painting and Finishing Shelves

You can more easily paint, stain, or apply varathane to your newly made shelves if you have a dozen or so stacking bars on hand. What are stacking bars? They are H-shaped pieces of wood that are cut from 1 × 2s and are 10″–12″ long (Illus. 300). Before using them, drill holes to facilitate a 2½″ finishing nail.

Illus. 298. Lay the solid nosing stock between the front edges of the shelves and then glue and clamp the stock and the shelves together.

Illus.299. Ripping the shelves apart with the radial arm saw.

Now, when you are ready to finish the shelves, nail a stacking bar to each end. When you have finished one side, just turn it over and do the other.

Two additional bonuses: You can now stack your freshly finished shelves horizontally to take up less space when drying, and by stacking them horizontally, you lessen the chances of paint drip or runs.

Shooting Board

A shooting board is a device that was originally used before the days of the power planer, thickness planer, and

Illus. 300. The stacking bars in place on the ends of the shelves prior to painting.

jointer. Shooting boards are simply boards with straight, true edges that are used to guide the hand plane. The shooting board shown in Illus. 301 and 302 is simple to use and allows you to easily hand-plane a straightedge on a small board for joining.

Shop Cleaning

A good shop-type vacuum is the best way to clean up your shop. Unlike a push broom, it creates little dust and, of course, can get into those little nooks and crannies that a broom can't. I am usually in my shop six days a week, so I generally dedicate my Saturday mornings to cleaning up.

One of what I consider the most important cleanup jobs is the cleaning of my power tools (Illus. 303). It is amazing how much damage sawdust can do to your tools. You will probably extend the life of these tools threefold by giving them a regular vacuuming. Pay particular attention to the motor housings. Put the vacuum nozzle up tight to the openings to clean out the dust and debris.

Sliding T Bevel

Whoever designed this tool (Illus. 304) deserves a Nobel Prize mainly for preserving peace in the workshop and preventing an awful lot of cursing. *No* shop should be without one.

The biggest advantage of a sliding T bevel is in its use to duplicate complex angles. You simply loosen the thumbscrew or clamping lever, set the handle and the blade flush against your workpiece, tighten it up, and set your mitre gauge or saw accordingly. This solves the problems of trying first to figure out the angle and then trying to figure out just where 37.36 degrees is on your mitre scale.

As an added bonus, the pointed end of the blade is exactly cut at 45 degrees.

Illus. 301. The shooting board being used to hold a small workpiece for hand-planing.

Illus. 302. The angle pieces are screwed to the shooting board for edge-planing.

Illus. 303. A regular vacuuming of your shop is a safety factor. Regular vacuuming of your tools and their motors will prolong their lives.

Illus. 304. The sliding T bevel will transfer the precise angle to your mitre gauge or your radial arm saw.

Solvents

Safely Disposing of Solvents

It's so easy to go into your local paint or hardware store, order a gallon or so of paint thinner or the like, use it, and then dump the used material down the drain. Right? Wrong. Please *do not* do that. Pour the waste into an empty plastic container, save it until it is full (store it outside), and then call your local environmental agency and ask them how to dispose of it. This applies not only to solvents, but to paint, lacquer, varnish, contact cement, thinner, wood filler, paint remover, or any other product that is labeled *toxic* or *hazardous*.

I don't want to get on my soap box here, but I do want to point out that as responsible woodworkers the only assurance that we and our children have to continue in our business or hobby is to look after our environment. Sounds trite? Maybe so, but let's continue our enjoyment of woodworking, and let's make sure that there are enough healthy trees around to do so.

Okay, I've said my peace. Now, here are a couple of **shortcuts** to temporarily dispose of some of those hazardous materials. Pour your used material into a container of cat litter (Illus. 305). Let it dry. When you have a sufficient quantity, then call the agency for safe disposi-tion instructions. Oh, by the way, *do not* use sawdust as an absorbing agent. Sawdust could spontaneously combust.

Another solution is to "paint" the material on the walls of an old barn or shed and let the sun dispose of it.

Probably, however, the best solution is to give consideration to the relatively new "environmentally friendly" materials that are safe and water-soluble. All you purists better get ready to adapt to these new products as they are becoming very popular.

Properly Storing Solvents

I have yet to see a home workshop that does not have an assortment of cleaners, paint thinners, lacquers, paints, and solvents, etc., that are not sitting on open shelves. All of these are dangerous materials and should be treated with the highest of respect. Most of them are toxic, flammable, explosive—or all three. Ideally, they should be kept locked away and out of reach of young, curious hands and should be stored outside and isolated.

Well, keeping the solvents away from youngsters should not be a problem. Isolating them outside is a problem for those of us who live in the Northern climates. The products will probably freeze in the winter or go below the usable temperatures, which will render them useless.

Ideally, these products should be stored in a *safe* cabinet—a steel, airtight, fireproof cabinet such as is seen

Illus. 305. You can safely dispose of most toxic shop liquids by pouring them onto cat litter, and then bagging the litter, storing it outside, and calling your local hazardous waste agency.

in industrial plants. Needless to say, this is not practical for the home woodworker.

The next best thing, then, is a small metal cabinet such as an old filing or stationary cabinet that can be locked (Illus. 306). The lock should keep the kids out of it. The cabinet should be well marked to characterize its contents (flammable, toxic, explosive, etc.) and should be placed away from any source of direct heat. The purpose of the *steel* cabinet is that if a fire should break out within it, it will not spread as quickly.

Spirals, Making

Some neat things such as salad bowls, decorative cones, etc., can be made from spirals, but laying out the design and cutting them has until now been somewhat difficult.

To draw a spiral, wrap a piece of string around a nail and tie the loose end to a pencil. Using the pencil, start drawing a circle from the nail that is fixed to the middle of your workpiece (Illus. 307). These are the cutting lines. Select the proper band-saw blade, tilt your table to the desired angle that you want the bowl or cone to be, and proceed to cut from the outside line.

Illus. 306. Solvents, lacquers, and other flammable or toxic material should be stored safely outside or in a locked steel cabinet.

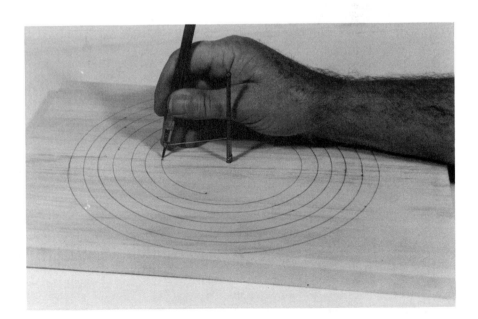

Illus. 307. Drawing spirals for bowl-making on the band saw.

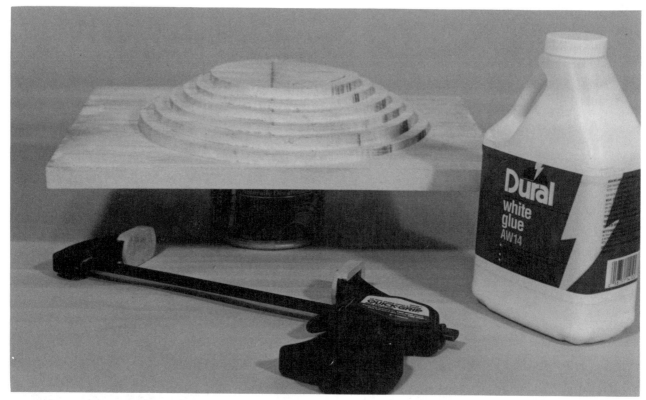

Illus. 308. When the cut is complete, place the workpiece over an appropriate sized tin can. Stretch the piece over it, and then glue and clamp it.

Once the cut is complete, turn off the saw and *slowly* start to retract the blade by backing up through the cut. Place a dowel or a tin can under the center of the workpiece, and carefully pull the coil down, clamping it to a secure surface (Illus. 308). A little glue before clamping will hold it all together.

Spokeshave

The spokeshave is similar to a drawknife and is a useful tool to have in your tool drawer (Illus. 309). The blade on it is adjustable, so that you can vary the depth and the angle of the cut.

The spokeshave is a tool that was devised many years ago to taper the spokes on wooden wagon wheels. Over the years, as its use became more prevalent, the design was

altered and spin-offs have evolved. New models came out with inward- and outward-shaped blades, angled blades for corners, and router-type blades.

Spray Painting Small Parts

Method #1

The problem with spray-painting small parts is that the air pressure behind the spray tends to blow the parts all over the place. This usually happens with a spray gun *or* an aerosol spray can. The other problem is that you usually have to do one side at a time.

Next time you have some of these small parts to paint, tap a small nail into the bottom of them, or use their packaged screws to secure them and then set them on a

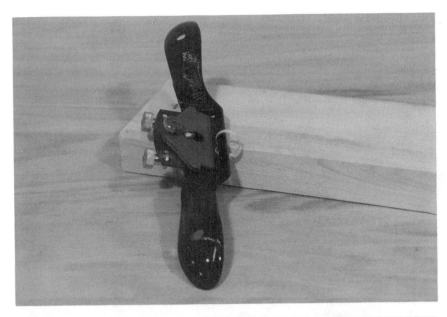

Illus. 309. The proper use of a spokeshave.

Illus. 310. Spraying paint on small parts is easier when they are sitting on a piece of fly screen.

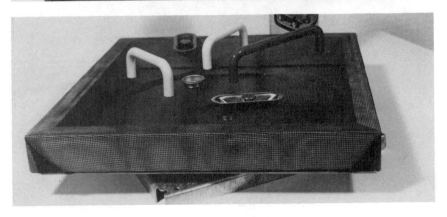

Illus. 311. The fly-screen frame is adapted to fit on a lazy Susan mechanism.

piece of nylon fly screen (Illus. 310). A push pin might work if they are wooden parts.

The fly screen should be stapled to some sort of frame for stability. The advantage of the screen is that you don't get the usual accumulation of paint that sticks under the sprayed part.

Method #2

Rubbermaid has an inexpensive rotating spice-bottle rack available that acts like a lazy Susan. Lazy Susan units are also available at your local hardware store (Illus. 311).

Build your screen frame so that it will fit on the upper portion of the lazy Susan turntable.

After you have arranged the small parts on the fly screen as described in the previous section, simply rotate it to ensure an equal finish on all sides of the parts.

Squaring

Here are a couple of **shortcuts** to determine whether or not your project corners are square and true. These methods will mostly apply to larger projects where a builder's square won't reach.

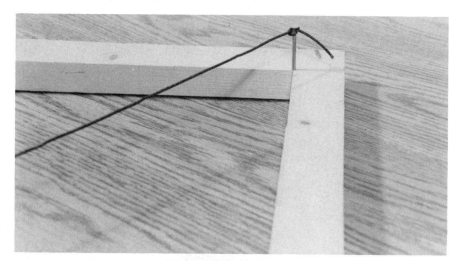

Illus. 312. Using a length of string to verify squareness.

Illus. 313. The 3–4–5 method being used to check for square.

Illus. 314. Applying stain with a plastic spray bottle will ensure an even application and the use of less stain.

In the first method, with a tape measure or a string, measure diagonally across two opposite corners (Illus. 312). Mark the string and measure the other two corners. The measurements should be identical.

The second method is called the 3–4–5 method and it is really very simple (Illus. 313). Start at one corner of the piece. At the right of the corner, make a mark *exactly* at 3″. At the left of the corner, make a mark *exactly* at 4″. Now, measure diagonally across to the two lines. This measurement should read 5″ *exactly*. Double-check by repeating this at the opposite corner.

Stains

Wiping and Applying Stains

A quick and easy way to *evenly* apply an oil-based or water-soluble wiping stain is with a pump-type sprayer (Illus. 314). They are usually available at your local hardware stores for a few dollars.

The beauty of these sprayers is that the stain is applied uniformly. If properly applied, there will be no overlapping or dark spots to worry about. And there's a bonus: You will use a lot less stain.

Before using the sprayer on your workpiece, try it on a piece of scrap so that the nozzle can be properly adjusted. What you want is a fine mist that will spread evenly. Hold the sprayer 12″–15″ away from the surface. Do about one square foot at a time. Spray it and then wipe it down. A slight overlap on the next section will blend the stain. *Do not saturate* the board with the spray. Very thin applications are better. This will give you a better idea as to the density and coverage for the desired end result.

A word of *caution:* Do this in well-ventilated areas and wear the recommended safety gear.

Water-Soluble Wood Stains

Welcome to the 21st century and kiss the oil- and solvent-based inflammable, toxic stains goodbye. I have tried the new water- or latex-based stains and they work beautifully (Illus. 315). What's more, they don't overly raise the grain, contrary to expectations. These stains go a lot further than the oils and may be mixed with one another to produce more subtle shades. They can also be mixed with the new water-soluble varathanes for a one-step finish or you can mix them with compatible latex paints to give a translucent pastel finish. All in all, these stains are a great breakthrough in finishing.

The big advantages of these stains, though, are the water cleanup and the ease of application. You can brush them on, roll them on, wipe them on with a damp cloth, or even spray them on. The method that I prefer is to use a

Illus. 315. A selection of the many water-based wood stains that are now replacing the oil-based types.

scrap of foam rubber as an applicator. It applies the stain evenly and it's disposable.

A typical water-soluble wood stain is the Flecto Diamond stain that is compatible with Flecto's Diamond varathane finishes. Trust me, these water-soluble stains and finishes work well and, in most cases, better than the old traditional finishes.

One word of caution, however: *Do not* use steel wool to smooth between coats. Remember, you are working with a *water*-soluble material and it will react with the steel wool. The black flecks or rust spots will prove this to you.

Stationary Power Tools, Keeping Them Stationary

Many home woodworking shops don't have the space to allow for a lot of stationary power tools. The answer, then,

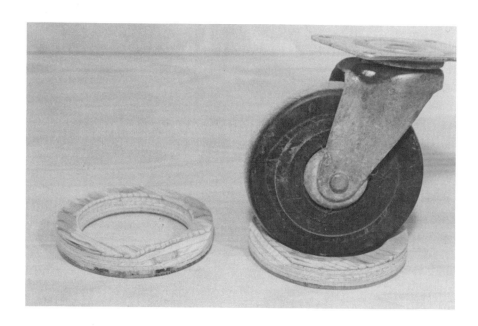

Illus. 316. Plywood doughnut wheel chocks like these will keep your mobile tool stands in position.

is usually to install casters on a power tool's base. This will allow the tool to be tucked out of the way until you are ready to use it.

Locking casters, however, are usually about 50% more expensive than ordinary ones and are a nuisance to engage. You usually have to bend over and lock each wheel individually.

Try this: Make a couple of ¾″ thick plywood doughnut wheel chocks (Illus. 316). The inside diameter of the "doughnuts" should be just big enough to allow the caster wheels to *almost* touch the floor.

Use your belt sander or your band saw to taper one side of the chock or the entire chock. This will make it easier to guide and run the machine into the chocks. The chocks will hold the machine and prevent it from moving.

There is one other thing to remember: If your machine has two fixed and two swivel casters on it, the chocks go under the swivel ones.

Steel Square

Definition of a Steel Square

The steel square is an invaluable tool in any workshop (Illus. 317). Usually, the body, as the long side is called, is 24″ long and the tongue is either 12″ or 16″ long. These measurements conform to the standard stud and joist placements. The body is generally 2″ wide and the tongue 1½″ wide. The outside corner is called the heel.

A builder's or framing square differs from a steel square in that it has a number of scales printed or etched on the body, the tongue, or both parts. These scales usually consist of a scale which tells how long a 45° brace should be to support a given shelf size; a board measure scale; an angle-cut scale; and a rafter scale. There are a number of books available to explain the various uses of these scales and how to read the scales on the square.

If, after testing your steel square, you find that for some unknown reason it is not true, there are a number of options, the last of which is to junk it. First, though, try this **shortcut**: After checking the square and determining that it is on the high side (for example, 90.5, 91, or 92 degrees), draw a straight line from the heel to the inside corner of the square (Illus. 318). With a pointed punch, and a fairly heavy steel mallet, hit a spot on the line close to the *heel*. Check the square for accuracy. Hit it again in the same spot if it needs it.

Conversely, if the square is on the low side (for example, 89.5, 89, or 88 degrees), do basically the same as above, *but* use the punch close to the inside corner.

Measuring with a Steel Square

The steel square is a versatile tool that no well-equipped shop should be without. It can find centers and make circles, arcs, angles, etc. Here are a few ways to make use of its versatility.

To draw a 45° angle, place your square on the work-

Illus. 317. The builder's square has etched scales and data on it.

Illus. 318. Truing up the steel square by peening on either the inside or outside corner.

piece flush with one side. Make a mark at, say, the 4″ line on the tongue. Now, make a mark at the 4″ line of the body. Draw a straight line between the two marks and you have a 45° angle.

To determine the diameter of a large circle, place your square on the surface with the heel flush with the edge. Make a mark where the tongue intersects with the edge of the circle and a mark where the body intersects. Draw a straight line across the circle to meet the two marks and you have your diameter. Measure the diameter, divide by two, and you have the radius and the centerpoint.

Illus. 319 illustrates how to use the steel square for determining pitch, rise, and run for use in roof or stair building.

Table Saw

Most of the **shortcuts** listed under Radial Arm Saw apply also to the table saw. Some of the shop tips and jigs for the band saw also apply to the table saw. I have chosen not to duplicate them for the sake of expediency. Refer to the sections Radial Arm Saw and Band Saw to pick those shortcuts that can be applied to the table saw.

Tape Measure and Inside Measurements

I have a problem when it comes to making precise inside measurements with a tape measure. Most tape measures have "Add 3 inches" printed on the case, some use 2½ inches, and some others have a small window on the top. When I look down on the tape measure, either the window always seems to be dirty or scratched or the cases seem to protrude to make accuracy difficult.

I've found a solution that works. I lay a combination square down, inside the area to be measured. I know that the blade is exactly 12″ long. Then I measure up to the blade and add the 12″ (Illus. 320). It works every time.

Thickness Planer

Making a Thickness Planer Work Better

We all know how a thickness planer works, but if you want your thickness planer to work *better* for you, maybe this will help.

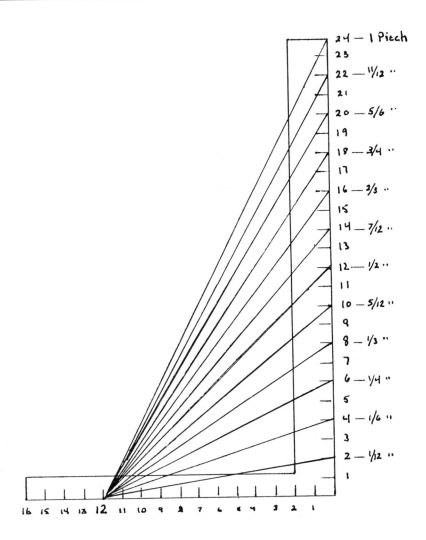

24 — 1 Pitch
23
22 — 11/12 ''
21
20 — 5/6 ''
19
18 — 3/4 ''
17
16 — 2/3 ''
15
14 — 7/12 ''
13
12 — 1/2 ''
11
10 — 5/12 ''
9
8 — 1/3 ''
7
6 — 1/4 ''
5
4 — 1/6 ''
3
2 — 1/12 ''
1

16 15 14 13 12 11 10 9 8 7 6 5 4 3 2 1

Pitch Scale

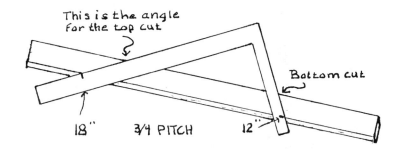

This is the angle
for the top cut

Bottom cut

18''   3/4 PITCH   12''

Scribing the cut angle on a rafter

Illus. 319. Using the steel square to determine pitch of a rafter or stair riser and to scribe for the top and bottom cuts of a rafter.

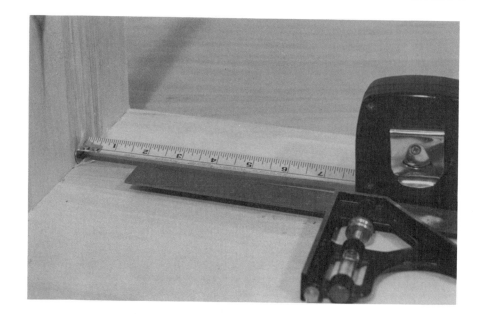

Illus. 320. Using a combination square and a tape measure will give you more accurate inside measurements. The measurement shown is 14".

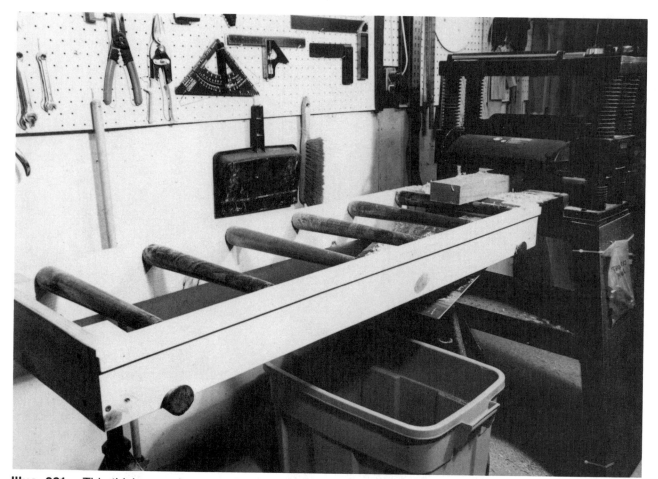

Illus. 321. This thickness planer out-feed table will usually prevent any cupping at the ends of the planed workpiece. Note the chute that allows shavings to drop into the box below.

Short of the heavy-duty industrial planers, most of the types that we, the lowly woodworker, would buy, are in the 10″–14″ width capacity. They are a relatively small machine that either comes with a stand or has a stand available as an option. Some are actually called portable. Calling them portable reminds me of the television industry when they would put hand grips on the sides of the 21″ television sets and call them portable, even though they weighed in at about 100 pounds.

Anyway, the greatest problem with thickness planers is the out-feed table. It's generally not long enough or doesn't have the stability to retain your workpiece in a truly level position as it's coming out of the machine. The result is a small cup at or near the end of the stock. Sometimes if the in-feed table is not long enough, a cup may also appear at the front of the stock. One way to solve these problems is to plane stock longer than what is required for your workpiece. Then, simply cut off the cupped portion. Another option, though, is to build an out-feed table that will prevent the cupping from happening at all.

The out-feed table shown in Illus. 321 and 322 is easy enough to build. I was able to scrounge six or so rollers from an old conveyer. I then built a frame of 1 × 4s and

installed the rollers so that they would protrude *just* above the frame. The adjustable supports were picked up at a surplus store. I added a piece of scrap ¼″ plywood to act as a chute and direct the shavings into a plastic bin. Now, there is no more end cupping and there are very few flying wood shavings.

Making Tapered Legs with a Thickness Planer

The jig in Illus. 323 and 324 will taper four or more table legs at a time. Basically, the jig is a box without a top. The sides are slotted to accommodate a sliding clamp that holds the legs tightly. You set your squared stock lengths in the box and add a shim under one end. Make sure that the shim is at the end of the stock. Run the stock through the planer, flip the pieces over, and repeat. Add a shim again and run the other two sides through. Always make sure that the rough stock protrudes *above* the box sides.

When the desired taper is attained on one side, simply turn the workpiece over and repeat the process (Illus. 325). If an all-around taper is required, the same methods are used.

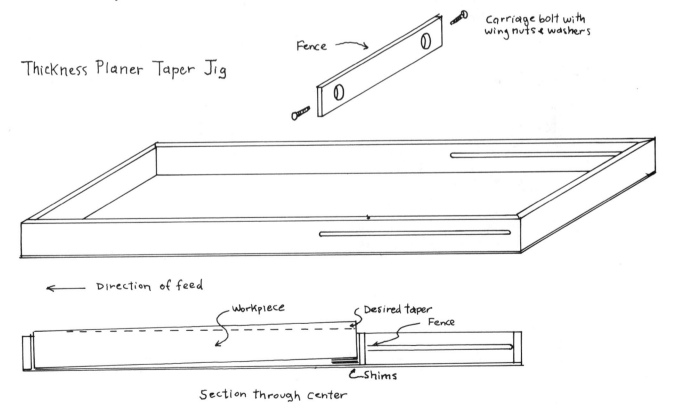

Illus. 322. Construction of the thickness planer taper jig.

Illus. 323. The taper jig. Note the slotted sides to accommodate the sliding clamp.

Illus. 324. Shims are used to raise the jig in stages until the desired taper is reached.

Try Square

In England, this tool (Illus. 326) is called a "trying square," and accurately so, because it is used to "try" the squareness of the workpiece.

There are three types of try square that I know of. The one thing that they all have in common is a flat 90° face (the inner edge). One type is flat up to the blade. The second is flat up to the blade and then turns 45° towards the back of the blade so that it can check mitres as well. The third type is adjustable and is usually called a combination square.

Illus. 325. The result: Four equally tapered legs that were made on the thickness planer.

Illus. 326. Three types of try squares: 1, a 12″ bevelled try square; 2, a 6″ try square; and 3, a combination square.

For crucial measurements, make sure that there are no dings on the face and that the blade is truly flat. The blade should be checked for tightness as well. Also, if you are going to etch your name or initials on the square for identification, do so on the body, *never* on the face or the blade.

To check the accuracy of a try square, or, for that matter, any square, place it flush against one edge of a square piece of stock that is no wider than the blade of the square. Draw a line. Now, place the square on the opposite edge and draw another line to meet the first one. If the lines meet, the board *and* the try square are true. If there is a difference, and, after checking with other squares it proves to be the fault of the square, throw it away. I don't know of a way to economically repair a try square.

Vacuum

(Also see Sawdust)

Picking Up Nails with a Vacuum

This little **shortcut** is effective and saves me a lot of bending and stooping. I came up with the idea when I was tearing down walls to build my new workshop. I was trying to be economical by saving the 2 × 4s, so, needless to say, I had to remove the nails from them. Being lazy, I just let the nails drop on the floor, thinking that I would sweep them up later. Well, a push broom just doesn't work. All it does is make dust and hardly moves the nails.

Then, I had a brilliant idea. Using some epoxy glue, I glued a fairly strong magnet to the suction part of my vacuum cleaner. I positioned it about ½″ above the bottom of the vacuum cleaner so that it would lift the nails off the floor and not jam them under it (Illus. 327). Now, I occasionally lift the wand, pluck off the nails and continue to vacuum.

Expanding on the above idea to pick up other material, attach a strip of magnetic plastic (the same material that's used for the refrigerator stick-ons) to the bottom of your regular vacuum cleaner (Illus. 328). Double-faced adhe-

sive tape will work. Now, that needle or pin lying on the carpet or the floor in the sewing room will be easier to pick up. Plastic magnet strips can be found at sign shops or plastics suppliers.

Veneer

Cutting Veneer (*Also see Plywood*)

Veneer should be cut with an extremely sharp knife. The problem, though, is keeping the blade sharp. Olfa has an inexpensive "break-off" knife (Illus. 329) that seems to fit this task perfectly. As soon as you feel some resistance when cutting, just snap off a piece of the blade. It's a worthwhile tool to invest in.

Working Safely with Veneer

When veneering workpieces such as a table or cabinet top, you should be careful to make sure that piece that you are veneering is thick or strong enough to take the stresses of the drying glue. The substrate should be more than ¾″ thick if it is softwood or at least ¾″ thick if it is a hardwood.

As an added safety precaution, a brace is generally put under but parallel to the veneer. To avoid making this extra substructure, simply veneer the underside of the work-

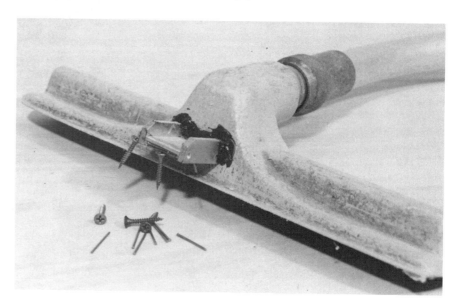

Illus. 327. A strong magnet attached near the bottom of the shop vacuum will pick up nails, screws, etc.

Illus. 328.   A plastic magnetic strip attached to your vacuum cleaner will do wonders in your sewing room.

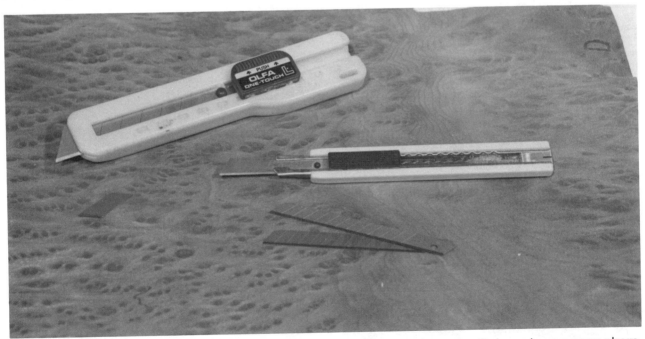

Illus. 329.   This "break-off" blade knife is ideal for cutting veneer, because you will always have a razor-sharp knife.

piece at the *same* time you are veneering the top (Illus. 330).

If you are using plywood as a substrate, it is imperative that you veneer the underside of it as well. For added strength, it is always best to make sure that the veneer runs cross-grain to the top and bottom surfaces.

Vise

Framing Vise

Stanley Tools has a terrific framing vise that can be used as shown in Illus. 331 and an up-graded model that comes complete with a frame for a mitre saw. The beauty of the one illustrated here is that it swivels 360° and it sits in a ball joint so that it may be tilted as well. It holds your workpiece securely enough to allow gluing and nailing or screwing right on the vise.

Vertical Planing Vise

The shop-made vertical planing vise shown in Illus. 332 and 333 is a great tool to have around the shop. It allows you to secure your workpiece so that you can work on its edge. The one that I have seen on various jobsites is made primarily for the planing of door edges. I modified this one by making it a sliding jig. This allows you to clamp workpieces of varying thickness. The wing nuts and washers make sure that the workpiece is held firmly.

Using two of these vises will keep your larger workpieces secure for planing or sanding.

Wheels, Shop-Made

Here is a quicker way for making a dozen or so toy wheels. Select a piece of wood stock that is about ¼″ thicker than the wheels you want to produce. It should be long enough to accommodate the required quantity.

Set up your drill press with the appropriate hole saw and set your depth adjustment to stop the drill press ⅛″ or so above the table. Drill your wheels. When you are finished, simply resaw the stock to the desired thickness.

For sanding, run the cutoff in the band saw and take off another ⅛″ or ¼″ from the top side. Clamp this to your workbench and install your wheels (Illus. 334). An orbital sander will do a fine job of finishing the surfaces, all at the same time.

Illus. 330. To prevent the workpiece from warping or twisting, veneer its underside as well. Here the underside has been done and the finishing surface is being prepared.

Illus. 331. Stanley Tool's framing vise swivels and tilts to accommodate awkward workpieces.

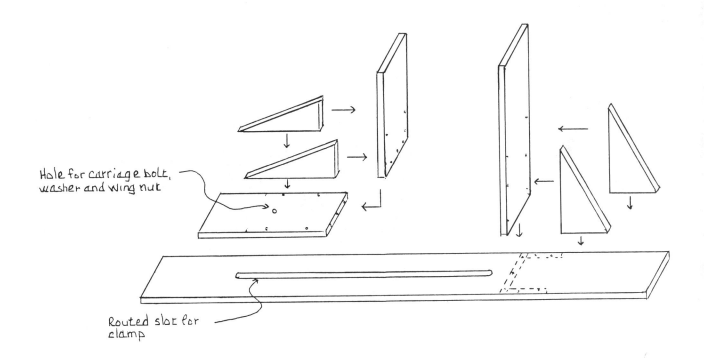

Hole for carriage bolt, washer and wing nut

Routed slot for clamp

Vertical Planing Vise

Illus. 332. Construction of vertical planing vise.

Illus. 333. This vertical vise will keep your workpiece secure and steady while you are working on its edges.

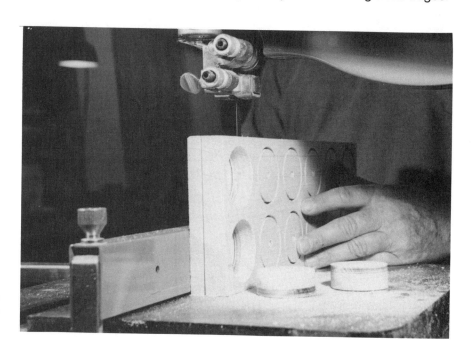

Illus. 334. Resawing re-leases these toy wheels for later finishing.

Illus. 335. This shop aid will allow the sanding of a dozen or more toy wheels at the same time.

Wood, Sources of

Wood can be salvaged from many unlikely sources. For example, how often have you seen an old black-and-white television console cabinet left at the curb, waiting for the garbage truck? The really old ones were usually made of solid mahogany, walnut, cherry, or oak.

Freight pallets that are sometimes discarded are usually made from birch, maple, elm, oak, or other hardwood (Illus. 336).

The Far East automobile manufacturers send engine blocks, motorcycles, and other heavy parts in crates usually made of lauan (a mahogany-like hardwood). I have recently heard of an individual who converted a Kawasaki motorcycle crate into a fine-looking stereo cabinet.

I'm not suggesting, for a moment, that you take your pickup truck and scour the neighborhood on garbage day just to pick up the jetsam. However, keep your eyes and ears open for opportunities. A little bit of time and effort, a thickness planer, and some imagination is all it takes to convert these discarded items into usable wood.

Wooden Balls, Shop-Made

Here is a way to make perfectly round wooden balls. A stationary or a portable belt sander is all that is required. The portable belt sander should be the type that can be bolted or clamped in an inverted position to your workbench.

First, you have to make a frame that is the size of your sander (Illus. 337 and 338). The walls of the frame should extend 3″ or 4″ above the belt surface. The inside of the front edge requires a small wedge that goes right across the frame. The entire box frame has to be made so that it remains stationary and is not moved by the belt. The

Illus. 336. This freight pallet is built from solid birch. If dismantled, it could make a fine cabinet carcass.

Illus. 337. An underside view of the wooden ball-making frame used for a portable belt sander.

Illus. 338. The ball-making frame for a bench-top sander.

Illus. 339. The hardwood cubes will turn into perfectly round balls after they come out of the sanding frame.

height of the walls is determined by the maximum size of the balls that you want to make. The walls must be able to *contain* them. Let's use 1″ balls as an example. The wall height should be at least 2″ above the base of the wedge. A top should be made as well.

Okay, the box frame is built. Now for the fun. To start the balls rolling, cut a couple of 1″ cubes of hardwood and place them in the box frame. Turn on the sander. It will probably take an hour or so, but you will end up with a couple of perfectly round balls (Illus. 339).

Wood Filler, Applying

Most woodworkers are quite familiar with the application of the various types of wood filler. We all have little accidents or make little mistakes that we have to hide. To make that joint look perfectly mitred, we fill in the cracks with wood filler.

The toughest mistakes to fix on the surface are dings or dents made by a hammer. It seems that the wood filler just won't stay put, no matter what you do. Here's the answer: Use your electric drill with a 1/16" bit and drill a couple of *shallow* holes in the dent (Illus. 340). These holes will allow the wood filler to grab onto something.

Wood Scraps, Using

First, never throw *any* piece of wood away. Sure, it can be used as compost, but that should be your last resort. I have a couple of scrap bins that I use for plywood and for solid stock (Illus. 341). I also have a couple of plastic milk cases that I throw my 2 by's (2 × 4s, 2 × 6s, etc.) into (Illus. 342). Any small cutoffs go into a bin that I built on casters. I roll it under my radial-arm-saw extension table, which is centrally located in my shop (Illus. 343).

I don't have a wood stove or a fireplace, but I do have a lot of friends who are more than willing to take my softwood scraps to be used as kindling.

Hardwood is another story. I'm a bit miserly when it comes to some of the more exotic hardwoods. I rarely give any scraps away. Most scrap pieces can be used for screw plugs or other decorative matching or contrasting parts.

Wood Stain

(See Stains)

Wood Storage

There is a right and a wrong way to air-dry or just store lumber or hardwood. The wrong way is to haphazardly stack the wood on a lumber rack. This will usually result in warped, twisted, or crooked material.

Try this little **shortcut** to store lumber properly: Next time you are out making a purchase at your favorite lumberyard, buy a bundle of laths. When your lumber arrives, lay out three laths (assuming they are 8′ long lumber) and place a layer of lumber perpendicular on top of them. Place three more laths on top of the first layer, etc. There should be a lath in the middle and one about a foot from each end. Use more than three laths if your stock is longer than 8′.

Now, the important part. The laths should all be in the same position; that is, if you are looking at a stack of lumber, the laths should form a straight vertical line. If the laths are not straight up and down, the result may be kinks in the boards.

Also make absolutely sure that the annual rings on the lumber arch upward (Illus. 345). It will allow moisture to drain down, rather than form a pocket which will result in a cup.

The reason, of course, for doing any of the above is to ensure free air circulation while acclimatizing the material and to further ensure that your material stays straight and true.

Woodworking Trivia

I just had to throw this in. In grade school (we called it grammar school), from grade 6 on all the boys in the school had to take woodworking class. For some unknown reason, in the mid 1940s it was called **sloyd**. Sloyd is the Scandinavian word for woodworking. By grade 8 (the first year of our high school) it was called manual training. In grade 10, it was called woodworking. I really don't know why it was given the Scandinavian name of sloyd, but if any of you have an answer, write to me.

Illus. 340. Drilling a couple of shallow holes in the dents will allow the wood filler to grab hold.

Workbench, Bench Hooks

Here's a tool that I haven't used since my old days in grade school, but it's still useful to have around the shop when you can't find those elusive bench dogs.

Using a good grade (clear) of ¾″ plywood, cut a piece 8″ × 12″ and sand its surfaces and edges smooth. Cut two pieces of ¾″ scrap plywood 8″ long × 1¼″ wide. Glue and screw one piece flush along the short edge of the plywood, turn it over, and do the same on the other side and the opposite end. Now you have a bench hook (Illus. 346).

"What do I use it for?" you ask. Well, you put it on your workbench with the bottom 1″ × 1¼″ piece hooked against the edge of the bench. Thus the name bench hook.

Illus. 341 (right). Large wood scraps are placed in a rolling bin for reuse on later projects.

Illus. 342. Smaller pieces are stored in plastic milk crates.

Now, you can use it for mitre- or square-cutting with your backsaw, or as a brace for chisel work or planing. Like most of my jigs, I drill a hole in it near the top so I can hang it up on a pegboard.

Here are instructions for building another type of bench hook. Follow the above directions, but on one side, or edge, make a 45° cut near the corner (Illus. 347). Right-handers should make the cut on the right side of the boards, and left-handers on the left side. This will not give you a perfectly mitred cut, but it will be close enough for those workpieces that don't have to be precise.

Workmate

Enlarging the Worktable of the Workmate

The Workmate® by Black & Decker is an invaluable tool to have around any home woodshop. I won't go into its many attributes here, except to say that it is a very versatile tool. However, it does have one drawback. The top surface is just a little small. Here's a method for enlarging it.

Illus. 343. This rolling wood scrap bin fits nicely under my radial-arm-saw-extension table.

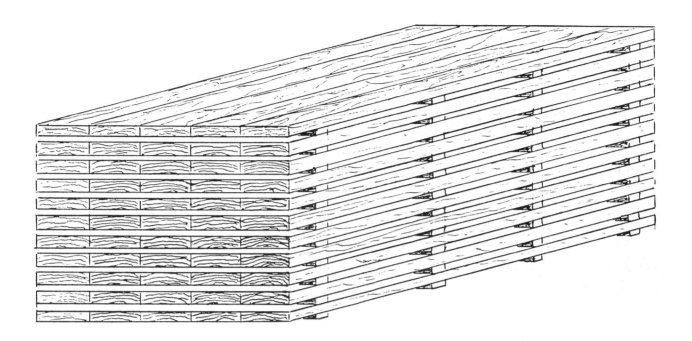

Air Drying Lumber

Illus. 344. Air-drying lumber with laths separating the boards for circulation.

Illus. 345. When air-drying lumber, the annual rings on the lumber should arch upward to prevent cupping and warping.

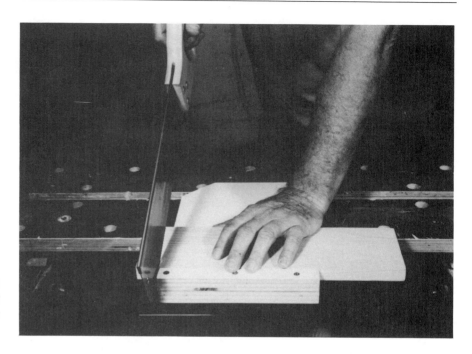

Illus. 346. The bench hook is an extremely handy jig for square-cutting, planing, or carving.

Illus. 347. Cutting a 45° angle off one corner of the bench hook will help you make a mitre cut freehand.

Use a piece of ¾″ plywood approximately 30″ × 30″. This would make a good-sized work surface (Illus. 348). On the underside of the plywood, glue and screw a strip of ¾″ plywood that is 4″ wide × 30″ long. Run it down the middle. Cut one more piece of ¾″ plywood that is 5″ wide × 30″ long. Before gluing and screwing it onto the narrower piece, check the thickness of the Workmate's jaws. Mine are ⅞″ plywood, so I had to shim my work surface with a piece of ⅛″ plywood. This T-shaped piece will now hold the work surface securely in the jaws of the Workmate. Sand and finish the top surface, and you have a portable workbench.

Illus. 348. This plywood work surface is easy to build and adds to the versatility of the Workmate®.

Nail Support Bin for the Workmate

Rubbermaid, among other manufacturers, sells clip-on containers that fit onto brackets. These brackets hook onto pegboards. This is very convenient when you are working within the confines of your workshop. However, during the warm months you may have several woodworking projects to do out of doors. Running back and forth to your workshop to get six or so screws or nails is not my idea of a good time.

The solution is to bring them with you. The Rubbermaid storage containers have a built-in clip on their backside, for hanging. Here's a way for hanging them on the cross-brace of your Workmate: Purchase aluminum angles from hardware stores or your local aluminum distributor (you might also try an aluminum window and door retailer). The 1″ × 1″ × ⅛″ angles are sold by either the weight or the foot and range in length from 8′ to 20′ or more. Rest assured, the unused portion will not be wasted (see Aluminum Angle).

Cut a length equal to the cross-bar on your Workmate. Turn your Workmate upside down. Set the aluminum angle on the underside of the cross-bar. Drill three or four holes that are the size of your pop rivets (blind rivets) and install the angle. When you turn the unit upright, you now have a bracket on which to install your nail or parts bins

(Illus. 349). This will save a lot of time when using your Workmate away from your shop.

Tool Rack for the Workmate

The tool rack shown in Illus. 350 is an easy-to-make accessory for your Workmate. The rack is made of ½″ plywood. Appropriate-sized holes are drilled to facilitate *your* selection of tools. The beauty of it is that it can easily be lifted off when not in use.

Workshelf for the Workmate

Some of the new models of the Workmate, usually the deluxe versions, come equipped with an integral workshelf. The shelf is usually between the step and the rear lower brace. This, however, is a fairly recent innovation. Thank you, Black & Decker, for listening to the consumer. The workshelf is an extremely handy unit for keeping parts, tools, nails, screws, etc., off the floor or ground.

For those of us who bought earlier models, a shopmade add-on is easy to make. Most of the Workmates that I have seen have horizontal corner brackets on them. These will support a sheet of ¼″ plywood or other rigid material cut to size (Illus. 351). That's all it takes.

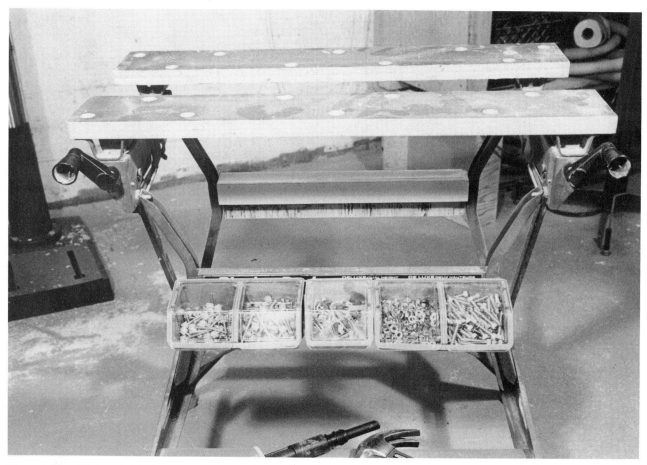

Illus. 349. This nail-bin hanger bracket is riveted to the Workmate with a cross-brace. Storage containers can be hung on it.

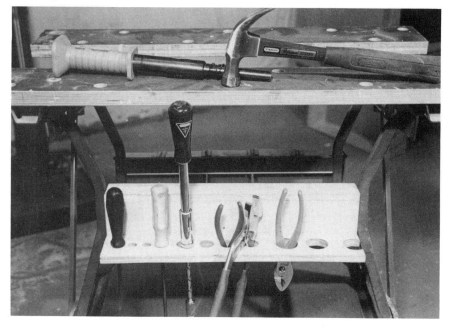

Illus. 350. To add versatility to your Workmate, add this clip-on tool rack.

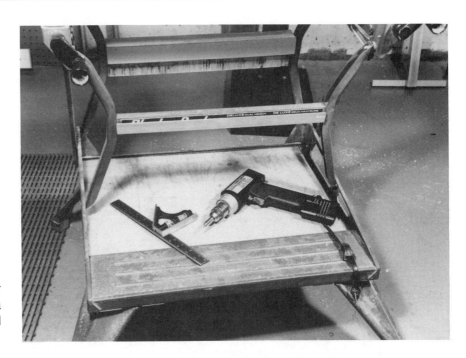

Illus. 351. Plywood or other rigid material can be used as a workshelf for earlier-model Workmates.

Workshop, Remodelling a

My previous workshop was 12′ × 20′, and it was adequate for the stationary tools that I had at the time. However, I lucked into some adjoining space that would triple the size of the shop. Needless to say, I jumped at the opportunity.

I thought that I would like to share some problems that I encountered when remodelling my workshop, along with my solutions. The first thing that I did was take photographs of the pegboard layout because I was planning to repaint it and I wanted to know where to replace the tools. Then, with a cross-section pad (grid sheet), I proceeded to do a rough sketch of how I wanted the new shop to be laid out (Illus. 352).

Some walls had to be knocked down, so I was careful to save the existing panelling and the 2″ × 4″ studs and ceiling and floor plates. These would come in handy later.

Prior to moving any equipment into the space, I swept and vacuumed the area and then washed the concrete floor with TSP (trisodium phosphate) to remove any grease or oil (Illus. 353). I then painted the floor with the new Flecto Diamond paint®. This is the water-soluble varathane finish that used to be available only as a clear finish for wood, but is now available in a wide range of colors. This took a total of (I kid you not) six hours for two coats of paint.

I then insulated the perimeter walls with 1″ thick Truefoam® (Styrofoam) and proceeded to reuse the wall panels that I had removed in demolition. I used the same Truefoam on the ceiling to absorb some of the noise.

Now, it was a matter of the electrical work. Using the rough sketch as a guide, I laid out the positions of the outlets and the lighting. Don't be too fussy about the electrical outlets, because Powerbars™ can make up for a lot of mistakes (Illus. 354). A normal duplex outlet (referred to as a two-outlet plug fixture) can look after 20 additional outlets (10 on each power bar), providing, of course, that the bars are equipped with their own circuit breakers.

There were only four incandescent light fixtures in the new space, so I went hunting for some more. I found a building where they were doing some renovations and finagled a couple of four-tube fluorescent fixtures which a buddy of mine installed (Illus. 355). He was also instrumental in doing the wiring and the hookups. Thanks, Jack.

Task lights were installed over most of the stationary tools to eliminate the shadows (Illus. 356), and a sliding (drapery) track light was installed to brighten up the shadowed area on the workbench.

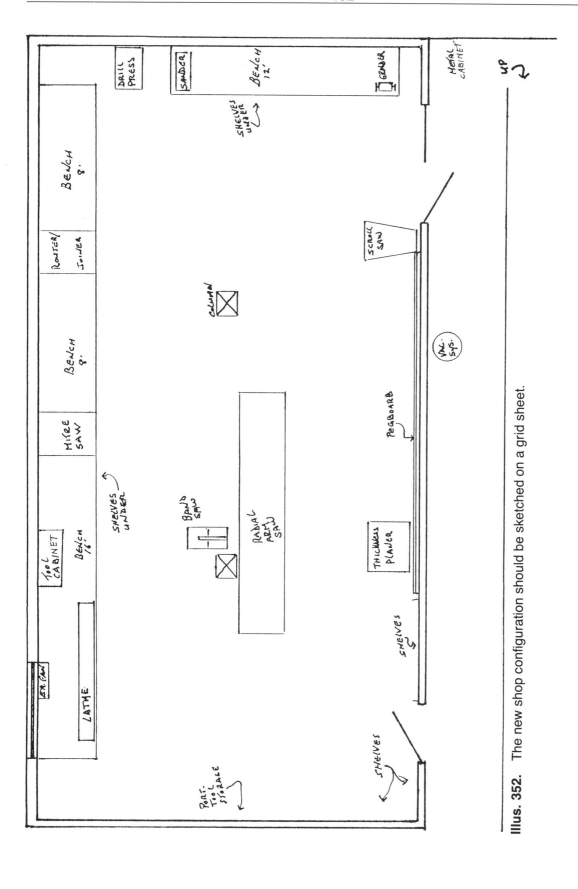

Illus. 352. The new shop configuration should be sketched on a grid sheet.

Illus. 353. Using TSP before painting will remove any grease or oil spots on a concrete floor.

Illus. 354. Power bars with their own circuit breakers can save a lot of money on electrical installation.

Illus. 355. Using recovered fluorescent fixtures will save a lot of money. These used ones were purchased at bargain prices from a building contractor.

Illus. 356. Task lights will brighten up specific work areas.

I used my original shop-built dust collector (vacuum), but I had to reroute the piping and put in new hoses and gates (Illus. 357). My buddy rewired the system to give me a more central on/off switch right by my radial arm saw.

The new area had a window, although a small one. I took advantage of this outside exposure. A friend of mine gave me a surplus hamster-cage-type exhaust fan, which I put to use by knocking out two panes of glass and fitting in the fan. A hinged, insulated, lift-up door was fitted to the fan casing to prevent any back-draft and to reduce the noise level (Illus. 358).

At an auction sale, I was able to pick up a number of shelf units similar to those used in stores, which I imme-

Illus. 357. The built-in shop vacuum has an on/off switch that is handy to use on most of my stationary power tools.

Illus. 358. This window-fitted exhaust fan is insulated to cut the noise level and to keep the cold out in the winter months.

Illus. 359. This shelving was picked up at an auction at a very low price.

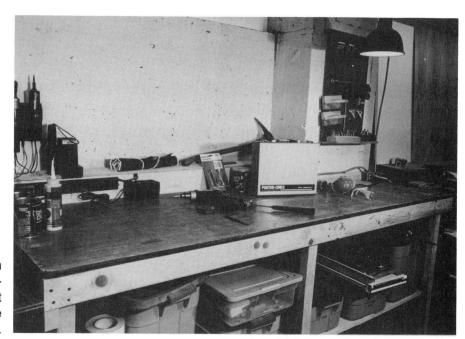

Illus. 360. The workbench tops are from old banquet tables that were bargained for at a flea market. The table frames are the old wall studs.

Illus. 361. Stationary power tools should be placed logically according to their order of use. Here you can see that the thickness planer is used as the first step and the radial arm saw as the second.

Illus. 362. This rather unattractive box unit is a sawdust collector for my radial arm saw. The vacuum gets most of the dust; the rest falls into the box.

diately put to use for storing my parts bins (Illus. 359). The additional pegboard was picked up used at a very reduced price.

Workbenches are the focal point of any workshop. My workbench is now close to 36′ in length. It is basically constructed of recovered 2 × 4s, the ones that held up the old walls. I also used three 36″ × 8′ banquet tabletops to complete the benches (Illus. 360). I bought these tabletops at a bargain at a flea market.

Placement of the stationary tools was next (Illus. 361). I tried to do this in a logical fashion based on the natural process of raw lumber to finished workpiece. The thickness planer is close to the door, and the radial arm saw is adjacent to it, because cutting is usually the second step.

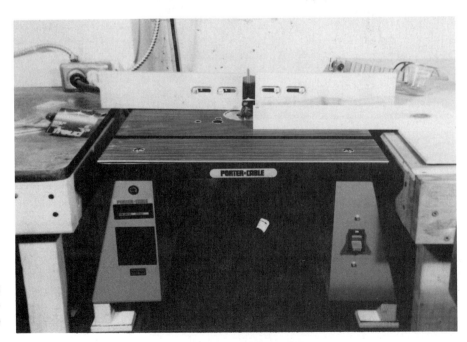

Illus. 363. Tools such as this router/shaper table work better when they are level with the workbench.

Illus. 364. The small belt sander, a real dust maker, is connected directly to my central shop vacuum.

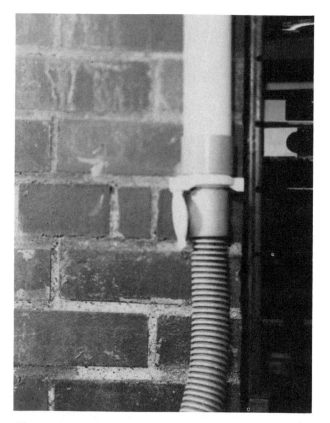

Illus. 365. A vacuum valve and a length of hose located close to the workbench allow me to connect my portable tools.

The band saw is right next to the radial arm saw. The drill press is off by itself. The mitre saw is built into the workbench and the surface of the saw is level with the bench to facilitate long pieces of stock. The lathe is off to one corner on the end of a workbench.

I built a large, ugly but practical box behind my radial arm saw and hooked up the vacuum system to it (Illus. 362). What the vacuum doesn't get, the box will. There is a hinged door at the bottom back of the box to make it easy to remove the excess sawdust.

The router table is set in between two benches but is level with both, again to facilitate the longer pieces of material (Illus. 363).

Most of my sanding is done with portable tools, but I do have a small 1″ belt sander, which is close to a vacuum hookup (Illus. 364). The bench-top grinder/disc sander is also close at hand.

Oh, one more thing: I made sure that I had a centrally located vacuum valve (Illus. 365) close to the workbench so I can connect my portable tools.

The new workshop seems to work thus far (Illus. 366 and 367). Nothing is permanently fixed, so, after a few months have passed, if a change is required, it will be easy to make.

Illus. 366 and 367.   Two views of my remodelled shop.

Illus. 367.

Glossary of Woodworking Terms

Abrasive   This term is generally used to refer to sandpaper. However, it is an all-encompassing term that may include sharpening stones, pumice powder, rottenstone, steel wool, synthetic pads, or any product used to abrade, smooth, or polish.

Adhesive   A general term referring to a material that will bond, either temporarily or permanently, two or more pieces of wood. Some types of adhesives used in woodworking are glue, double-faced tape, rubber cement, hot-melt glue, contact cement, epoxy cement, etc. The terms adhesive and glue are synonymous.

Air-Dried Wood   Hardwood or softwood that has been naturally dried by exposing it to outside air. The wood is usually stacked with spacers between each piece to allow air to circulate.

Arborite®   A plastic laminate. (See also Laminates.)

Annual Rings or Growth Rings   These are the rings as seen in a cross-section of a tree. They represent the new annual growth of a tree.

Astragal   A small moulding that can be flat or T-shaped, plain or ornamented.

Backing or Balancing Sheet   Material that is equal in thickness and nature to the face sheet. It is applied to the back of the core material to promote stability and prevent warping.

Banding   This is a relatively thin material, generally matching the face surface, that covers the exposed edges of a table, shelf, gable, etc.

Batten   A strip of wood placed over joints for added strength and/or appearance.

Bead   This is a small, half-rounded plain or ornamented moulding that is used for decorative purposes.

Beam Compass   The beam compass is used for drawing or measuring larger circles. The two points of the compass are usually adjustable and connected by a solid piece of material such as a dowel.

Bird's-Eye Wood   Wood with circular or elliptical areas that resemble the eyes of birds. A sometimes desirable feature in hardwoods. It is most often found in sugar maple (bird's-eye maple).

Bleeding   A condition in which gum, resin, or creosote exudes from some woods, usually softwoods. It is most prevalent in spruce.

Blemish   Any undesirable mark on the faces of wood.

Blind Dovetail   (See Dovetail, Blind.)

Board foot   The term used for the measurement of hardwoods and softwoods. A board foot (bf) is 12″ wide by 12″ long by 1″ thick. This term is used for unfinished (undressed) wood. If this term is used for dressed lumber, it will be based on the undressed dimensions.

Bole   A trunk or branch that is large enough to be used for lumber or veneer.

Bolt   A threaded metal, or other material, device that is

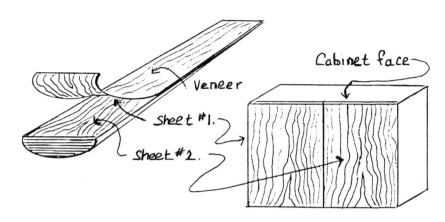

Illus. 368. Book-matching.

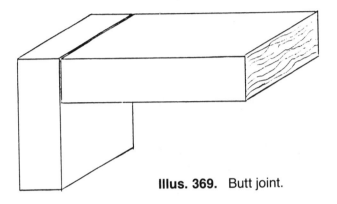

Illus. 369. Butt joint.

usually used with like-sized nuts to complete the fastening procedure.

Book-Matching   Generally, a term used with reference to veneers. Book-matching is a flitch or set of veneer sheets that are cut sequentially from the same log (Illus. 368). When laid out side by side or end to end, a repeat grain pattern is produced.

Bowing   The warping of wood. Bowing refers to a bend in the horizontal plane of the board.

Box Nails   Small fine, common nails used in rough box- or crate-making.

Brad   A very fine wire nail, generally thinner than a finishing nail, that is used in cabinetry and picture-framing.

Bullnose   The rounded edge of stair treads or the rounded edge of a surface in cabinetry.

Burl   A distortion of the wood grain caused by dead branches. It is often a desirable trait in some woods because it adds to the figuring.

Butt Joint   The weakest of all wood joints (Illus. 369). The two ends, faces, or sides of the mating workpieces are simply glued together without any other form of fastening.

Butt Hinge   The type of hinge that is usually found on interior or exterior doors. The hinge is square or rectangular in shape, the plates require recessing into the frame, and the door and the hinge pin are exposed.

Carcass   The framework of a cabinet, including the top, side, back, and end panels, not including drawers, etc.

Casing   The interior framework of a cabinet. (See also Carcass.)

Caulk   A variety of materials or compounds that are used to seal joints in cabinetry or construction. The toothpaste-like material is "squeezed" into and around the joints, usually to prevent moisture or air from entering.

Chamfering   Rounding off the sharp edge of wood. This can be done with a router bit or with sandpaper.

Check   A lengthwise split in a board, usually across the growth rings.

Circumference   The distance around the outside line of a circle.

Closed Grain   Grain usually found in slow-growing hardwoods. The term refers to woods that have rather indistinguishable growth rings.

Coarse Grain   Grain usually found in faster-growing softwoods. The annular rings of these woods are highly distinguishable.

Coarse Texture   This refers to wood having large pores. Some forms of oak would be considered coarse-textured.

Compass   The compass is a tool used to either measure or draw a circle.

Cope   Cutting away of one piece of wood to receive the moulded portion of another.

Cord   The measurement of (usually) logs or firewood. A cord of wood is a stack that measures 4′ high × 4′ wide × 8′ long.

Core   The inner piece of wood between veneers or laminates. (See also Substrate.)

Cornice   The horizontal top mouldings in cabinetry, furniture, and architecture.

Counterbore   To drill a screw hole that is slightly smaller in diameter than the screw. This allows the screw to enter the wood and secure it without splitting the wood.

Countersink   Usually a shallow, tapered hole that will allow a wood screw to sit flush with the surface. A flat-bottomed countersink is used to recess a roundhead screw or bolt head.

Crook   A deviation in the trueness along the edge of a board.

Crosscut   The cutting of wood perpendicular to the grain.

Cubit   An ancient term of length, currently considered to be equal to 18″.

Dado   There are three definitions of dado: 1, the base of a Greek order column; 2, the lower, thicker part of a wall, usually covered in a material other than that of the top portion; 3, a flat-bottomed cut in wood that is lower in depth than the surrounding area.

Deciduous   The term used to describe trees that shed their leaves seasonally.

Delamination   The separating of veneers or other laminates from their core or substrate.

Dimension Lumber   The "dressed" size of softwood or hardwood.

Dovetail Jig   A jig or tool that sets up the proper, balanced spacing to make dovetail joints with a router.

Dovetail Joint   A series of triangular-shaped slots cut into the end of a workpiece (Illus. 370). Identically shaped tails made in the joining piece at right angles marry the two to make a decorative and secure joint. The dovetails are usually made on a jig with a router or by hand with a backsaw or dovetail saw.

Dovetail, Blind   Similar to the regular dovetail joint described above, but the tails (dovetails) are not cut deep enough to be exposed on the outside edges.

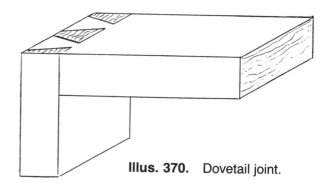

Illus. 370.   Dovetail joint.

Dowel   A cylindrical length of wood.

Dowel Joint   A short piece of dowel that is used to "pin" two pieces of wood. Identical holes are drilled in each joining piece. The dowels are inserted in the holes, glue is added, and the pieces are clamped together until set.

Dressed Wood   Wood that is rough-cut from a tree and is cut into various thicknesses. The wood is then rough-cut into various standard widths. The wood is then finally "dressed," that is, put through a thickness planer to make it relatively smooth on one, two, or four sides. The rough dimensions of the board are referred to, not the dressed dimensions.

Dry Rot   Decay caused by a fungus. This usually starts in moist wood. The fungi then supply their own moisture and proceed into the dry areas of the wood.

Drywall   A paper-covered sheet of a mineral called gypsum. The sheets are more commonly seen in 4″ × 8″ dimensions. There are standard thicknesses. Drywall is generally used in place of plaster for the surfacing of interior walls. Drywall is also known as plasterboard, GWB, gyproc, gypsum board, and wallboard. Gypsum board is the accepted generic term in the United States; gyproc in Canada.

Eased Edges   These are the slightly rounded edges that you find on common lumber. The purpose is to remove the sharp edges that are normally produced in milling.

Enamel   An oil-based paint that was usually available only in a high-gloss finish that was opaque but today is available in finishes from gloss down to matte. Clear and semiclear densities are also available. Enamels may be thinned and cleaned up with turpentine.

Epoxy   An extremely versatile adhesive that has high shear strength. Epoxy is a two-part adhesive (a resin and a hardener) and must be mixed 50/50 just prior to use.

Epoxy Paint   A very hard, durable paint finish for both interior and exterior use. It is an excellent finish for concrete or wooden floors.

Face   The face side is the side of a board that shows the most desirable surface for its intended purpose.

Figure   This is the pattern produced naturally in the grain of the wood.

File   A metal, serrated tool used to remove material (wood, metal, plastics, etc.). The serrations vary in depth and closeness depending on the intended use of the tool.

Filler   (See Wood Filler.)

Finger Joint   A series of deep grooves cut into the edge of a piece of wood to receive similar grooves in the piece to be joined (Illus. 371). The purpose of this type of joint is to provide a larger surface area for better glue adhesion.

Flat Cut   The method of cutting logs into boards. The log is cut lengthwise into the desired board thicknesses. This method wastes more wood than the conventional quarter-cutting method. However, it does produce a more attractive figure in the wood grain. Flat cut also refers to the type of veneer cut. Flat-cut veneer usually produces a more highly figured strip.

Flitch   Generally used in referring to sheets of veneer that are cut and stacked in a set to produce book-matching. (See Book-Matching.) In fact, a flitch is the squared or rounded piece of wood that veneer is cut from.

Flute   A hollow or a groove that is cut longitudinally for decorative purposes.

Formica®   A brand name that refers to various laminated plastic products. (See Plastic Laminate.)

Full Sawn   Lumber that is cut to full size, for example, 2″ × 4″.

Gable   The side and back panels of a cabinet or bookcase.

Gel stain   A wood stain with a jelly-like consistency. According to manufacturers, it is easier to apply and does not need mixing or stirring.

Gateleg   This usually refers to a type of table that has legs and their supports hinged to the basic table frame. The leg swings out horizontally (like a gate) to support a vertically hinged tabletop extension.

Glue   (See Adhesives.)

Grading of Lumber   Lumber, whether it be softwood

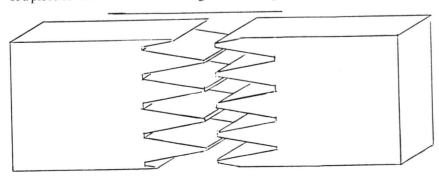

Illus. 371.   Finger joint.

or hardwood, is always graded to an association standard. This guarantees the purchaser that any lumber bought within a particular grade will be consistent. A stamp or seal type mark will appear on every board, which will indicate the name of the mill, the local association, and the type, quality, and dryness of the material.

Grain   The "lines" in wood that seem to indicate layers. These, in fact, are the edges of the annual rings that run longitudinally because of the way that the board is cut.

Green Wood   Freshly cut wood that has had no intentional drying and has a high moisture content, usually 25%–30%.

Grit   This may refer to the grit of sandpaper or the grit of sharpening stones. The lower the number, the more coarse the grit. The numbers may run from 30 to 4,000.

Growth Rings   (See Annual Rings.)

GWB   An abbreviation used by architects, designers, and engineers for gypsum wallboard. (See also Drywall)

Gyproc   (See Drywall.)

Hardwood   The botanical term for broad-leafed, flower-bearing trees that has, in fact, nothing to do with the density or hardness of the wood.

Hard Wood   The correct way of referring to hard, dense woods such as walnut, rosewood, etc. However, common practice over the years has been to use hardwood.

Heartwood   The middle or core of the tree. The wood from this area is generally darker and more figured than the sapwood.

Inlaying   A technique in which the surface is recessed to accept a thin piece or pieces of wood that are usually different than the under-surface.

Jig   A commercial or shop-made tool, aid, or accessory that will help in performing a woodworking operation faster and more accurately. It can be designed to be used only once or repeatedly.

Joint   When two pieces of wood are permanently connected, the point of connection is called the joint. There are many different types of joints, for example, dovetail, mortise-and-tenon, and dado joints.

Kerf   The space made by the thickness of a saw blade after cutting (for example, a circular-saw blade's kerf is ⅛″).

Key Joint   A mitred joint that has a kerf cut into the fitted edges (Illus. 372). A spline is then fitted and glued into the kerf.

Kiln   An oven in which lumber is dried to reduce its moisture content. This stabilizes the lumber dimensionally.

Kiln-Dried   Lumber that has been placed in a kiln to remove a large percentage of its water content. The result is a more stable board that is less apt to warp or twist.

Knot   A knot on a board indicates that a tree branch was growing in that location.

Lacquer   A resinous or synthetic finish for wood that has a very high gloss surface. Lacquer may be clear or colored. True lacquer is a resin-based material. Today,

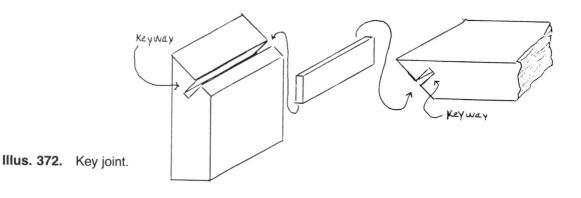

Illus. 372.   Key joint.

though, there are a number of synthetic lacquer-like materials that are far more durable and easier to repair if damaged.

Laminate   This refers to wood that is thicker than veneer and is fastened together usually with glue. True lamination has all the wood grain running parallel to each laminated piece.

Laminates   The term "laminates" usually refers to plastic laminates such as Formica® or Arborite®. The term in its true sense, however, describes a material that consists of many layers, for example, plywood.

Lamination   The joining together (by the use of glue or other fastening devices) of two or more thicknesses of wood.

Lap Joint   A wood joint wherein one or both mating pieces are dadoed to fit. The purpose of the lap joint is to provide a larger area for gluing, and thus a stronger joint.

Laths   Strips of unfinished wood, commonly 1½″ wide × ½″ thick, that are commonly used to support a plaster wall. The laths are nailed horizontally or diagonally to the wall studs and spaced about an inch apart.

Marquetry   The art of inlaying wood strips, squares, or other shapes into the surface of a substrate.

Measuring Lumber   Lumber thickness is usually measured by the *four* system. For example, a 1″ thick board is called four/four lumber and written 4/4. Lumber that is 1½″ thick is written 6/4.

Melamine®   (See also Plastic Laminate.) Melamine is a very thin plastic laminate that is generally used only on vertical surfaces or other areas that are not subject to a lot of hard use.

Melamine Paint   A very durable paint that uses the same plastic materials as those found in melamine. This paint can be used to restore plastic laminate countertops, etc.

Micarta®   (See Arborite, Formica, and Laminates.)

Mitre   In joinery, this refers to the ends or the edges of two pieces of wood that are cut at an angle (usually 45°) for the purpose of joining.

Moisture   The water content of wood in terms of weight, usually expressed in percentages, for example, a 30° moisture content.

Mortise   This is a recess of a particular shape that is cut into a board to receive a tenon from another board to form a mortise-and-tenon joint.

Moulding   Wood that has been shaped along its edges or face to give it an ornamental appearance.

Mil   A diameter measurement usually for determining the thickness (diameter) of wire. One mil is ¹⁄₁₀₀₀ths of an inch.

Nails   Metal fasteners used in woodworking. They are usually made of steel wire that is cut and formed. One end is pointed, the shape of which is determined by its intended use. The other end may have a range of shapes that vary with the application. The thickness and the length are expressed in either inches, penny size, or millimetres.

Nominal Size   The dimensions of a board that has been cut, but before it has been planed or shaped.

Nosing   A board that has had its edge shaped for a particular use, such as a stair tread. (See also Bull Nosing.)

Nut   A threaded metal (or other material such as plastic, nylon, etc.) fastener of various shapes and sizes. It is usually used in conjunction with a *bolt*.

Old Growth   The term "old growth" usually refers to trees harvested from naturally established stands where the trees had to compete with each other for nourishment. These trees usually have long knot-free trunks and are highly desired by woodworkers.

One-Step Finishing   (See Varnish Stain.)

Paint Thinner   A term that usually refers to mineral spirits such as turpentine and Varsol®.

Panel   A term usually used in furniture-making that refers to a thin sheet of wood that is set or recessed into a frame.

Pitch   An accumulation of resins in wood. These may be in the form of pockets, streaks, or seams.

Pith   The first annular ring on a tree.

Plaster   A mixture of either lime or gypsum that is mixed with water to form a thick paste, and then applied to walls. The plaster is laid on top of lathes and is trowelled to a smooth finish.

Plasterboard   (See Drywall.)

Plumb   Truly vertical, 90° off horizontal.

Plumb Line   Usually a strong cord attached to the middle of a weight. The cord is held or fixed to a horizontal member so that the weighted end hangs down, thus indicating a vertical line.

Pocket-Screwing   A method of fastening a table or cabinet top to the horizontal support rails (Illus. 373). A hole is drilled into the inside edge of the rail. The hole is drilled on an angle (usually about 15°) so that the screw will go through the rail and into the under surface of the top.

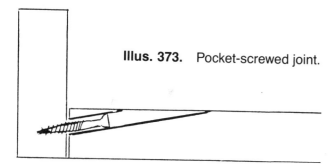

Illus. 373.   Pocket-screwed joint.

Polyurethane   A synthetic, plastic-based varnish or lacquer that is used as a finishing material for wood. It is available as a solvent or water-based and in a variety of textures. Polyurethane is an extremely durable wood finish that avoids most of the problems generally associated with varnish or lacquer.

Primer   A special coat of paint or other material that is used to bond subsequent coats to the substrate.

Putty   A pasty substance used for filling gaps or flaws in wood.

Quarter Sawing   This is a method of cutting logs into boards that is generally thought to be less wasteful than flat-cutting. The log is cut through its diameter twice to produce four quarter logs. The boards are then cut from each quarter. This method is usually reserved for the utilitarian types of wood because it does not enhance the grain figure. It is also known as rift-cutting.

Rabbet   As used in wood joinery, a rabbet is a notch in the edge or a slot in a piece of wood that is made to receive another piece.

Rail   A cross member used in cabinetry as part of the framework.

Raised Panel   A panel that is usually of equal thickness to the frame that it sits in. However, the panel edges are tapered inward to allow the panel to be rabbeted into the frame.

Rasp   A very coarse-toothed file that is used for very rough removal of material.

Recess   (See also Rabbet.) A slot or a groove cut into wood. It can be either a rabbet or a dado joint.

Resawing   A process in which thinner pieces are cut from a larger piece of wood. As an example, let's assume you have a 4″ × 4″ piece of hardwood and need four pieces of wood that are 1″ × 1″. A wide blade in a band saw would accomplish this.

Resin   A: A thick, sticky liquid found in pockets of some softwood trees. B: A synthetic material used in the production of some adhesives.

Reveal   A recess that is intentionally made to show the division of two or more planes of wood.

Rod   A measurement of distance that equals 5½ yards or 16½ feet.

Rotary Cutting   The cutting of veneer by rotating the log against a knife. The knife is set in a way that peels a continuous strip from the log.

Rough Lumber   (See Nominal Size.)

Rounding Off   (See also Chamfering.) A method of removing the sharp edges from cut wood. Rounding off can be achieved by means of a router with the appropriate bit installed. It may also be done with a power sander or by hand sanding.

Sap   The fluids of a tree with the exception of the resins.

Sapwood   The living outer dimensions of a tree.

Scribing   A method of marking wood so that it will mesh with an uneven surface.

Sealer   Liquids, either clear or opaque, that are applied to wood prior to applying a finish. The purpose of the sealer is to fill the pores in the wood and thus give a smooth finish.

Seasoning   A term usually synonymous with air-drying, but which refers generally to any means of wood drying.

Spalted Wood   Partially decayed wood that is characterized by irregular dark-zone lines.

Span   The distance between the outstretched thumb tip and the little finger, now considered to be 9″.

Stain   (See Wood Stain.)

Stile   In cabinetry, the vertical support members in the framework.

Substrate   The core or base material onto which a veneer or other type of finishing surface is applied.

T Nut   A threaded fastening device with a toothed flange that is recessed into wood. The flange grips the wood surface to prevent turning. The T nut facilitates the fastening of two or more pieces of wood with a threaded bolt.

Template   Usually a rigid pattern that is used to transfer its shape onto another object by tracing it.

Tenon   In wood joinery, a tenon is a projection of wood cut to a particular shape so that it fits tightly into a recess in a second piece of wood called a mortise to form a mortise-and-tenon joint.

Toenailing   Toenailing is a method of fastening wood members, usually in construction. For example, if a vertical 2 × 4 is being toenailed to a floor plate, the nails are driven through the 2 × 4 on an angle of about 30°.

Tongue   A projection, usually on the edge of a board, that will fit into a recess of similar shape on another board.

Tun   A tun is a large barrel that holds 252 gallons.

Tung Oil   A varnish-like liquid used in wood finishing that may be clear or tinted with a wood stain. Tung oil dries to a very hard finish.

Turpentine   A form of mineral spirits that is used for thinning enamel-based paints, etc. (See also Varsol.)

Turps   An abbreviated name for turpentine.

Urethane   (See Polyurethane.)

Varnish   A liquid preparation comprised of resins dissolved in oil, alcohol, or both. The material is used in wood finishing and can be applied with a brush or a spray.

Varnish Stain   Usually a mixture of varnish and an oil stain that is used as a shortcut in wood finishing to change the color of wood. This material is also available in a polyurethane base. It is also known as One-Step Finishing.

Varsol®   The name Varsol has become synonymous with mineral spirits and paint thinner. The term is more commonly used in Canada.

Wallboard   (See Drywall.)

Warp   A general term used to describe a piece of wood that is not truly flat in all planes.

Wood Filler   A product, available in a number of different forms, that is used to fill holes, gaps, flaws, or mistakes in wood. The material is the consistency of a thick paste and can usually be stained or painted to match the surrounding area.

Wood Stain   Liquid material used to alter the natural color of wood before finishing. It can be oil- or water-based, translucent or opaque, included in a varnish or urethane base for a one-step finish.

Appendices

WEIGHTS AND MEASURES

Unit	Abbreviation	Equivalents In Other Units of Same System	Metric Equivalent
Weight			
Avoirdupois			
ton			
short ton		20 short hundredweight, 2000 pounds	0.907 metric tons
long ton		20 long hundredweight, 2240 pounds	1.016 metric tons
hundredweight	cwt		
short hundredweight		100 pounds, 0.05 short tons	45.359 kilograms
long hundredweight		112 pounds, 0.05 long tons	50.802 kilograms
pound	lb *or* lb av *also* #	16 ounces, 7000 grains	0.453 kilograms
ounce	oz *or* oz av	16 drams, 437.5 grains	28.349 grams
dram	dr *or* dr av	27.343 grains, 0.0625 ounces	1.771 grams
grain	gr	0.036 drams, 0.002285 ounces	0.0648 grams
Troy			
pound	lb t	12 ounces, 240 pennyweight, 5760 grains	0.373 kilograms
ounce	oz t	20 pennyweight, 480 grains	31.103 grams
pennyweight	dwt *also* pwt	24 grains, 0.05 ounces	1.555 grams
grain	gr	0.042 pennyweight, 0.002083 ounces	0.0648 grams
Apothecaries'			
pound	lb ap	12 ounces, 5760 grains	0.373 kilograms
ounce	oz ap	8 drams, 480 grains	31.103 grams
dram	dr ap	3 scruples, 60 grains	3.887 grams
scruple	s ap	20 grains, 0.333 drams	1.295 grams
grain	gr	0.05 scruples, 0.002083 ounces, 0.0166 drams	0.0648 grams
Capacity			
U.S. Liquid Measure			
gallon	gal	4 quarts (2.31 cubic inches)	3.785 litres
quart	qt	2 pints (57.75 cubic inches)	0.946 litres
pint	pt	4 gills (28.875 cubic inches)	0.473 litres
gill	gi	4 fluidounces (7.218 cubic inches)	118.291 millilitres
fluidounce	fl oz	8 fluidrams (1.804 cubic inches)	29.573 millilitres
fluidram	fl dr	60 minims (0.225 cubic inches)	3.696 millilitres
minim	min	1/60 fluidram (0.003759 cubic inches)	0.061610 millilitres
U.S. Dry Measure			
bushel	bu	4 pecks (2150.42 cubic inches)	35.238 litres
peck	pk	8 quarts (537.605 cubic inches)	8.809 litres
quart	qt	2 pints (67.200 cubic inches)	1.101 litres
pint	pt	½ quart (33.600 cubic inches)	0.550 litres
British Imperial Liquid and Dry Measure			
bushel	bu	4 pecks (2219.36 cubic inches)	0.036 cubic metres
peck	pk	2 gallons (554.84 cubic inches)	0.009 cubic metres
gallon	gal	4 quarts (277.420 cubic inches)	4.545 litres
quart	qt	2 pints (69.355 cubic inches)	1.136 litres
pint	pt	4 gills (34.678 cubic inches)	568.26 cubic centimetres
gill	gi	5 fluidounces (8.669 cubic inches)	142.066 cubic centimetres
fluidounce	fl oz	8 fluidrams (1.7339 cubic inches)	28.416 cubic centimetres
fluidram	fl dr	60 minims (0.216734 cubic inches)	3.5516 cubic centimetres
minim	min	1/60 fluidram (0.003612 cubic inches)	0.059194 cubic centimetres
Length			
mile	mi	5280 feet, 320 rods, 1760 yards	1.609 kilometres
rod	rd	5.50 yards, 16.5 feet	5.029 metres
yard	yd	3 feet, 36 inches	0.914 metres
foot	ft *or* '	12 inches, 0.333 yards	30.480 centimetres
inch	in *or* "	0.083 feet, 0.027 yards	2.540 centimetres
Area			
square mile	sq mi *or* m²	640 acres, 102,400 square rods	2.590 square kilometres
acre		4840 square yards, 43,560 square feet	0.405 hectares, 4047 square metres
square rod	sq rd *or* rd²	30.25 square yards, 0.006 acres	25.293 square metres
square yard	sq yd *or* yd²	1296 square inches, 9 square feet	0.836 square metres
square foot	sq ft *or* ft²	144 square inches, 0.111 square yards	0.093 square metres
square inch	sq in *or* in²	0.007 square feet, 0.00077 square yards	6.451 square centimetres

METRIC SYSTEM

Unit	Abbreviation	Approximate U.S. Equivalent			
Length					
		Number of Metres			
myriametre	mym	10,000			
kilometre	km	1000	6.2 miles		
hectometre	hm	100	0.62 mile		
dekametre	dam	10	109.36 yards		
metre	m	1	32.81 feet		
decimetre	dm	0.1	39.37 inches		
centimetre	cm	0.01	3.94 inches		
millimetre	mm	0.001	0.39 inch		
			0.04 inch		
Area					
		Number of Square Metres			
square kilometre	sq km *or* km²	1,000,000			
hectare	ha	10,000	0.3861 square miles		
are	a	100	2.47 acres		
centare	ca	1	119.60 square yards		
square centimetre	sq cm *or* cm²	0.0001	10.76 square feet		
			0.155 square inch		
Volume					
		Number of Cubic Metres			
dekastere	das	10			
stere	s	1	13.10 cubic yards		
decistere	ds	0.10	1.31 cubic yards		
cubic centimetre	cu cm *or* cm³ *also* cc	0.000001	3.53 cubic feet		
			0.061 cubic inch		
Capacity					
		Number of Litres	*Cubic*	*Dry*	*Liquid*
kilolitre	kl	1000	1.31 cubic yards		
hectolitre	hl	100	3.53 cubic feet		
dekalitre	dal	10	0.35 cubic foot	2.84 bushels	
litre	l	1	61.02 cubic inches	1.14 pecks	2.64 gallons
decilitre	dl	0.10	6.1 cubic inches	0.908 quart	1.057 quarts
centilitre	cl	0.01	0.6 cubic inch	0.18 pint	0.21 pint
millilitre	ml	0.001	0.06 cubic inch		0.338 fluidounce
					0.27 fluidram
Mass and Weight					
		Number of Grams			
metric ton	MT *or* t	1,000,000			
quintal	q	100,000	1.1 tons		
kilogram	kg	1,000	220.46 pounds		
hectogram	hg	100	2.2046 pounds		
dekagram	dag	10	3.527 ounces		
gram	g *or* gm	1	0.353 ounce		
decigram	dg	0.10	0.035 ounce		
centigram	cg	0.01	1.543 grains		
milligram	mg	0.001	0.154 grain		
			0.015 grain		

Index

A

Abrasives, 12–14, 200
   grading system, 12, 14
   new types, 12–13
ABS, 118
Acrylic plastics, *See* Plexiglas
Adhesives, 14–17, 200
   epoxy, mixing, 15
   glue, removing, 14
   proper application, 16–17
Adze, 17
Air-dried wood, 200
Aluminum, grinding and filing, 17
Angles, drawing, 18
Annual rings, 200
Arborite, 200
Astragal, 200

B

Backing or balancing sheet, 200
Banding, 200
Band saw, 19–34, 97, 169. *See also* Bench-Top Power
   Tools
   backtracking, 21, 22
   bearing wheels, 26, 27
   bevel-cutting, 22
   bimetal blades, 23
   blade guard, 32, 33
   blade tension, 26
   circle-cutting, 24, 25
   compound mitres, cutting, 25
   cool blocks, 28–29
   crosscuts, long, 29–30
   cutting accurately, 26–27
   dowels, crosscutting, 28
   features, 19–20
   flush fence, 27, 28
   guide blocks, 27, 28, 29
   out-feed roller, shop-made, 30, 31
   relief cutting, 31, 32
   resawing, 32
   rip fence, commercial, 32, 33
   rip-fence addition, 28
   scoring for a straight line, 33–34
   tuning and adjusting, 26
   types, 19, 20
   V block, 28
   wheel roundness, 26
Band-Saw Blades
   bi-metal, 23
   carbide-tipped, 23
   rounding, 22–23
   selecting, 23
   tensioning, 23–24
Bar clamps, gripping, 34
Batten, 200
Bead, 200
Beam compass, 200

Belt sander, 124
Bench hooks, 185, 186, 188
Bench-top power tools, 35–40
    band saw, 35, 36
    belt/disc sanders, 36
    bench grinder, 36, 37
    drill press, 37–38
    lathe, 38
    mitre saw, 36–37
    router/shaper table, 38, 39
    scroll saw, 39
    table saw, 40
Bench vise, 40
Bird's-eye wood, 200
Biscuit joiner, 124
Bleeding, 200
Blemish, 200
Blind Dovetail. *See* Dovetail, blind
Blind Riveter. *See* Pop riveter
Board foot, 200
Bole, 200
Bolt, 40, 200
Book-matching, 200, 201
Bowing, 200
Box nails, 200
Brace, 41
Brad, 200
Builder's square, 169
Bullnose, 200
Burl, 201
Butt hinge, 201
Butt joint, 201

C

Carcass, 201
Casing, 201
Caulk, 42, 201
Centers, drawing, 42
Chalk Line, 42, 43, 44
Chamfering, 201
Check, 201
Chisels, maintaining, 44, 45
Circular saw, 45, 46, 124
Circular-saw blades, cleaning, 45, 46

Circumference, 201
Clamps
    alligator, 65
    bar, 65
    C-clamp, 65
    clothespin, 65
    framing, 61
    hand, 65
    long-reaching, 46, 47
    mini, 46, 47
    paper clip, 65
    protecting workpiece from, 46, 47, 48
    rubberband, 46, 47
    spring, 65
Closed grain, 201
Coarse grain, 202
Coarse texture, 202
Compass cutter, 47, 48
Compasses
    architects', 48–49
    beam compass, 49, 50
    circle-drawing, 49
    draftsman's, 48, 49
    free-arm, 48, 49
    with screw gears, 48–49
    shop-made, 49, 50
Cope, 202
Cord, 202
Core, 202
Cornice, 202
Counterbore, 202
Countersink, 202
Crook, 202
Crosscut
    with a band saw, 29, 30
    definition of, 202
Cubit, 202
Cutting tools. *See also* Hand Tools
    backsaw, 66
    coping saw, 66
    crosscut saw, 66
    Dozuki saw, 66
    fretsaw, 66
    hacksaw, 66
    keyhole saw, 66
    knife, utility, 66
    mitre saw, 66
    ripsaw, 66

D

Dado, 202
Deciduous, 202
Delamination, 202
Dents, filling, 184, 185
Depth gauge, 50, 51
Dimension lumber, 202
Dimples, removing, 51
Doors, installing, 51
Dovetail jig, 202
Dovetail joint, 202
Dowel, 202
Dowel joint, 52, 202
Drawer handle jigs, 52, 53
Drawknife. *See* Spokeshave
Dressed wood, 202
Drill, 124, 125
Drill bits
    sharpening, 53–54
    truing, 54
Drilling techniques
    around corners, 54
    holes, in tight spots, 55
Drill press, 55, 56, 57
    angle jigs for a, 55
    bits, tightening, 55, 56
    drilling spheres, 56
    lathe, as, 56, 57
    table, raising, 57, 58
    table, setting angles on a, 56, 57
Dry rot, 202
Drywall, 202, 203
Dust, 58, 194. *See also* Sawdust, Shop Cleaning, and
    Vacuum Cleaning

E

Eased edge, 203
Edging. *See* Shelves
Electric drill. *See* Drill
    Press and Portable Drill
Enamel, 203
Engraving tool, 125

Environment, respecting, 10, 11
Epoxy glue, 15, 203
Epoxy paint, 203
Epoxy plastic, 118

F

Face, 203
Fastening tools. *See also* Hand Tools
    nail gun, 67
    riveter, 67
    staple gun, electric, 67
    staple gun, manual, 67
Ferrules, 58–59
Figure, 203
Files
    bastard-cut, 68
    cleaning, 58, 59
    definition of, 203
    grinding, 18
    diamond (triangular), 68
    needle, 68
    rat-tail, 68
Filters, disposable, 59
Finger joint, 203
Flat cut, 203
Flitch, 203
Flooring, workshop, 59, 60
Flute, 203
Foam, cutting, 60, 61
Folding rule, 61
Formica, 203
Framing clamps, 61
Framing nailer, shop-made, 61–62
Framing square, 169
Framing vise. *See* Vise, framing
Fretsaw. *See* Coping Saw
Full sawn, 203

G

Gable, 203

Gateleg, 203
Gel stain, 203
Geometry, 62, 63, 64. *See also* Mathematics
Glue, 203
Glue gun, 125
Grading lumber, 203, 204
Grain, 204
Green wood, 204
Grinding wheel, protecting, 18
Gripping tools. *See* Hand Tools
Grit, 204
Growth rings. *See* Annual Rings
GWB, 203
Gyproc. *See* Drywall

Hardwood, 204
Heartwood, 204
Heat gun, 126
Hinges
    blacklap, 77
    brass-butt, Colonial, 77
    butt, 77
    cabinet, 77
    concealed, 77, 78
    hammered strap, antique, 77
    piano, 77, 78
    recessed 90°, 77
    SOSS, 77, 78
    strap, 77, 78
    strap/butt gate, 77
Hole saw, 78–81
    making rings, 78
    plugs, releasing, 79, 80
    self-ejecting, 80
Honing. *See* Sharpening

Hammers. *See also* Hand Tools
    ball-peen, 68
    carpenter's nailing, 68
    framing, 68
    mallets, 68
    sledgehammer, 68
Handsaws
    Japanese, 63, 64, 65
    shop-made, 63, 65
Hand tools, 64–76
    chisels, 66, 67
    clamping, 64, 65
    cutting, 66, 67
    fastening, 66, 67
    filing, 67, 68
    gripping, 67, 68
    hammering, 67, 69
    levelling, 69, 70
    marking, 69, 70
    measuring, 69, 71
    nailsets, 72, 74
    pliers, 68, 69, 71
    prying, 72
    punches, 72, 73
    scraping, 72, 73
    screwdrivers, 72, 74
    smoothing, 74, 75
    turning, 74, 76
    wrenches, 74, 76

Inlaying, 204

Jigs
    angle, band saw, 20, 21
    angle, drill press, 55
    angle-cutting, 18
    circle-cutting, 24, 25
    coping saw, 50
    for copying parts, 25–26
    definition of, 204
    dovetail, 202
    drawer handle, 52–53
    framing nailer, 61–62
    hole-spacing, 123
    mitre, 132, 133
    mitre-gauge-extending, 97, 100
    mortise-and-tenon, 133, 134

polygon angles, 120
radial-arm-saw swing fence, 134, 135
router cross-grain, 142, 143
square-cutting, 188
thickness planer,
taper, 173, 174
vertical planing, 178, 179, 180
Joint
  definition of, 203
  identifying, 80, 81

K

Kerf, 204
Key joint, 204
Kiln, 204
Kiln-dried, 204
Knife, break-off, 176, 177
Knot, 204

L

Lacquer, 204, 205
Laminate, 205
Laminating, safety techniques for, 81
Lamination, 205
Lap joint, 205
Lathe, 82–91
  bowls, turning, 82, 83, 85
  calipers, 85
  center finder, 86
  chisels, 85
  description and use, 82–85
  drill press as, 56, 57
  duplicator, 86
  guard, 86–88
  life, prolonging, 86, 87
  motor, 84
  plain spur, tailstock, 84
  pulley drive, 84
  sanding, 89–91
  sanding drums, 88
  spur center, headstock, 84

  swing, 83
  tool rest, 84
  tools, 85
Laths, 205
Legs, chair and table, fitting, 42, 43
Levelling scribe, 90, 91
Levels
  box beam, 69, 70
  contractor's, 69, 70
  electronic, 69, 70
  fence post, stud, 69, 70
  line, 69, 70
  pocket, 69, 70
  stud finder, 70
  torpedo, 70
Lighting in the workshop, 91
Lumber, grading, *See* Grading

M

Mallet, shop-made, 91, 92
Marking gauge, 92
Marking tools
  carpenter's pencil, retractable, 70
  draftsman's pencil, 70
  felt-tip marker, 70
  lumber crayons, 70
  marker, water-soluble, 70
  scratch awl, 70
Marquetry, 205
Mathematics/Geometry
  arc, 93
  circle area, 93
  circle circumference, 93
  cube area, 93
  dividing a line, 94
  ellipse, making, 95–96, 99
  equilateral triangle, making 94
  hexagon within circle, making, 95, 96
  octagons, making, 95, 96, 97, 98, 99
  parallelogram area, 93
  pentagon within circle, making, 94, 95
  polygon area, 93
  rectangle area, 93
  square area, 93
  trapezoid area, 93

triangle area, 94
Measuring lumber, 205
Measuring tools
    angle finder, 71
    bevel, sliding, 71
    calipers, 71
    draftsman's protractor, 71
    folding rule, 71
    marking calipers, 71
    square, adjustable, 71
    square, steel, 71
    tape measure, 71
    thickness gauge, 71
    try square, 71
    yardstick, 71
Melamine, 118, 205
Melamine paint, 205
Metric system, 212
Micarta, 205
Mil, 205
Mitre gauge
    extending a, 97, 100
    fitting a, 97, 98, 100, 101
Mitres
    definition, 205
    hand-cutting, 98, 100, 101
Mitre saw, 36, 37, 126, 127
Moisture, 205
Mortise, 205
Moulding, 205
Murphy's Woodworking Laws
    clamps, 102
    ladder, 102
    nail, 102
    screw, 102

N

Nailing techniques
    for close quarters, 103
    when close to edges, 102, 103
    correct, 104, 105
    guards, 103, 104
    toenailing, 104, 105
Nails
    common, 106
    cost, keg, 105–106

    definition of, 205
    penny system, 106
Nailsets, 137
Nominal size, 205
Nosing, 205
Nut, 205
Nylon plastic, 117, 118

O

Oil stain. *See* Stains
Old growth, 205
One-step finishing. *See* Varnish Stain
One-two-three blocks, 100
Orbital sander, 127

P

Paint
    amount, estimating, 110, 111
    brushes, cleaning, 107, 108, 109
    mixing small amounts, 107
    polyurethane, water-soluble, 106, 107
    rollers, cleaning, 108, 109
    roller trays, cleaning, 110
    for shop floors, 106, 107
    thinner, recycling, 111, 112
Paint thinner, 205
Palm sander, 127, 128
Panel, 205
Patterns, transferring, 112
Pegboard
    hooks, securing, 113, 114
    placement, installation, 112, 113
    uses, 113
Pencils, how to use, 114
Pitch, 205
Pith, 206
Planer, 127, 128
Planes
    boards, smoothing edges, 116
    bench, 115

block, 115
chamfer, 115
compass, 115
fillister/rabbet, 115
fore, 115
grooving/trenching, 115
jack, 115
jointer, 115
moulding, 115
nosing, 115
rabbet, 115
router, 115
smooth, 116
spokeshave, 115, 116
trying, 115, 116
Plaster, 206
Plasterboard, 206
Plastics. *See also* Plexiglas
bending, 116, 117
cutting, 116, 117
history, 116, 117, 118
safety techniques, 118
types, 117, 118
Plexiglas, welding, 119
Pliers
end nippers, 71
groove-joint, 71
needle-nose, 71
side cutters, 71
slip-joint, 71
ViseGrips, 68
Plumb, 206
Plumb line, 206
Plywood, preventing tear-out in, 119
Pocket-screwing, 206
Polygons, 119, 120
Polycarbonate, 118
Polyethylene, 118
Polystyrene, 118
Polyurethane, 118, 206
Polyvinyl acetate, 118
Portable drill
depth stop, 122
holes, perpendicular, 122, 123
holes, repeat, 123
Portable power tools
belt sander, 124
biscuit joiner, 124
circular saw, 124
drill, 124, 125
engraving tool, 125

glue gun, 125, 126
heat gun, 126
jigsaw, variable-speed, 126
mitre saw, 126, 127
orbital sander, 127
palm sander, 127, 128
planer, 127, 128
random orbital sander, 127, 128, 129
reciprocating saw, 129
router, 129
selecting, 129–130
staple gun, electric, 125
Primer, 206
Prying tools
crowbar, 72
nail puller
Wonder Bar, 72
Pulleys, sizing, 130
Punches
flat-end, 73
pointed, 73
round-end, 73
screw-hole centering, 73
Putty, 206
PVC, 118

Q

Quarter-sawing, 206

R

Rabbet, 206
Radial arm saw
angle gauge, 121, 131
crosscutting, 136
cut depth, adjusting, 131, 132
extension table, 132
mitre cuts, jig, 132, 133
mortise-and-tenon jig, 133, 134
sawdust collector for, 197
setting up, 134

square, checking for, 130–131, il 131
stop block, 134, 135
swinging fence, 135, 136
Rail, 206
Raised panel, 206
Random orbital sander, 127, 128, 129
Rasp
  definition, 205
  shop-made, 136, 137
Recess, 206
Reciprocating saw, 129
Refinishing methods
  bleaching spots, 139
  paint strippers, 137, 138
  polyurethane, water-soluble, 140
  safety precautions, 137, 138
  sanding, 140
  stains and finishes, 139, 140
Resawing, 206
Resin, 206
Reveal, 206
Riveter, 121, 122
Rod, 206
Rotary cutting, 206
Rotary tools, 141, 142
  dental bits for, 141, 143
Rough lumber, 206
Rounding off, 206
Router
  cross-grain jig, 142, 143
  trimming laminates, 142, 143
  types of, 129
Rust, preventing, 142, 143

S

Safety, Workshop, 10–14
Sanders
  belt, 123, 124
  orbital, 127
  palm, 127, 128
  random orbital, 127, 128, 129
  safety guard for, 143, 144
Sanding discs
  refurbishing, 144, 145
  removing, 145
Sandpaper, 14
Sap, 207

Sapwood, 207
Sawdust-Collection Systems, 145, 146–147, 148, 194, 197
Scrapers and spatulas, 73
Screwdrivers
  drill driver, 74
  Phillips, 74
  reusing, 147, 149
  reversible, 74
  Robertson, 74
  slot-head, 74
Screws
  countersinking, 147, 149
  hardwood, driving into, 148, 150
  measuring, 149, 150
  pilot holes for wood screws, 150, 151
  selecting, 151
  tight spots, driving into, 149, 150
Scribing, 207
Scroll saw, sanding with a, 151, 152
Sealer, 206
Seasoning, 206
Sharpening Techniques, 154–156
Sharpening tools
  combination benchstone, 75
  filestones, Arkansas, 75
  filestones, India, 75
  oilstone, India, 75
  slipstones, carbide, 75
  slipstones, round-edge, 75
Shelf brackets, making, 156–157
Shelves
  making, 157
  painting and finishing, 157, 158, 159
  stacking bars, 157–158, 159
Shooting board, 158, 159, 160
Shop cleaning, 159, 161
Silica gel, 142
Silicone, 118
Sliding T bevel, 159, 161
Smoothing tools
  bench plane, 75
  block plane, 75
  jack plane, 75
  rabbet planes, 75
  router plane, 75
  smoothing plane, 75
  spokeshave, 75
Solvents, 162, 163
  disposal, 162, 163
  storage, 162, 163

Spalted wood, 207
Span, 207
Spirals, making, 163, 164
Spokeshave, 164, 165
Spray-painting small parts, 164, 165, 166
Square, steel. *See* Steel square
Squaring, 166, 167
Stain, 207
Stains
   water-soluble wood, 139, 167, 168
   wiping and applying, 166, 167
Staple gun, 125
Stationary power tools, 168, 169
Steel square
   builder's/framing, 169
   measuring with a, 169, 170
   pitch, determining with a, 171
   truing, 169, 170
   try, 174, 175, 176
Stile, 207
Substrate, 207

T

Table saw, making mitre cuts with a, 132, 133
Tape measure, and inside measurements, 170, 172
Template, 207
Tenon, 207
Thickness planer
   more effective, 171, 172, 173
   tapered legs, making with a, 173, 174
T nut, 207
Toenailing, 104, 105, 106
Tongue, 207
Try square, 174, 175, 176
Tun, 207
Tung oil, 207
Turpentine, 207
Turps, 207

U

Urethane, 207

V

Vacuum, cleaning with a, 58, 145, 146, 147, 159, 161, 176, 194
Varnish, 207
Varnish stain, 207
Varsol, 207
Veneer
   cutting, 176, 177
   working safely with, 176, 178
Vises
   framing, 178, 179
   vertical planing, 178, 179, 180

W

Wallboard, 207
Warp, 207
Weights and Measures, 210
Wheels
   shop-made, 178, 180, 181
Wood sources, 181
Wooden balls, shop-made, 181, 182, 183
Wood filler
   applying, 184, 185
   definition of, 207
Wood scraps, using, 184, 186
Wood stain, 207
Wood storage, 184, 187
Woodworking trivia, 184
Workbench, Bench hooks for, 185, 186, 188
Workmate
   nail support bin, 189, 190
   tool rack, 189, 190
   workshelf, 189, 191
   worktable, enlarging, 186, 187, 188
Workshop
   flooring, 59, 60
   lighting for, 91
   remodelling a, 191–199
   safety techniques for, 10–14
Wrenches, 76

Acknowledgments

Many thanks to the following companies and people for their help and assistance in putting this book together.

American Tool Companies, Mississauga, Ontario

Black & Decker Canada, Toronto, Ontario, Canada

Delta International Machinery (Division of Pentair Canada, Inc.), Guelph, Ontario

DeWalt Industrial Tool Company, Brockville, Ontario

East/West Distributors, Ltd., Richmond, British Columbia

Flecto Coatings, Inc., Toronto, Ontario

Freud Canada, Mississauga, Ontario

Hettich International, Concord, Ontario

IBM Canada, Halifax, Nova Scotia

Kodak Canada Limited, Toronto, Ontario

Lee Valley Tools, Ottawa, Ontario

Norton Canada, Ltd., Hamilton, Ontario

Olfa Knives (c/o Walter Absil Co., Ltd.), Montreal, Quebec

Rubbermaid Canada, Inc., Mississauga, Ontario

Michael Scott of Delta International

Sears Canada, Inc., Toronto, Ontario

Stanley Tools, Division of Stanley Co. of Canada, Inc., Burlington, Ontario

Vermont American–Canada, Mississauga, Ontario

Wedge Innovations, Inc. (Smart Level)

About the Author

Graham McCulloch is an architectural designer and woodworker who lives and works in Halifax, Nova Scotia, Canada. This is his second book on woodworking shortcuts. *Ingenious Shop Aids & Jigs* was the first.